World University Library

The World University Library is an international series
of books, each of which has been specially commissioned.
The authors are leading scientists and scholars from all over
the world who, in an age of increasing specialisation, see the
need for a broad, up-to-date presentation of their subject.
The aim is to provide authoritative introductory books for
students which will be of interest also to the general
reader. The series is published in Britain, France, Germany,
Holland, Italy, Spain, Sweden and the United States.

Donald Longmore

The Heart

**edited and illustrations designed
by M.J.Ross-Macdonald**

World University Library

Weidenfeld and Nicolson
5 Winsley Street London W1

Photoset by BAS Printers Limited, Wallop, Hampshire
Manufactured by LIBREX, Italy

Contents

1 Introduction

While art, theology, and philosophy have endowed the heart with every kind of lofty and noble attribute, science has tended to the opposite pole – until recently. For most of the last three centuries we have treated the heart as a mere pump, mechanically ingenious but conceptually simple. Behind this attitude lay the belief that we understood the activity of the heart in all but a few minor details. Such a belief, we now know, was ill-founded; it asserted that the heart was easy to explain in terms of nineteenth-century technology – a technology that had no mathematical way of examining the passage of information and that understood only the crudest servo (or feedback) mechanisms. In the last two decades we have begun to develop that kind of mathematics; it has given us new insight into the way in which complex processes are controlled, and we have applied that insight to the control processes of the heart. Here, as in so many other fields, medicine has benefited from the fallout of other technologies. The result has been a total revaluation of the heart's mechanism. We see it now as a pump, the subtlety and adaptability of which put it at the extreme limit of our mind's conceptual resolving power.

This change in attitude is part of a revolution discernible through the whole field of biology – analogous to the revolution that over-took physics at the turn of the century. Until that time, physics too seemed an almost completed subject. Almost all the directly observable aspects of energy and matter had been described, mathematically related, and reduced to coherent sets of laws; only a few gaps remained. In showing how those gaps could be bridged Einstein reopened the entire subject. Einstein's achievements never have been – and probably never will be – satisfactorily explained in lay terms. His mathematics is just not reducible to everyday language. Every attempt to reduce it destroys its beautiful compact-ness – and that compactness is an essential part of the service he performed for science. Nevertheless the student of science can grasp that Einstein provided a new language for physics. He devised new 'words', mathematical words, for describing events and relationships that, until then, were mere intuitions or inchoate perceptions. The average scientist simply fails to see events and relationships for which no words have yet been devised. He may have the same sorts of intuitions as the great trail-blazers of science but, unlike them, he lacks the power to devise a new framework of language in which discoveries can achieve conscious and communicable form. Let us look at our discovery of the heart in this light.

The most superficial reading of history appears to show a neat line of development in which unwarranted assumptions, packed with error, are gradually and painstakingly demolished to reveal a clean core of truth. Only when we dig beneath this surface do we find the usual mishmash of historical accident, beneficial prejudice, intrigue, and bloody-mindedness – all of them an essential part of the growth of science.

Most important among the early beliefs about the heart was the Aristotelian view that the heart was the seat of the senses. The modern story begins in sixteenth-century Padua. (For a full account read chapter 3 of Herbert Butterfield's *Origins of Modern Science* – see bibliography on page 248 to which I acknowledge a debt for some of the following material.) Padua was *the* medical university in Europe at that time; it was also one of the most Aristotelian. In fact Renaissance writers tended to sneer at Padua for its whole-hearted commitment to Aristotle. What they overlooked was the fact that Paduan Aristotelianism differed from the brand taught elsewhere. Other universities taught a highly christianised version as a preliminary to theology. At Padua they taught Aristotle neat – or at least through the commentaries of the Muslim Averroes – and as a preliminary to medicine, not theology. Moreover, since the early fifteenth century, Padua had been ruled by Venice, the most anticlerical state in Europe. The resulting freedom of thought attracted many of the ablest men of the time – among them Vesalius, Copernicus, Galileo, and William Harvey.

Origins of modern anatomy

It is ironic, then, that Aristotle was overthrown at Padua not (as elsewhere in the Renaissance) by a rekindled interest in Plato and Pythagoras but by the typically medieval method of commenting and further commenting on Aristotle. Throughout the fifteenth and sixteenth centuries Padua engaged in spirited debate on the whole business of scientific method; but the debate was conducted entirely within the terms of Aristotelian science. The works of Copernicus and Vesalius, both Paduans, were published in the same year, 1543, right in the middle of that debate.

Vesalius's great anatomical work, *De Humani Corporis Fabrica*, shows clearly the extent of the Paduan revolution of that time. It represents the triumph, or partial triumph, at least, of observation over authority. The authority in question was Claudius Galenus, known as Galen, a second-century Greek, physician to Marcus Aurelius. This extraordinary man proved that the nerves conducted a 'force of contraction' from the brain to the muscles. He dissected and described a large number of muscles and proved, contrary to earlier teaching, that each muscle contracted in only one direction. In fact he founded the sciences of neurophysiology and experimental anatomy. The influence of his guesses concerning the blood circulation, however, were more baleful, obstructing the progress of physiology right down to the time of William Harvey. Galen fell into two main errors (see figure 1·1). First, he thought the arterial and venous systems were quite separate – that the blood ebbed and flowed in each. Secondly, he thought that the lungs were merely bellows for forcing air into the left side of the heart, where it removed impurities and gave Vital Spirit to the blood, thus restoring

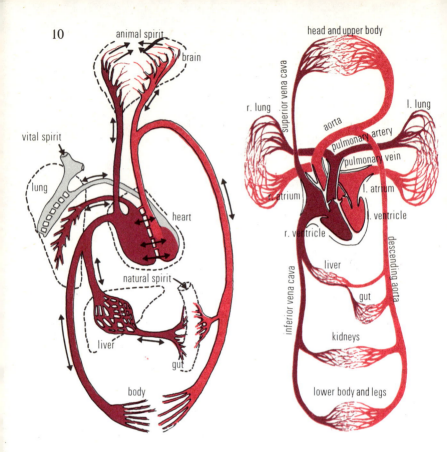

its colour. He identified the airway between lung and heart as what we now call the pulmonary veins. Vital Spirit was one aspect of *Pneuma*, or World Spirit. The other two aspects were Natural Spirit (which came from food via the liver to the blood) and Animal Spirit (which the blood fed to the brain and which the brain then discharged through the nerves to the muscles).

If we cut through Galen's archaisms by putting oxygen for Vital Spirit, energy for Natural Spirit, and nerve energy for Animal Spirit, we can see at once both how close his guesses were and how falsely he related them to the true functions of the blood. It was these false connections that impeded anatomy and physiology for

1·1 Galen's theory of the circulation (*far left*) is discussed at length in the text. It is contrasted with the true circulation, which shows how spent blood (darker) from the tissues collects on the right side of the heart, and passes through the lungs (where its CO_2 is removed and replaced by oxygen) to the left side of the heart, which pumps it back to the tissues. Also identified are vessels and structures that are frequently mentioned throughout this book.

so long. They trapped even Galen himself, for he was forced into a number of supporting errors consistent with his main error. First, he believed that the centre of the blood system was the liver, which turned food into blood. Secondly he believed that the heart imparted movement to the blood during its diastole, or filling phase – from which it followed that the pulse was the muscular expansion of the arteries, which (confusion worse confounded) produced the contraction of the heart by sucking the blood from it. (Actually these beliefs are not so surprising; diastole is the most dramatic of all the heart's movements even though it is, as we now know, a passive relaxation of muscle rather than an active move-ment. The expansion of the arteries is similarly dramatic.) Finally he was forced to postulate minute pores in the septum between the two halves of the heart in order to allow venous blood (rich in Animal Spirit) and arterial blood (rich in Vital Spirit) to commingle. More than twelve hundred years later we read of anatomists, baffled in their search for these nonexistent pores, praising God for his power to make blood pass in such rich quantities in both directions through holes too fine to be seen!

Yet, given a creator with such power, the Galenic view was coherent within itself and related neatly to a general medical theory that dealt with the body in terms of spirits and humours. Because of that coherence it exerted a compelling grip on men's minds, and it is against this general atmosphere of acceptance and completeness that we must weigh Vesalius's achievements.

In 1536, at the age of twenty-two, Vesalius was appointed pro-fessor of anatomy at Padua, the day after he graduated. At once he abolished the tradition whereby the professor read appropriate texts from Galen while a demonstrator dissected a corpse as a sort of animated 3D illustration; implicit in this sytem was the belief that if the demonstrator failed to reveal what Galen said was there, then he – not Galen – was to blame. Seven years later he published his monumental *De Fabrica*, summing up the knowledge he had gained, not from Galen, but directly from observation. The bones, muscles, nerves, brain, and blood system – all were shown with clarity and accuracy (figure 1·2). The text was strongly antigalenic and anticlerical: 'Not long ago', he wrote, 'I would not have dared to turn aside even a hair's breadth from Galen. But it seems to me that the septum of the heart is as thick, dense, and compact as the rest of the heart. I do not, therefore, see how even the smallest particle can be transferred from the right to the left ventricle through the septum.' He further showed that the thigh bone was straight (that is, you can run an imaginary straight line through it from top to bottom, passing through bone all the way), not curved as Galen had said. Sylvius, an orthodox anatomist and Vesalius's ex-teacher, dismissed this fact with the contemptuous remark that straight thigh bones resulted from the ridiculous contemporary habit of wearing tight breeches. (We should not smile too condescendingly at Sylvius, however; the cosy techniques used by medical orthodoxy to dismiss uncomfortable novelties are remarkably persistent.) Contrary to clerical teaching, Vesalius showed that men and women have the same number of ribs (confounding the myth that Eve was created from a rib of Adam's) and that there is no 'indestructible bone' from which the whole person could be recreated at the resurrection.

Attacked on both flanks, by the Church and by the medical old guard, Vesalius could not withstand the pressure. He resigned his chair and became medical adviser first to the Habsburg emperor Charles V and later to Charles' son, Philip II of Spain. In Spain he wrote: 'I still live in hope that some time or other, by some good fortune, I may once again be able to study that true Bible, as we count it, of the human body and of the nature of man.' It was never more than a hope. In 1564, at the age of fifty, he died.

Amid the praise that Vesalius is rightfully accorded it is often

TRIGINTA PARI-   VM NERVORVM
QVAE A' DORSALI ME-   DVLLA DORSI OSSIBVS
contenta originem ducunt, nuda delineatio   ea proportione expressa, qua superiùs ue-
næ cauæ & magnæ arteriæ delineationes   exhibuimus. Hæc trium subsequentibus
   Capitibus communium figura-   rum secunda numeratur.

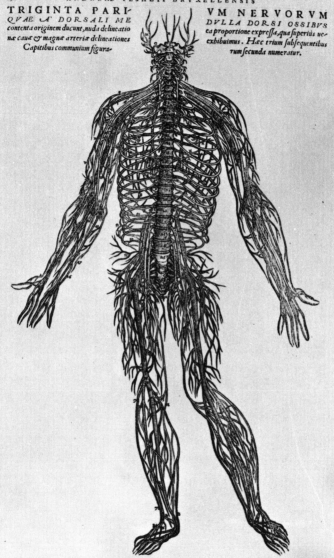

14

forgotten that his was a most incomplete revolution. He overturned Galen in so many details, and yet it never seems to have occurred to him that the whole of Galen's general theory of human physiology needed radical revision. (Vesalius continued to believe, for instance, that the blood ebbed and flowed in the vessels, being created in the liver and consumed elsewhere. He still believed that air went from the lungs to the heart.) Nor, to be fair to Vesalius, did the need for revision occur to later generations of anatomists, who accepted his 'modifications' of Galen without fuss. It is a remarkable testimony to the power of an accepted idea to blind us to the evidence of our senses. In fact, with hindsight, we can see that the problem was circular. Galen's physiology was 'right' because his theory of the blood was 'right' because his physiology was 'right' . . . and so on.

As long as this self-supporting argument remained persuasive it was impossible for physiology, and thus for medicine itself, to escape from error. What is digestion? Respiration? Excretion? What does the blood carry? Where does it pick up and offload its burdens? What are its other functions? These and similar questions lie at the very centre of physiology; but as long as the circulation of the blood was wrongly understood it was impossible to get answers to each separate question that would also fit into a single coherent framework.

The work of William Harvey

That is Harvey's achievement: to have seen the large framework. His predecessors at Padua had achieved part of the synthesis. Colombo, in 1559, established the 'smaller circulation' – right ventricle→lungs→left atrium and ventricle. Fabricius, in 1574, saw the valves in the veins but he missed their point completely; for him they merely checked the excess flow of the blood down the veins to the arms and legs. Both men interpreted their findings as faithful Galenic students. In 1593, another Italian, Cesalpino (not a Paduan), saw that the blood went *to* the heart in the veins, *away* from it in the arteries; but, incredibly, he never linked the two facts by asserting that the blood in the arteries drained through the tissues into the veins and so returned to the heart. Like many before him he used the word 'circulation' but only in the sense in which we speak of traffic circulation – akin to the Galenic ebb and flow.

Neither Colombo's nor Fabricius's discoveries were widely published. But Harvey must have heard of them when he studied under Fabricius at Padua between 1599 and 1602. After his return to London he took up a teaching post in anatomy at St Bartholomew's Hospital. He dissected human cadavers as well as living dogs, pigs, snakes, frogs, fishes, lobsters, shrimps, insects, slugs, and oysters. He minutely examined the valves of the veins and the heart. He studied variations in structure or activity caused by sickness, posture, medicine, and toxins. He became the world's leading authority on the heart and blood and, through his writings, remained so long after his death.

By 1619 he was convinced of – and began to teach – the following points: 1. The systole (contraction) of the heart fractionally precedes the pulse; thus the heart is a muscular sac that squeezes out the blood rather than sucks it in; 2. That the pulse is the result of this outflow from the heart, not of an active muscular expansion of the arteries; 3. That there are no pores in the septum between the right and left sides of the heart; thus (see figure 1·1) *all* the blood in the right ventricle is sent through the pulmonary artery to the lungs, then via the pulmonary veins to the left atrium, from there to the left ventricle, from there via the arteries and arterioles, through the tissues and into the veins, which drain back into the right atrium, the collecting chamber of the heart; 4. That the blood in the arteries is thus the same blood as that in the veins; 5. That

1·3 Four diagrams from Harvey's book show experiments that could have been done at any time from Galen's day onward. Figura 1 shows how the veins distend in a tourniqueted arm – obviously, reasoned Harvey, because the blood being pumped out from the heart through deep-lying arteries cannot return through constricted superficial veins. The other figurae show how the valves in the veins (swellings labelled B, C, D ... etc) help this return flow.

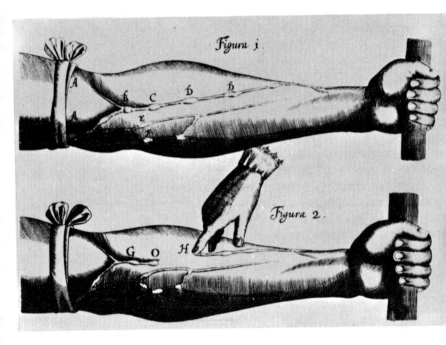

the dynamic centre of the system is the heart, not the liver.

He supported this revolutionary thesis not only with details from his enormous experimental knowledge and with simple demonstrations such as any man could perform (see figure 1·3) but with a clinching mathematical argument. In any given hour, he showed, the heart pumps out a quantity of blood whose weight is greater than that of a man and several times greater than the quantity of nourishment taken in a whole day. Only a circulatory theory could explain where all that blood came from or went to. At the urging of his colleagues he published his theory in *Exercitatio Anatomica de Motu*

In Figura 2, for instance, when the vein is constricted at H before the tourniquet is tightened, the valve at O prevents blood from flowing back between O and H – even when (Figura 3) the experimenter tries to massage it back beyond O. But when he massages in the reverse direction (L to N, Figura 4) he finds he can empty the vein. By such rigorous yet simple proof, Harvey showed that venous blood can flow only one way – toward the heart.

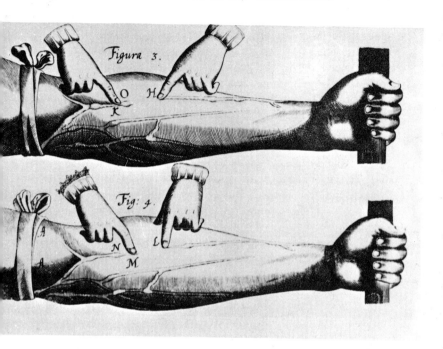

Cordis et Sanguinis in 1628. Within forty years not a single Galenical anatomist was to be found in any European centre of learning.

Harvey owed his success to his thoroughly modern practice: he refused to assign a definite function to a structure until it was confirmed by experiment – and preferably given a quantitative or mathematical form. But the success of his theory – its extraordinarily rapid spread – has other causes. *De Motu Cordis* came out at a time when mechanics and astronomy were revolutionising earlier beliefs about the nature of matter and the universe. Again the revolution involved the overthrow of Aristotelian notions, and again Padua was one of its centres.

In Aristotle's universe things moved because of 'inherent tendencies'. Objects fell to the ground, for instance, because all matter possessed an inherent tendency to seek the centre of the universe (the centre of the earth). The stars, sun, moon, and planets, locked fast in their crystal spheres, rotated about that same centre because rotation was 'inherent' in all spheres. Such theories were demolished by the work of men like Copernicus and Galileo (both Paduans) and others, such as Kepler. Newton, of course, was later than Harvey. The new theories saw the world not in terms of mystical innate tendencies but of measurable forces, of attraction, of impetus; in short, they saw the world as a *machine*. And when Harvey spoke figuratively of the heart as 'a piece of machinery in which though one wheel gives motion to another, yet all the wheels seem to move simultaneously' he struck exactly the right chord in his readers' minds. Like the universe, the human body could be seen as a piece of clockwork.

In a way Harvey was too successful, seen, that is, from our standpoint in the 1970s. The view of nature as a simple machine was eagerly seized by philosophers – by Descartes in particular. It soon passed into general currency, and for almost three centuries stood as one of the central dogmas of science, including medicine. In its time it was one of the most potent and enriching ideas of all, and many advances can be traced to its influence: the laws equating all forms of energy, the molecular theory in chemistry, the field equations relating electricity to magnetism, the theory of evolution, mendelian genetics, the statistical view of social behaviour, the vaccine-and-drugs revolution in medicine – all these are aspects of the universe-as-machine outlook.

The modern view

But, just as Aristotelianism, with its insistence on observation and deduction, contained the seeds of its own destruction, so the mechanical hypothesis, with its built-in imperative to seek ever subtler evidence of cause-and-effect relationships, foundered in the welter of complexity it laid bare. The signs were to be seen first in mathematics with its 'nonsensical' new geometries; then in physics, in that great period between Einstein's theory of relativity and Heisenberg's discovery that uncertainty is part of the very fabric of nature. These various upsets all share one singular feature: common sense, our everyday experience of cause and effect, is no longer a certain guide to understanding the intimate behaviour of matter. Biology is only just beginning to feel the effects of this reversal; it is of a similar order though it has arrived by a different route.

Its pioneers were not biologists but mathematicians, men like Boole, Turing, and Norbert Weiner. Their subject was the 'statics and dynamics', so to speak, of information. Weiner, in particular, studied the mechanisms of decision and control in complex, self-organising systems – machines, social institutions, and living organisms; he coined the word *cybernetics* to cover this new approach in science. And since it is so new, we face enormous difficulties in assimilating it or in stating its principles briefly. It amounts to a fundamental reordering of our whole framework of thought. Perhaps I can best explain its significance by contrasting this new framework with the old.

In the former, mechanistic view of the universe, phenomena were related in a simple linear manner – cause and effect. To take some elementary examples in medicine: Bacteria (causes) produce diseases (effects). Diseases (causes) produce a rise in body temperature (effect). Temperature rises produce sweating and flushed skin, which, in turn, produce drops in temperature. That is a simple linear chain. Practically the whole of science has been discovered and taught in this way, so that one's knowledge of the universe could, schematically, be written out on thousands of paper ribbons, each starting with a cause and ending with an effect.

Now as long as we are dealing with small parts of a system this is a perfectly valid framework in which to operate. But – and this is the prime dogma of cybernetics – when we deal with whole systems, or even with subsystems above a given level of complexity, such a framework is not merely inadequate, it can be dangerously misleading. For, common to all linear chains is the concept of an 'inside' and an 'outside'; the first cause is outside the system, the resulting chain of effects inside. In the example above, for instance, most doctors would think of bacteria as belonging outside the system (that is, the patient) and the effects as being inside. This approach is valid if the doctor's interest centres on curing the patient's fever; but dangerously simplistic if his field is broader – if, for instance, he is studying the total environment in which diseases arise as well as their medical, social, and industrial consequences. In such a study it is meaningless to assign to bacteria the outside role; there *is* no outside.

That is what cybernetics has taught us. When we study large, self-organising systems we must, so to speak, collect all the paper ribbons and glue them end to end in a many-dimensioned array of loops, branches, and subloops – a maze with no defined beginning or end.

The heart, like all other organs of the body, is just such a system. And the story of its scientific analysis and investigation aptly illustrates both the initial potency as well as the ultimate bankruptcy of the simple cause-and-effect approach. Because Harvey looked for measurable causes and effects he succeeded in determining the true role of the heart. And because success is contagious, all later cardiologists looked at the heart in the same light. They added enormously to his basic discovery – particularly around the turn of the century, in elucidating the heart's conductive mechanism (see figure 6·4). In no instance, however, did they actually reverse one of his major conclusions. But our very success in pursuing this line of inquiry has brought us to the point where useful information is ceasing to come in. As long as we think within a simple, mechanistic framework and call the heart (as one eminent cardiologist has done) a 'simple pump', we will gain little new knowledge about its function. In fact, we already know so much about it at this level of simple observation that, we may be sure, the really important questions have yet to be asked.

Those questions involve complexity – the complexity of many intricately related systems. The heart is a community of complex cells; it is surrounded by other such communities of equivalent complexity. Together they add up to the total complex system of a human being who, in turn, is a member of the complex community of mankind that survives in a complex environment.

Such a system is total. It has no outside. Or, to put it another way, all the relevant factors are inside. There is no absolute starting point – no point we could call a primary cause, from which all else stems. We may start where we choose. In this book I have chosen to start with a mature heart in a mature system.

2 The invisible dance

Everything that we do results in a series of complex events inside the body – the nervous system sends messages to different parts of the body, the heart adjusts its output, the glands secrete, and so on. To describe in detail all these processes would fill hundreds of books. This pinpoints one of the most urgent problems in biology today. We need a new way of relating what the great biochemist Sir Gowland Hopkins called 'the invisible dance of molecules' to the easily recognisable, general properties of whole organisms. We need a set of related, hierarchical descriptions at various levels of detail which, like a nest of chinese boxes, contains and enlarges upon its predecessors.

We are going to face that problem in this chapter because it is here that we study the molecular dance which the heart exists to support – indeed, that support is its only function. For instance, several dozen pages hence I will be describing a faulty heart valve. It takes no medical knowledge to comprehend: the valve is, quite simply, too stiff and does not close properly. But the results of this defect, first in the heart, then the lungs, the liver, the kidneys, the control centres of the nervous system, and finally in every tissue in the body – to understand all this calls for a clear grasp of how these tissues depend on one another in health.

The common denominator of their interdependence is the blood –a liquid tissue.

Single-celled organisms live only in a watery environment. When they are exposed to the air, as during dispersal, they develop a thick, impervious wall which protects them until they can return to a watery environment. Such protection is necessary because life in water is much more congenial than in air. For example, temperature fluctuations are less, and there are usually soluble foods ready to hand. Waste is disposed of by diffusion. In the case of air-breathing, terrestrial animals consisting of many cells, the environment of their cells is actually more or less the same as sea water

2·1 The interdependence of five organs or tissues that form the interface between man and his environment; black arrows show where substances and energy enter or leave the system; red arrows mark blood routes. The liver rather than the heart is at the centre of this system.

was millions of years ago; they are bathed in a watery fluid containing dissolved gases, salts and foods. As we shall see, this fluid around every cell passes in and out of the blood vessels.

The blood supplies, in remarkably constant proportions, a rich soup of nutrients and dissolved gases. It regulates the water content of the tissues and removes their waste products. It neutralises acids or alkalis. It helps to regulate temperature. It seals wounds and fights off invaders. We shall look at this last property in chapter 7 when we discuss heart transplantation, for it is most relevant there. All the other properties are aspects of the simulated primeval sea we maintain within. The blood achieves these feats partly by its innate composition and partly through its four interfaces with the outside world (see figure 2·1): the lungs, the gut, the kidneys, and the superficial tissues. Through these organs and tissues, molecules and heat energy can pass to and from the environment.

The centre of this system is not the heart but the liver. For, as long as we focus on events at the molecular level, we can justifiably call the heart a 'mere' pump. The subtlety of its construction and the diversity of its response to changes within this system do not belong to this part of the story; for the moment, then, we will relegate it to the minor role of pumping blood past these four important interfaces and through the liver. A schematic circuit of this kind is given in the figure; it summarises much of what follows.

2·2 The famous Krebs cycle, discovered in 1937 by Hans Krebs (Nobel prize, 1951), shows how glycogen and fat are metabolised to yield energy (as ATP), CO_2 and water. In the absence of oxygen, glycogen can be converted to lactic acid in order to yield energy. In short, all intermediate and end products of energy metabolism are acidic.

The food we eat is unacceptable to the body without drastic modification. It comes in large, more or less solid lumps, much of it insoluble in water. The protein is foreign and must be taken apart into its basic amino acids before we can use it for building body protein. The fats and carbohydrates come in large unwieldy molecules which must be similarly dismantled before the body can tolerate them. And the vitamins, minerals, and essential salts are locked up inside animal or vegetable cells that must be broken open and dissolved before the body can absorb them. Only water and small, soluble molecules can pass straight through the gut into our bloodstream. It is the job of the gut, in the first place, to achieve this dismantling. The veins from the gut go directly and exclusively to the liver, which takes the small, dismantled molecules, stores some, destroys others, and releases the rest for general use in the body. The liver has its own arterial supply too. Through this flows not only its own quotas of oxygen and nourishment but a whole range of harmful products. Some are toxins from wounds and infections; some are byproducts of metabolism itself (that is, the total process whereby food is turned into tissue or energy); some are soluble toxins that enter the blood through the stomach wall – alcohol, for instance; some are dead or degenerate blood cells. All of these are rendered harmless in the liver. With superb economy it turns – to take one example – some wastes into bile which, secreted into the digestive system, helps in the breakdown of fat globules.

The products of this activity, whether they are stored in, or rebuilt by, or directly released from the liver, eventually find their way into the body's tissues. In Hopkins's phrase, they join the molecular dance. Some of the products go to make protein. The discovery of how this happens is one of the triumphs of our decade and one of the most remarkable feats in the long history of science. But there are so many good modern accounts of it, both

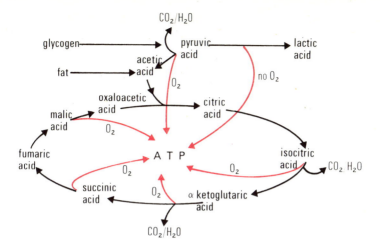

in books and journals (see bibliography), that the story needs no retelling here.

As for fats, their story is rarely told in any detail outside specialist books on physiology and biochemistry. Perhaps it is because the function of fats is either more obscure than that of protein and carbohydrate or seems just humdrum. Even young schoolchildren can learn to equate protein with bodybuilding, carbohydrate with energy; but once you have got beyond the part played by fatty tissue in conserving body heat and water you come straight to its role in the chemistry of the cell membrane, the production of surface active agents, and other such obscurities.

But the story of carbohydrates, which was to the 1930s what DNA was to the 1950s and 1960s, is less frequently told these days. For that reason alone it is worth recapitulating. In addition, the energy-yielding ability of carbohydrate lies at the very centre of our present theme. After all, when a tissue needs extra energy it usually needs it pretty fast and it is the job of the blood, which circulates through the periphery of your body on average every four minutes, to deliver it.

Carbohydrates, fully digested, are turned into glucose. The liver converts the glucose to glycogen, or animal starch, and stores it. The liver can also make glycogen from protein and fat. This glycogen is widely distributed throughout the body but the chief reservoirs are the liver and the muscles. When somebody exerts his muscles the glycogen is transformed by a series of energy-yielding steps into pyruvic acid. The further history of this acid is summarised in figure 2·2. As can be seen, the pyruvic acid is converted first into acetic acid and then by a complex cycle of seven acids into CO_2 and water, yielding the energy-rich compound ATP (adenosine triphosphate – about which more will be said in a moment). It takes some moments for the extra CO_2 in the bloodstream to reach the brain centres which control the breathing and heartbeat; meanwhile the muscles continue to work in relative oxygen starvation. In these conditions the pyruvic acid is converted, without need of oxygen, into lactic acid – again yielding ATP.

ATP is the universal energy carrier. It takes part in every energy transformation throughout the entire plant and animal kingdom. It is not, of course, the only such carrier. Indeed, every molecule involved in metabolism is at some stage either a source of or a sump for energy; nevertheless ATP is an important product of every energy-yielding reaction. Its potential is summed up in figure 2·2, which shows how each transformation between adenosine and mono-, di-, and triphosphate either absorbs or yields energy.

In the muscle the ATP breaks down to ADP or lower and provides energy that allows the basic filaments of muscle to climb along one another and so produce a contraction. The process is mechanically analogous to the way an ear of barley will climb up the inside of your sleeve if you shake your arm – but its details are not relevant here. All this time the muscle glycogen is being depleted. The muscle restocks itself by converting glucose from the blood. The blood glucose, in turn, is replenished from the liver glycogen – which, in its turn, is made up by digestion and the reconversion of most of the lactic acid that was produced by the muscle.

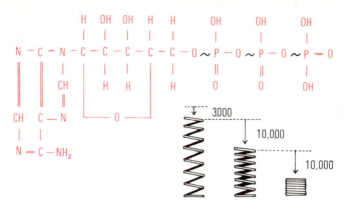

Activity makes acid

One word has turned up again and again in these last few paragraphs and it features overwhelmingly in the energy-yielding diagram: acid. In short, the products of metabolism are acids of one kind or another – lactic acid, acetic acid, the whole citric acid cycle, and even CO_2, which forms carbonic acid (H_2CO_3) with water:

$$CO_2 + H_2O \rightleftharpoons H_2CO_3.$$

All acids dissociate to a greater or lesser degree, yielding a free radical with a negative charge and hydrogen ions with a positive charge. Carbonic acid, for instance, dissociates thus:

$$H_2CO_3 \rightleftharpoons H^+ + HCO_3^-.$$

Hydrochloric acid thus:

$$HCl \rightleftharpoons H^+ + Cl^-.$$

It is the degree of dissociation that determines the strength of an acid, not the number of hydrogen atoms in its molecule. Thus although carbonic acid has two hydrogen atoms per molecule, it dissociates only weakly; whereas hydrochloric acid, with only one hydrogen atom, dissociates almost completely. In a very strong acid, like hydrochloric, there is between 0·1 and 0·01 gm of H^+ ions per litre. In a weak acid, like carbonic, there is only 0·000001 gm/litre. Water has 0·0000001 gm/litre. And in a strong alkali solution there is only 0·00000000000001 gm/litre of H^+ ions. Clearly these figures as they stand do not offer a very handy scale for expressing the strength of an acid. If we take their logarithms, we get a better scale: from -1 to -14. By convention we can reverse the sign to give from 1 to 14; and this is, in fact, the well known pH scale for measuring the acidity or alkalinity of a liquid. Water, with a pH of 7, defines the neutral point. The reversal of the sign explains the seeming paradox that the lower pH values represent *greater* acidities; hydrochloric, strongly acidic, has a pH between 1 and 2; carbonic, weakly acidic, is about pH6; highly caustic alkalis approach pH14.

The pH range of the blood that is compatible with human life is 7·0 to 7·8, and only in terminal illness does it stray outside those limits. Its healthy range is even narrower: 7·36 to 7·44 arterial and 7·31 to 7·39 venous. (Remember this when in the following pages we talk about 'acidosis' in the blood; it is a purely relative term since the blood is always slightly alkaline.) All this is in marked contrast to the pH range in more primitive life forms, even among the vertebrates. In some fish, for instance, the *normal* pH is anything between 7 and 9. Compared with all other animals humans are far less tolerant of changes in the internal milieu. The necessity of maintaining a very delicate internal balance and the violence of our reaction (from coma to tetany) when it is upset is part of the price we have paid for intellectual progress.

How is this remarkable constancy maintained? The body has three systems for regulating pH: buffer systems in the blood itself; the kidney, which can selectively pull H^+ ions out of the blood and push them into the urine; and the lungs, which get rid of CO_2.

To understand the mechanisms behind these three systems look back at the tell-tale double arrow in the equation that governs the dissociation of carbonic acid:

$$H_2CO_3 \rightleftharpoons H^+ + HCO_3^-.$$

This arrow indicates that the equation goes both ways and that the entities on either side are in equilibrium. For instance, if we added a strong acid to a carbonic solution the preponderance of H^+ ions would drive the equation backward so that little or none of the carbonic acid would be dissociated. The full equation, remember, is:

$$CO_2 + H_2O \leftrightharpoons H_2CO_3 \leftrightharpoons H^+ + HCO_3^-.$$

Thus any addition to any of the reagents will drive the total equilibrium forward or back. More CO_2, for instance, produces more H^+ ions:

$$CO_2 + H_2O \leftrightharpoons H_2CO_3 \leftrightharpoons H^+ + HCO_3^-.$$

The removal of water has the reverse effect:

$$CO_2 + H_2O \leftrightharpoons H_2CO_3 \leftrightharpoons H^+ + HCO_3^-.$$

All the reactions we are about to study have this reciprocal nature; until you get into the way of feeling these equilibria surging backward and forward, the system is difficult to master.

The interdependence of the three pH regulators is summarised in figure 2·4. The upper part is schematic but includes all the essentials; the more complete version below is for those who find details easier to comprehend than generalisations. The blood buffers of which potassium haemoglobinate (KHb) is typical, mop up any H^+ ions in excess of normal levels. The radicals left behind (HCO_3^- for bicarbonate and X^- for lactate, pyruvate, citrate, and all the others) attach to potassium in the cell or to sodium outside it. Thus, because the stronger acids (HX) form more H^+ ions than the weak carbonic, there is a general tendency to inhibit HX dissociation in favour of $H^+ + HCO_3^-$ dissociation. In short, the blood buffers drive the equilibria away from strong acid toward weak acid. The lungs, by removing CO_2 (and a little water), push the

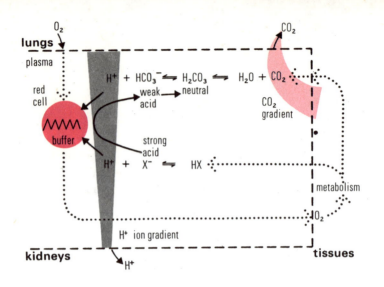

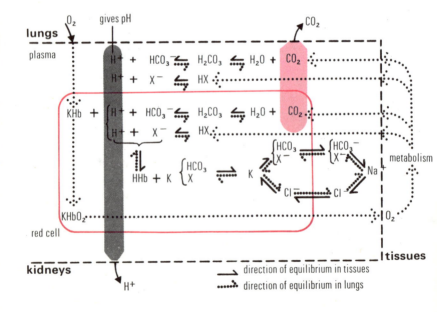

2·4 How the blood, lungs and kidneys interact to control the acidity 31
(i.e. the H⁺ ion concentration) of the blood. The lower figure
is a fuller version of the upper one. The red blood cell buffers
the blood by temporarily mopping up H⁺ ions – which are permanently
eliminated in the kidney. The lungs get rid of CO_2, which helps
drive the equilibria toward neutral H_2CO_3.

reaction further: from weak acid toward neutral. And the kidneys, by removing H⁺ ions, have the same effect.

Each of these mechanisms can compensate for failures in another. Thus diseased or damaged lungs can fail to extract enough CO_2, causing a 'respiratory acidosis'; the kidneys then overexcrete H⁺ ions, causing a 'renal alkalosis' which compensates the acidosis and keeps the pH normal. Conversely, if the kidneys over- or under-excrete H⁺ ions, causing a renal alkalosis or acidosis, the lungs under- or overextract CO_2, causing a compensatory respiratory acidosis or alkalosis. And if the tissues themselves over- or under-produce acids, causing metabolic acidosis or alkalosis, the lungs and kidneys compensate by over- or underactivity. (Medical students reading this should be warned that many authors lump the renal conditions in with the metabolic ones – complaining even as they do so of the intellectual confusion this can cause.) These intricate balancing mechanisms show to what remarkable lengths the body will go in order to maintain the constancy of its internal milieu. Even patients who are desperately ill can show a completely normal pH. And, of course, a sound heart and circulation is the pivot of the whole system.

Feeding the tissues

So much for the regulators which maintain the general chemical environment of the metabolism. What of its physical environment – the hydrostatic forces and osmotic pressures that push the nutrients through the tissues and pull out the wastes? What role does the heart play here?

Picture a small piece of tissue traversed by a number of blood capillaries, as in figure 2·5. At any given moment only a few of the capillaries in such a network are carrying blood; the remainder are closed down at the minute precapillary sphincter at the arterial

2·5 In a typical capillary bed blood flows from the arterioles (A) to the venules (B) through thoroughfare channels (C) and capillaries (D). The flow of the blood through the capillaries is intermittent, being regulated by precapillary sphincters (E), which respond both to nerve stimulation (nerves are shown in black) and to local build-ups of waste products. Arteriovenous shunts (F) provide a means of bypassing the capillary circulation when the blood is needed more urgently elsewhere. Muscles, which are absent in capillaries and in parts of the thoroughfare channels, are shown as stripes around the vessels. The section shown represents less than a tenth of a cubic millimetre of tissue.

end of each vessel. At times of crisis these sphincters can come under the overriding control of the nervous system and the circulating hormones; usually, however, they are controlled by local reflexes in response to a very localised build-up of metabolic waste products. Such a build-up causes the sphincter to relax, allowing blood to flow inward and irrigate the area, bringing nutrients and carrying off wastes. As the wastes are cleared, the sphincter again contracts, shutting off the blood once more. Three minutes is the average time for such a cycle in resting tissue.

There is no anatomical difference between the two ends of a capillary; under a microscope they cannot be told apart. So there are no actual structures that pull the nutrients out of the bloodstream or pull the wastes back into it. The process depends entirely on the varying balance between the blood pressure outwards from the capillary and the osmotic attraction into it (see figure 2·6). At the arterial end the blood pressure is still high – higher, in fact, than the osmotic forces that tend to pull water back into the capillary. The result is a net export of fluid into the tissues – carrying with it nutrients, amino acids, hormones, enzymes, salts, electrolytes, and dissolved oxygen. At the venous end, however, the blood pressure has dropped and the osmotic forces can exert themselves and pull back some of the fluid into the bloodstream – carrying with it unused nutrients, hormones, etc. plus dissolved CO_2, urea, acids, and other waste products. Only the protein cannot get back, for it exerts an even higher osmotic pull than the capillary blood. It is either used or drains away with the rest of the fluid via the lymph channels, which, ultimately, drain back into the veins at the base of the neck. To sum up: the capillaries irrigate the tissues and remove some of the wastes, the remainder together with some of

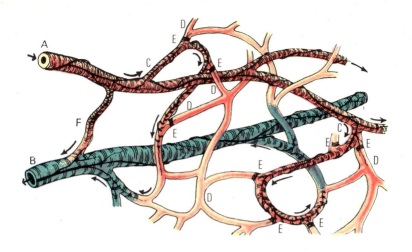

2·6 The interplay of hydrostatic and osmotic forces expels the serum containing amino acids, food, gases and water into the tissues at the arterial end of the capillary and pulls the serum containing unused nutrient and wastes back into the capillary at its venous end. This is not a static situation: you must imagine this capillary shutting down after a few minutes while a nearby one, running in a different direction, opens up. That one, too, will shortly close down while yet another opens up … and so on. This arrangement ensures that no cells are permanently near either a venous or an arterial end.

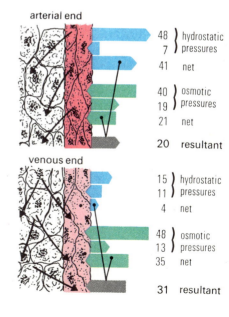

arterial end

48	}	hydrostatic
7	}	pressures
41		net

40	}	osmotic
19	}	pressures
21		net

| 20 | | resultant |

venous end

15	}	hydrostatic
11	}	pressures
4		net

48	}	osmotic
13	}	pressures
35		net

| 31 | | resultant |

the fluid drains back to the bloodstream via the lymphatics.

This vital movement of fluid into and out of the tissues depends absolutely on the flow of blood; so here is another life process that pivots about a healthy heart and circulation. If pressure is too high, the arterioles can constrict and so provide the peripheral tissues with an adequate flow of blood in the normal pressure range. And even if the pressure is slightly low, the system can adapt: the arterioles relax so as to maintain normal peripheral conditions even though central pressures are low. In fact many doctors treat moderately low blood pressure as the ideal state of health – though in some countries, Germany in particular, they treat it as a disease (rarely with any benefit to the patient, though the drug houses don't complain). Severely reduced blood pressure reduces the return to the heart. As a result, according to laws that we shall study in chapter 4, the heart's output drops further, lowering the pressure still further. This downward death spiral is so rapid that the patient is dead at the centre before the results begin to show in his tissues out at the periphery.

Now let us look at the organs that achieve the superb balancing feats we have so far reviewed: the heart, lungs, liver, and kidneys. It may seem a paradoxical arrangement of material to look at a mature, functioning system in chapter 2 and then in chapter 3 to watch that system grow from its simplest origins. But the reader will find its growth a lot easier to follow if he already understands some of the end points. Only the main features are covered in this chapter. More recondite matters, such as the surface active properties of blood vessels and lung tissue, the hydrodynamics of blood flow, the electrical axes of the heart, or homeostatic control, are dealt with later.

The heart (shown with the lungs in figure 2·7a) is a four chamber pump. Two smaller upper chambers, called atria, are topping-up pumps for the two larger lower chambers, called ventricles. Blood passes from the veins into the right atrium and on through a large three leaflet valve, the tricuspid, into the right ventricle. When the ventricle is nearly full the atrium contracts and tops it up, pre-stretching the muscle to its optimum contractile state. When the right ventricle contracts, the rise in pressure forces the tricuspid to shut; the tendinous cords (or heartstrings) – shown cut away in the figure – act like the cords of a parachute and prevent the valve from inverting back into the atrium. The same rise in pressure forces open the three much smaller leaflets of the pulmonary valve and pushes the blood out into the pulmonary artery. As the effort is spent, the pressure in the ventricle falls below that of the recently ejected blood, and the pulmonary valve is forced to close. This closure is not caused by a backward *flow* of blood – let me stress that now. The actual mechanism will be described in chapter 3; but it is important to grasp from the outset that the blood never reverses its course – never even halts – in any of the large vessels, including the heart.

Fractions of a second later the tricuspid valve opens and the cycle begins again. The blood in the pulmonary artery passes on through the lung capillaries, giving up its CO_2 and taking on more oxygen. As it does so it changes from its purplish venous colour to the lively red of arterial blood. It returns through the left atrium, which, like its counterpart, tops up its ventricle. This, the most powerful chamber of the heart, pumps the blood out through the aortic valve into the aorta and provides the pressure which, as we saw, is vital to the proper nourishment of the tissues. The heart itself is supplied with blood via two coronary arteries, which branch out at the very root of the aorta and run down over the surface of the heart, pushing a network of arterioles and capillaries deep into its muscle. Some of this blood drains back directly into the ventricles but most makes its way, via the coronary veins, to the lowest pressure area in the venous side of the heart – the right

2·7a The heart-lung complex, here shown in this oblique view of a cutaway chest. Part of the heart wall has also been cut away to show its four valves and the interior of three of its chambers. The lungs are partly cut away to show the paths through them of bronchi (yellow), and their associated veins and arteries. All the parts except the tendinous cords (which prevent the mitral and tricuspid valves from inverting into the atria) are labelled and identified in the drawing and key (*below right*).

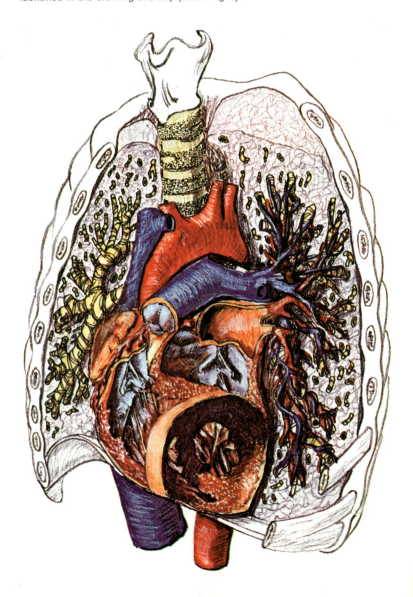

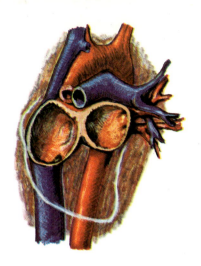

2·7b Left The figure shows the back walls of the two atria, which in figure 2·7a are concealed by valves. It also, incidentally, shows the parts left in the recipient in a heart-transplant operation (see chapter 7). Contrary to the convention used elsewhere in the book the pulmonary arteries in both figures are blue, the veins red – indicating the nature of the blood they carry.

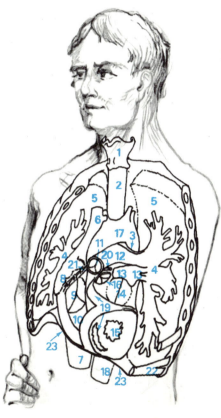

1 larynx

2 trachea

3 left bronchus

4 bronchi, arteries, veins

5 lungs

6 superior vena cava

7 inferior vena cava

8 front (=right) atrial appendage

9 tricuspid valve

10 front (=right) ventricle

11 pulmonary valve

12 pulmonary artery

13 pulmonary veins

14 mitral valve

15 back (=left) ventricle

16 aortic valve

17 ascending aorta

18 descending aorta

19 interventricular septum

20 back (=left) coronary artery

21 front (=right) coronary artery

22 ribs

23 diaphragm

atrium. Its opening into the atrium, known as the coronary sinus, is concealed in the figure; it lies on the floor of the atrium, immediately behind the bottom-most of the three leaflets of the tricuspid valve. (Note: some writers talk of 'coronary' others of 'cardiac', others of 'heart' veins; yet others distinguish between coronary veins emptying into the coronary sinus and cardiac veins emptying elsewhere. For simplicity's sake I use 'coronary' throughout.)

The cycle is so triggered that the two atria contract simultaneously, followed by the simultaneous contraction of the two ventricles. In the average 70 kg male (this trim paragon of physiology is used as a standard throughout this book; all figures, unless otherwise stated, refer to him) the average cycle lasts 0·86 sec, giving a pulse rate of 70 per minute. With each cycle each side of the heart pumps 80 ml of blood, making a total of 5·6 litres, or about 90 per cent of the total blood volume, each minute. The actual volumes of the ventricles when they are distended to optimum prestretch (to be defined in chapter 4) are over 80 ml – 100 ml for the left ventricle and 120 ml for the right ventricle; this slack capacity is taken up when there is an extra call on the heart, during exertion or after a shock, for instance.

The normal pressures in each ventricle are also different. During filling they are close to zero – that is, they fill passively, offering no resistance to the output from the atria. At the height of contraction the powerful left ventricle exerts a pressure equal to 120 mm Hg (millimetres of mercury). This very transient pressure, which lasts less than 0·1 sec, is transmitted to the arterial system; but as soon as the aortic valve closes, the systemic pressure falls to around 80 mm Hg. This lower pressure, which lasts for most of the cycle, is the important one for it sustains the flow throughout the system. The right ventricle, which has the much easier task of pumping blood through the lung capillaries, works at correspondingly lower pressures: from 0 to 12 mm Hg (at rest).

At the end of the finer bronchioles of the lung – they are much too fine to be shown in the figure – lie minute air sacs called alveoli. The total number of alveoli in both lungs is estimated at 750 million (see figure 3·20). Their combined surface area is 55 square metres – more than twenty-five times the area of the skin. The membrane around each alveolus is not continuous but is frequently supplanted by the membrane of the blood capillaries. The capillaries are only 5 to 10 microns in diameter – about the same as a single red blood cell (a micron is 10^{-6} metre); the membrane is a mere 0·1 micron thick. The reader might imagine that this network, through which the red cells must literally squeeze, would offer high resistance to the blood. In fact, because the network has so many branches (end to end they would measure several hundred kilometres), it offers remarkably little. The 12 mm Hg pressure in the pulmonary artery is high enough to push 5·6 litres of blood through this network each minute – and 12 mm Hg is little more than a sixtieth of an atmosphere!

Another result of this lower resistance is that the blood gets through the lungs very quickly. The average time spent in there by a red blood cell is about 0·8 sec – almost exactly the interval between successive heart-beats. From this it follows that there is only 80 ml of blood in the lung at any given moment (again at rest). Thus if we take a typical sequence of heart-beats and number them 1, 2, 3, ... blood passes from the right ventricle to the lungs on beat 1, from the lungs back to the heart on beat 2, and from there to the system on beat 3. To put it another way: The deoxygenated blood in the right atrium is reoxygenated and back on its way to the tissues in only 2·5 seconds. And this is in the body at rest – during exertion this period can be cut to about one second.

Those who have done experiments on diffusion in the laboratory may by now be wondering how the passage of gases between the blood and lung interior is so quick. Granted that the surface area

2·8 The core (*below*) and part of the outside (*right*) of a single human liver lobule. To picture the full lobule imagine the space between them doubled and filled with tubes and cells in the pattern indicated. The actual diameter of a lobule is about 1 mm. Blood from the gut (A) and arteries (B) drains into the liver sinusoids (C) where it is processed by liver cells (uncoloured). Products leave via three routes: the venule (D) that links ultimately with the hepatic vein, the bile duct (E), and the lymph ducts (F).

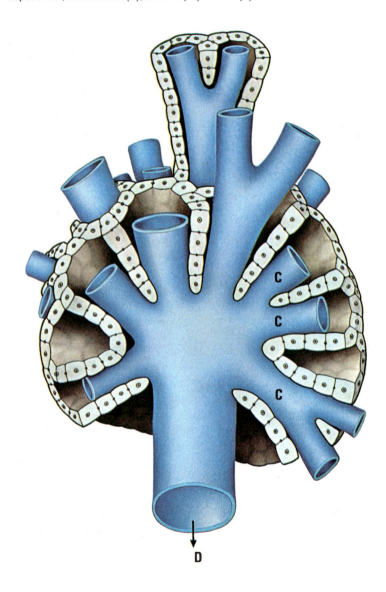

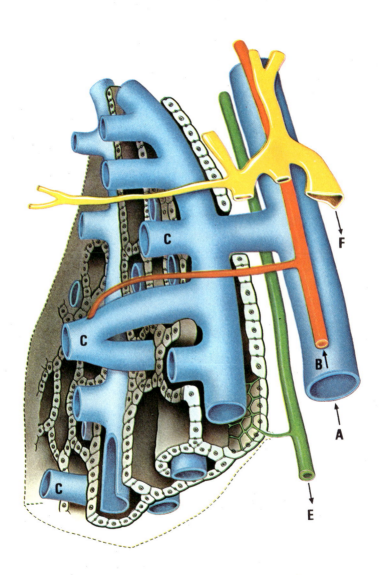

of the lungs is huge and that the membrane is only 0·1 to 0·2 microns thick, nevertheless how do 20 ml of these two gases change places in only 0·3 second and at the relatively high temperature of about 38°C? In the laboratory we would expect to allow at least twenty seconds to achieve the same volume of exchange. The answer lies in the extraordinary power of haemoglobin, the red pigment of the blood cells, to throw out CO_2 and snap up oxygen. It can do this sixty times faster than blood plasma.

The 5·6 litres of blood which leave the heart every minute go to nourish the tissues and collect their wastes. In most tissues this is achieved by the process of capillary irrigation, which we have already studied (pp. 32-3); exceptions are the cornea and humours of the eye, cartilage, and bone, all of which rely on the diffusion of plasma from more distant capillaries. With some tissues the blood has a more intimate involvement, one that is beyond the simple service of collection and delivery. These are the endocrine organs, sources of most of the body's hormones, and the nerve centres, which control and regulate our other activities. Discussion of these belongs to later chapters. Then there is the liver and the kidneys, whose functions we have already touched upon.

The liver circulation (figure 2·8) is straightforward. It has two inputs: food-rich but oxygen-poor blood via the portal vein from the gut, and its own arterial supply via the hepatic artery, an indirect offshoot of the aorta. The portal vein is an anatomical freak in the human. It begins, like all other veins, in a capillary bed, in this case the bed of the gut. These gut capillaries join together in the normal fashion to form the vein itself; but then, like an artery, it begins to branch out again, through capillary-like channels which ramify throughout the liver tissue.

The basic unit of liver tissue is the lobule (part of one is shown in the figure). In man they are roughly spherical and measure about 1 mm across. You will see that arterial blood and venous blood

2·9 The three histograms on the left make the point that 90 litres of blood yield 83 litres of tubular filtrate of which 82 litres are reabsorbed in the tubules, leaving only one litre of urine. The other histograms show some important constituents of the filtrate. Their total quantities (in grams per 83 litres) are listed above each bar; the quantities excreted in that one litre of urine (again in grams) are shown below the red bars. For instance, all glucose and nearly all sodium are reabsorbed; no sulphate or creatinine is. This reveals the amazing concentrating power of the kidney. Take urea, 27 grams of which are present in 83 litres of filtrate (just over $\frac{1}{3}$ gm/litre); in urine 20 grams of it are present in a single litre — a sixty-fold concentration.

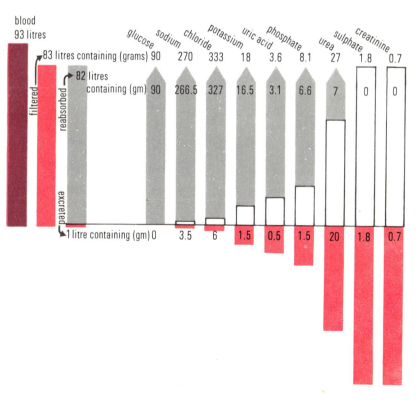

	glucose	sodium	chloride	potassium	uric acid	phosphate	urea	sulphate	creatinine
83 litres containing (grams)	90	270	333	18	3.6	8.1	27	1.8	0.7
82 litres containing (gm)	90	266.5	327	16.5	3.1	6.6	7	0	0
1 litre containing (gm)	0	3.5	6	1.5	0.5	1.5	20	1.8	0.7

blood
93 litres

filtered / reabsorbed / excreted

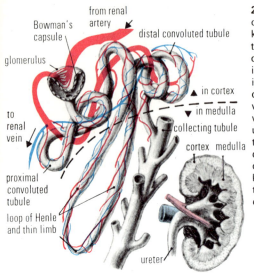

Bowman's capsule

from renal artery

distal convoluted tubule

glomerulus

in cortex

to renal vein

in medulla

collecting tubule

cortex medulla

proximal convoluted tubule

loop of Henle and thin limb

ureter

2·10 The anatomy of a nephron, of which there are a million in each kidney. Blood at high pressure passes through the glomerulus, where many of its constituents are forced out into the tubule. The text describes in detail how some of those constituents are reabsorbed in the various tubules while others, the waste products, are passed on to the ureter. The inset figure identifies the larger-scale features. The colour of the blood vessels is conventional, though in fact the kidneys, which absorb 20 per cent of the total resting circulation, consume very little oxygen.

do not actually meet until they both discharge into the sinusoids of the lobule; at this stage the arterial pressure is so low that there is no risk of cross-flow from arterial to venous systems. Both drain through the sinusoids to the venous capillary at the centre of the lobule. All lobular capillaries drain ultimately into three hepatic veins. These short veins run straight into the inferior vena cava, which is surrounded on three sides by the liver and which runs immediately to the heart. The hepatic veins are unusually well furnished with a muscular coat, used for regulating their diameter, and thus the flow of blood through the liver.

The picture, then, is clear: blood enters the liver, is processed, and passes out. A simple circuit. The kidney is not nearly so straightforward. It is as though a housewife, wanting to sweep and dust a room, emptied it of everything portable – small furniture, pictures, carpets, crumbs, dust, and all – and then carried back everything except the crumbs and dust. That, by analogy, is what the kidneys do to the blood.

The basic unit is the nephron (figure 2·10). It has two main parts: the glomerulus, which allows any substance with a molecular weight below about 70,000 to filter out; and the tubule, whose various parts actively transport back those filtered substances wanted by the body. As figure 2·9 shows, about 98 per cent of the glomerular filtrate is reabsorbed in this way.

There are about a million glomeruli in each kidney, making a total filtration area for both kidneys of 1·5 square metres. Each glomerulus has a diameter of about 250 microns and is traversed by fifty or so capillaries, each separate from the other and each bedded in the capsule lining like (as one kidney specialist puts it) 'fingers in a glove'. Thus only one micron of delicate membrane separates the capillary from the space labelled Bowman's capsule, which is where the filtrate collects. All the blood that enters the kidney, except for a tiny proportion that goes to nourish its own tissues, passes through these capillaries. This explains the fact that the kidneys can clear some toxins from the incoming blood in a single pass.

The filtrate in the Bowman's capsule passes out into the proximal convoluted tubule (14 mm long, 15 to 25 microns internal diameter). Here it meets the blood it has just left back in the glomerulus, but at a much lower pressure, though still separated by the thinnest of membranes. In the glomerular capillaries the pressure was 75 mm Hg – high enough to force a lot of fluid and smallish molecules (biologically speaking) through the membrane filter; many such substances are listed in the chart in figure 2·9. But the blood that leaves the glomerulus is at a much lower pressure, about 5 mm Hg. The blood, deprived of much of its fluid and smaller molecules, exerts a high osmotic attraction, about 30 mm Hg. It is here that the cells lining the tubules come into play. Without them the filtrate would diffuse back passively until it and the blood on the other side of the tubule wall were in osmotic equilibrium; the body would lose much valuable protein (which, having a high osmotic pull of its own could not diffuse back) as well as electrolytes and glucose while regaining a lot of unwanted urea, creatinine, and

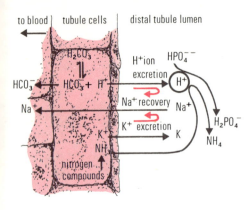

to blood | tubule cells | distal tubule lumen

2·11 How the cells of the distal tubule control blood pH. They actively excrete H^+ ions in exchange for valuable sodium (Na^+). If there is not enough sodium for this purpose, they will then excrete potassium (K^+) ions instead. To 'make room' for more H^+ ions in the urine they also excrete ammonia (NH_3) to buffer the H^+ by forming ammonium (NH_4); this complements the phosphate buffer system in the urine (HPO_4 to H_2PO_4).

other wastes. The tubules prevent all this from happening. The proximal part transports back all the glucose and all the potassium, plus 80 per cent of the sodium, together with some water and urea, both of which flow back passively. It also digests the filtrate proteins, excreting them back into the blood as amino acids. Since about 25 per cent of the plasma protein (i.e. 50 gm) is daily filtered, broken down and reabsorbed in this way, the kidney plays an important and hitherto unsuspected part in regulating the quantity and quality of circulating protein.

The loop of Henle plays an important part in conserving water. Only birds and mammals have this loop and only they among vertebrates can make concentrated urine. The mechanism is highly ingenious. The thin limb of the loop creates a region rich in electrolytes. The loop as a whole descends from the outer parts of the kidney, the cortex, into the medulla. This medulla is also traversed by the collecting tubules, which contain urine from which electrolytes have been extracted. Thus electrolyte-poor urine comes in contact with electrolyte-rich filtrate. The rich filtrate exerts considerable osmotic pull on the urine, which thus yields its water and becomes more concentrated. The water in the thin limb, in turn, is pulled back into the blood by the even greater osmotic attraction of the proteins in the blood plasma. A beautiful feat of conservation!

The action of the proximal tubule and Henle's loop represent the coarse adjustment of the filtrate. The fine adjustment, particularly of electrolytes, is carried out in the distal tubule. It is here that H^+ ions are excreted (figure 2·11) – or rather exchanged for Na^+ ions in the filtrate. If the body is depleted of Na^+, the distal tubule will excrete K^+ ions in order to recover Na^+ from the urine. It also manufactures ammonia and excretes it into the urine in order to buffer the H^+ ions and so make room for yet more H^+ ions.

And all this activity ultimately depends on the heart, and the pressure it maintains in the blood stream.

The reader should now have a sense of the total communion between every organ or tissue and the heart and blood, perhaps also have an uneasy feeling that the balance between normal and abnormal is extremely fine. But it would be wrong to presume that, being fine, the balance is also precarious. We have so far looked at only one of the thousands of ways in which our bodies compensate for disorder: the regulation of blood pH.

In the following chapter we shall see how some of those disorders – specifically those of the heart and circulation – arise. Then we shall be able to study more deeply these self-regulating systems. After all, the heart itself, considered as a piece of dead meat in an anatomist's hand, is a very dull organ. But in the living body, where it has to grow up and respond to a wide variety of physical and nervous stress, and where often by its own failure it is unable to pump enough blood to the organs which depend upon it, it is fascinating.

3 How the heart is formed

The system whose development we are going to watch is, by and large, the system we studied in its mature form in the previous chapter. Its first rudiments can be seen as early as day eighteen – well before the mother can be really certain she is pregnant. At that age the embryo is a lumpy disc just under a millimetre in diameter, attached to a yolk sac of about the same dimension; a short body stalk, soon to become the umbilical cord, attaches it to the wall of the uterus. In time this point of attachment will develop into the deep, interpenetrating, fingerlike protrusions of the true placenta – allowing a great increase in surface area that will, in turn, increase the passage of food and wastes between the mother and her developing baby. Even at this very early age a little diffusion of this kind is already taking place, but the embryo's main food supply is from the yolk sac.

And because of this the embryo has reached a kind of crisis. Of its tens of thousands of cells many will soon be too far from the yolk sac for simple diffusion to keep them adequately supplied with nutrient. Before this crisis becomes acute the embryo will develop a radically improved transport system of contractile tubes to carry nutrients, first from the yolk sac, then from the placenta to these distant tissues, and to remove their wastes. Such an explanation may sound teleological, as though this tiny organism had some sort of consciousness of its future needs and developed so as to anticipate them. Every medical student on his first encounter with embryology finds some such belief hovering at the back of his mind; and, without elaborate circumlocution, it is impossible to write about embryological development without slipping into a teleological sort of grammar. Again and again we shall see developments that anticipate some ultimate function: lungs that will not feel the air for months, a gut and liver that can digest and process milk proteins long before the first swallow, blood channels that can take the full output of the heart though in foetal life they take but a fraction of

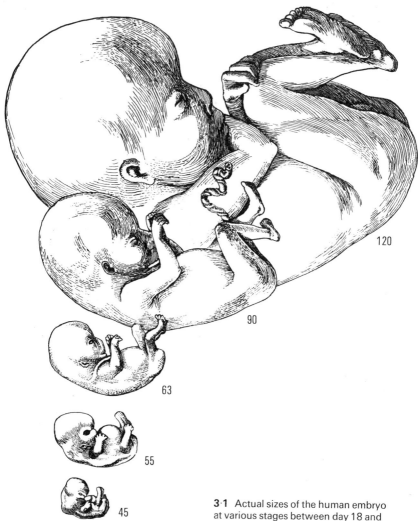

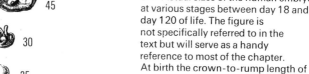

120

90

63

55

45

30

25

18

3·1 Actual sizes of the human embryo at various stages between day 18 and day 120 of life. The figure is not specifically referred to in the text but will serve as a handy reference to most of the chapter. At birth the crown-to-rump length of the baby is slightly more than three times that of the 120-day-old.

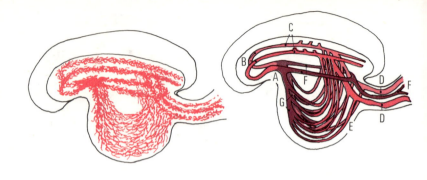

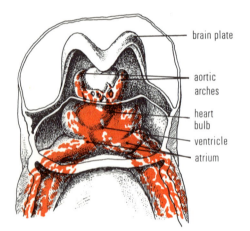

brain plate

aortic arches

heart bulb

ventricle

atrium

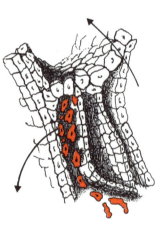

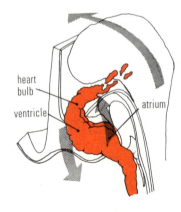

heart bulb

ventricle

atrium

3·3 These views of the heart between days 18 (*above*) and 21 (*left*) complement the drawings in figure 3·2. They show how jelly-filled 'islands' fuse to form the primitive heart tube. The arrows show the directions in which this part of the embryo moves as the primitive brain rapidly enlarges.

3·2 Left The plexiform growth of blood vessels in the 17 to 18 day human embryo is shown on the far left. The right-hand figure shows the structural plan we abstract from the real system. (For clarity, most figures in this chapter have undergone an equivalent degree of abstraction.) When the innumerable channels of the plexus have united, the jellylike substance that will slowly form into blood is squeezed forward from the primitive heart (A), through the twin aortic arches (B), and along the dorsal aortas (C), which divide into the umbilical (D) and vitelline (E) arteries. The umbilical (F) and vitelline (G) veins complete the circuit. The colouring is conventional and bears no relation to the actual degree of oxygenation of the primitive 'blood'. The crown-to-rump length of the embryo is less than 2 mm.

it, and so on. The fact is that every one of the systems we are going to study exists in a kind of anatomical limbo: in its form it harks forward to a job that does not yet exist; genetically it harks back hundreds of millions of years to a mature system that was analogous in structure and function. That is why, as we shall see, the most concise explanation of the status of the embryo (or foetus, as it is known after the third month of life) is often to be found far back in the evolutionary past. In the prime dogma (or oversimplification) of the embryologists: ontogeny recapitulates phylogeny; the development of an individual retraces the evolutionary development of the species.

This brings us back to the transport tubes which the embryo is going to need in its third week of life. Most of the body's organs begin as little islands of differentiated cells that rapidly grow into colonies and, by continued growth and differentiation, form the complex structures of the mature organ. The blood vessels, for that is what these transport tubes will become, are no exception. They begin as tiny islands (though 'lakes' would be a better word since they are actually jelly-filled cavities) spread throughout the embryo – in the wall of the yolk sac, near the head, down the developing nerve cord, and in the body stalk (figure 3·2). Around day eighteen these islands develop into short branching tubes which fuse to form a plexus or network. Their walls develop a muscular ability to contract, which they do at first spasmodically and then in regular waves (peristalsis) that pass along their length.

In this way they squeeze the jellylike contents to and fro. This movement of the jelly plays a central part in moulding the blood vessels. Like any other fluid the jelly will take the easiest channel through these plexuses. The channels thus favoured will grow at the expense of the rest, so that a single tube will appear to form from within the plexus, the remainder appearing to wither.

In the budding heart, however, there is no time for this kind of selection to operate, for the plexus there grows and fuses quickly into a single large chamber – large, that is, by comparison with the other developing vessels; by day twenty it is, in fact, still much smaller than this full stop.

The evolution of the heart

It is here that we must pause and take our first look at the evolution of the heart in order to understand the extraordinary contortions it is soon to undergo. The twenty-two day heart harks back to the four-chambered heart of the common ancestor of all fishes, amphibians, reptiles, birds, and mammals (figure 3·4); it lived about 450 million years ago. In this hypothetical ancestor the blood from the tissues followed a straight line course: into the venous sinus, which pumped it into the atrium, which pumped it into the ventricle, which pumped it into the arterial cone, which pumped it forward through twin sets of six aortic arches that ran between the gills, and so back to the tissues.

During the course of evolution this ancestral heart underwent a series of modifications. First, the atrium and ventricle enlarged; the venous sinus grew relatively smaller; and the arterial cone became partly merged with the ventricle. The atrium moved forward to lie above (in terms of fish posture; in human terms we would say behind) the ventricle. These changes brought certain mechanical advantages. Two chambers offered less resistance than four; being larger and more powerful they could pump more blood; moreover, each could develop a separate function: the atrium became a topping-up pump to stretch the ventricle, which

common ancestor (450+)

3·4 The evolution of the mammalian four-chamber heart from the primitive heart of the ancestral vertebrate; the figures in parentheses give approximate dates in millions of years from the present. The common ancestor had a straight-through flow from the venous sinus (1), via the atrium (2) and ventricle (3), to the arterial cone (4), and so to the tissues. The venous sinus and arterial cone gradually dwindled in importance while the atria and ventricles enlarged, developing two chambers each (a) and (b).

fish (400)

amphibian (300+)

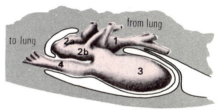

mammal & bird ancestor (220+)

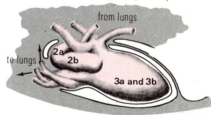

became the main pump. Such a system is inherently more flexible than a straight line four-chamber pump—for reasons that will become clear later when we look at the control of the heart rate.

One obvious result of these changes was a dramatic increase in size. The straight-through heart supported animals a few inches long. The two-chamber heart made five- to ten-fold increases in size possible.

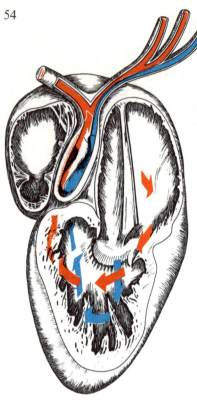

3·5 Separation of the arterial (red) and venous (blue) blood in the common ventricle of the frog; the bulbous ridge in the arterial cone assists this separation, so that venous blood is diverted toward the pulmonary artery for reoxygenation, while arterial blood, newly oxygenated, is diverted toward the tissues.

The two-chamber heart is characteristic of fishes. The next stage, the three-chamber heart, is characteristic of amphibians and nearly all reptiles. It came about over 300 million years ago. Basically it was a continuation of the earlier change. The atrium moved even more forward (upward in human terms) and developed a wall, or septum, down its middle, dividing it into a left and right atrium. Again, the two chambers developed separate functions. The right atrium took over the former atrial function of collecting the de-oxygenated blood from the system, the left atrium developed a special vein from the skin (in amphibians) or the lung (in reptiles) where the blood was oxygenated. Thus the right atrium contained deoxygenated blood, the left atrium oxygenated blood.

It might be objected that since both atria emptied into a common

3·6 A 100 million years of evolution lie between the amphibian arterial system and that of the mammals, who, with the birds, are the only animals to achieve complete separation of oxygenated (red) and deoxygenated (darker) blood. The six aortic arches (numbered in the amphibian) are relics of the six arches that run between the gill clefts and the spiracle of primitive fish. The pulmonary artery is marked p.a. Note that in each case the head end gets the most-oxygenated blood; such a relationship is set up very early in the embryo and is never subsequently eroded.

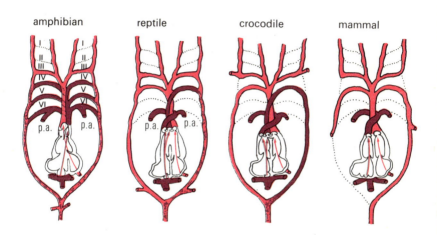

amphibian   reptile   crocodile   mammal

ventricle, which ejected into a common arterial system, the advantages of keeping fresh and spent blood separate were nullified. Not so (see figure 3·5). What had been rows of simple flap valves in the arterial cone of the fish became, in the amphibian, enlarged and fused, forming a sort of flexible baffle plate to divert the outflow into two channels, one to the vith (tailmost) pair of the aortic arches, the other to whatever remained of the arches I to v. The enlarged base of the arterial cone – now called the heart bulb – was so constructed that it diverted oxygenated blood from the left atrium towards arches I to v and deoxygenated blood from the right atrium towards arches vi, the pulmonary arteries. Of course, some mingling was bound to occur, but in modern amphibians and reptiles, anyway, it is remarkable how separate the two streams are kept. (Interestingly enough, amphibians that have regressed to a completely aquatic life, such as the lungless salamanders, have lost this three-chamber modification and gone back to a more fishlike arrangement.) Without this efficient separation there could have been no efficient oxygenation of the blood, and land-based (i.e., air-breathing) life would have been impossible.

About 220 million years ago, well before the great age of pre-historic reptiles, certain early members of the class *Reptilia* developed a true four-chamber heart in which a septum divided the ventricle into a right and left chamber. From this specialised group a clear line emerged leading to the crocodiles (the only surviving reptiles with a four-chamber heart) and the birds. It was once thought that the mammals, too, emerged from this line; but the fourth chamber of the mammalian heart comes, not from a division of the common ventricle, but out of an enlargement of the heart bulb. So it is now assumed, on these and other grounds, that the mammalian line emerged slightly earlier than the crocodile and bird line.

Even in the crocodile the separation of arterial and venous blood is incomplete, for, as figure 3·6 shows, the left systemic arch, carrying venous blood, joins the aorta, carrying arterial blood. Only in birds and mammals is this arch suppressed and the separa-tion of the two circuits complete. In turn this made gas exchange yet more efficient. Increased efficiency made for more wieldy and more flexible organisation. Among developments that belong exclusively to birds and mammals is the ability to control the internal body temperature to within fractions of a degree, which frees them from total dependence on ambient temperatures. Of course, the possession of a four-chambered heart and the ability to control temperature are not directly related; but both belong to a wider series of refinements that enable us to class birds and mammals at the top end of the evolutionary scale of complexity.

The complexity of the evolving heart can be related to every point along that scale.

The embryo heart

The heart's development is well nigh impossible to describe in words, and the result, even when well done, is tedious to all but those whose interest is professional. In the text which follows I shall therefore rely heavily on the accompanying figures.

Refer first to figure 3·7 on page 59, which shows the changes between day twenty-two and day thirty-two. Roughly this corresponds to the evolutionary change from a four-chamber through a two-chamber to a three-chamber heart. The four-chamber heart at day twenty-two consists of the venous sinus, the atrium, the ventricle, and the arterial cone. From day twenty-four to twenty-five the atrium moves upward; simultaneously the embryo's head folds forward, pushing the ventricle down until it lies in front of the atrium; also simultaneously the arterial cone moves to the embryo's right, so that, when seen from the front, the original straight tube has grown into a mangled S lying on its side.

Meanwhile a septum has grown across the floor of the cavity which contains the heart (the pericardial cavity); the two branches of the venous sinus lie below this septum and thus outside the heart proper. At the top end of the cavity the arterial cone is already dividing into a number of aortic arches.

The first primitive vascular circuit is now complete. Jelly, which already has the first few elements of blood within it, is now being pumped forward from the ventricle by rhythmic peristaltic waves, through the first few aortic arches, down the length of the embryo, to the fast dwindling yolk sac and the fast growing placenta. Urged onward by this arterial pressure, the same fluid, now bearing nutrients, is passing back up the umbilical veins and the vitelline veins from the yolk sac, to the right and left branches of the venous sinus, which drains directly into the atrium. Along the embryo, too, cardinal veins have developed in order to drain the bulk of its tissues back into the atrium.

At this stage the atrium, which is as large as the ventricle, is a true priming pump; later, when the ventricles are relatively much larger, it is reduced to a simpler topping-up pump. The first crisis, that of feeding tissues too distant and too active to be satisfied by simple diffusions, is over. Though perhaps it would be more meaningful to say that the embryo now passes into a state of perpetual impending crisis. These next few weeks are the really tricky ones as far as its development is concerned. Changes that took millions of years to evolve now take place within days. They proceed so quickly that the slightest mistiming of a sequence may lead to a permanent anomaly that only the surgeon can put right.

One feature of this primitive system is worth emphasising. The nutrient-rich blood from the yolk sac and placenta goes directly to the heart, nourishing no tissues on the way. From the heart it is pumped forward to the head, the site of the future brain and of many of the endocrine glands (which produce the chemical messengers and regulators called hormones). Thus the most important region of the embryo, and the one most sensitive to oxygen lack, is also the most favoured in its blood supply. It is a relationship that persists throughout embryonic, foetal, and independent life.

By day twenty-seven the simple circuit is beginning, once again, to be inadequate to meet the demands of the rapidly growing embryo, which now measures close on 4 mm from crown to rump. Throughout its tissues new arterial and venous systems are proliferating from new plexuses; these form innumerable junctions (or anastomoses) with each other and with the earlier vascular circuit. The further development of the heart must enable it to meet this ever-increasing load.

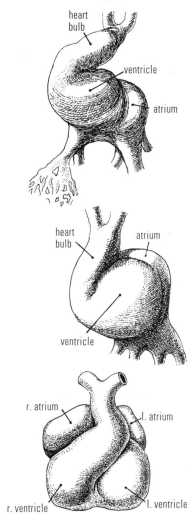

3·7 Changes in the heart's external appearance between day 22 (*top*) and day 32 (*bottom*); also (*top*), part of the plexiform venous system. Basically the atrium rises and spreads so as to sit above and partly envelop the ventricle. Although on the figure they are labelled right and left at day 32, the atria and ventricles are at this stage only just beginning to divide into these separate chambers.

Before we turn to that development, however, there is one loose end to clear up: the six aortic arches we met when we looked at the evolution of the heart. The human embryo, tradition says, develops all six, beginning with I at day eighteen and ending with VI at day twenty-seven, by which time I and perhaps II are already either insignificant or have disappeared. V also dwindles pretty quickly;

in fact some workers strongly deny that v exists at all in man. This whole business of aortic arches is fraught with controversy. While I was checking some of the details of this chapter with an eminent professor of anatomy, he gave me his opinion that the aortic arches are 'fairy tales'. So my use of the labels I to VI is tinged with a certain measure of cynical disbelief; but I will continue to use them for two reasons: in the first place, if the reader is a medical student, he will probably be required to learn these fairy tales as gospel, and secondly, since arches do undoubtedly form and so must have *some* label, and the traditional I to VI seems as good as any.

This leaves only III, IV, and VI to develop into the mature system. III and IV become part of the mature aorta; VI is the one to watch, for it develops extensions that grow down into the lungs, whose buds are beginning to show by day twenty-eight. (We will return to I and II later, in a different context.)

This stage of embryology is remarkable. The embryo is now less than half a centimetre long; its mother has only very recently become certain that she is carrying it. Yet already we can speak not merely of such gross structures as its heart, or head, or tail, but of such minutiae as its aortic arches, its lung buds, its oesophagus, its ventricle and atrium. Now we must narrow our focus even more and look at developments within these two last named chambers, for by day forty-eight they will have to develop into a true four-chamber heart supplying lung and systemic circuits that, but for one small channel, are totally separate. (During the same time an entirely new venous system will also have to develop; but that is a different story.)

Events between day twenty-seven and day thirty-four are really a consolidation of earlier progress. The two-chamber heart grows larger and the contortions that produced its mangled S shape continue (figure 3·7), so that the S is no longer recognisable. As part of this process the heart bulb enlarges out of the lower end of

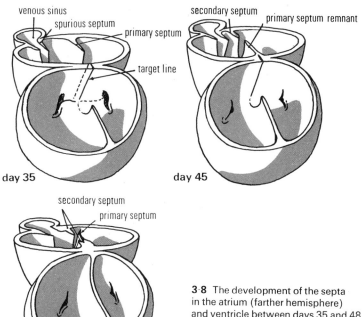

day 35

venous sinus
spurious septum
primary septum
target line

secondary septum
primary septum remnant

day 45

secondary septum
primary septum

day 48

3·8 The development of the septa in the atrium (farther hemisphere) and ventricle between days 35 and 48 (very schematic). The sequence is discussed fully on pp. 61–5.

the arterial cone and becomes, in effect, a third chamber.

The atrium is now near its final position above and behind the heart. During the following months the blood vessels that run into it will enlarge and become part of it; in the mature heart the only remnants of the week four atrium are the little ear-like appendages (or auricles) which lie over the top of the ventricles.

The enlargement of the heart bulb has an important anatomical consequence. In the next few weeks it is going to turn into what most books call the 'right' ventricle (as, indeed, I have called it up until now). In fact, as can be seen from figure 2·7 it is at the front of the heart; its enlargement pushes *the* ventricle (hitherto called the 'left' ventricle) to the back. Hereafter, then, in this book I shall ignore a bad convention, which has misled more surgeons than I

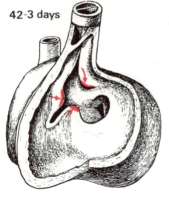

42-3 days

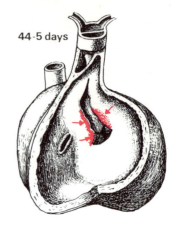

44-5 days

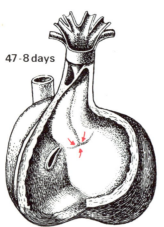

47-8 days

3·9 These diagrams recapitulate part of the sequence given in figure 3·8 and show how the septum growing down the arterial trunk meets the septum that separates the heart bulb from the ventricle. The heart bulb becomes the front ventricle (shown cut away), the ventricle becomes the back ventricle. Note how the septum in the arterial trunk has to twist so as to keep the outflow from these two ventricles separate.

care to think of, and call these features by their correct names: front ventricle and atrium (formerly 'right') and back ventricle and atrium (formerly 'left'). The pedantic will point out that the front chambers are slightly rightward of the back ones. To which it must be said that if something is 80 per cent front and 20 per cent right, you do more justice to call it 'front' than 'right'.

Day thirty-four sees the start of the next remarkable cycle of change: the development of septa down the middle of the atrium and between the ventricle and the heart bulb. These developments are shown both schematically and in something like their true complexity in figures 3·8 and 3·9. As can be observed, the process differs in the atrium and the ventricle – and for very good reasons.

I would like at this initial stage to point out that for easy comparison the hearts are all drawn the same size, though the volume of the heart at day forty-eight is nine times greater than at day thirty-five. Thus, many of the changes that appear to be a withering away are, in fact, the result of differential growth – one structure remaining minute while structures around it grow manyfold. The apparent disappearance of the spurious septum in the atrium is initially the result of differential growth, though ultimately it does become incorporated into the atrial wall. The division of the atrio-ventricular opening into two openings (which will house the mitral and tricuspid valves) is also achieved by differential growth. The top and bottom limbs of this opening grow inward, their edges forming cushions which, when they meet, 'stick' together and fuse. At the same time the ventricle and heart bulb, whose walls surround the two holes that are left when the slit fuses, are growing. As a result the two holes move farther and farther apart. The vertical centreline of the now fused atrio-ventricular opening becomes the target line of the septa growing down across the atrium and up between the ventricle and heart bulb.

Differential growth, however, cannot explain the extraordinary events in the atrium. There a primary septum begins to grow down toward the target line; but no sooner does it get there than it begins to vanish from its starting point, unsealing what was sealed. It may also vanish from the target line (authority is confused here), leaving a tiny bar of primary septum marooned across the middle of the atrium. Immediately a secondary septum begins to grow down as if to seal the hole thus created; and simultaneously a counterpart begins to grow up from the target line as if to meet it; but they never do meet. The lower part of this secondary septum meets with and incorporates the marooned remnant of the primary septum and stops. There is now a hole between the front and back atrium, which the primary remnant can, but does not, seal. The arrangement looks like a flap valve that will allow blood to pass from front atrium to back but not in the reverse direction. And, as we shall see when we look at the foetal circulation as a whole, that is precisely what it is.

Here is a feature that has no evolutionary counterpart (in other words, ontogeny, here, does not recapitulate phylogeny). No mature animal could have had such a system and been viable. It is an entirely embryonic feature that meets purely embryonic needs.

The septum which divides the ventricle from the bulb is, at first sight, a simpler affair. In fact, it is part of an extremely complex sequence of events which embraces the entire outflow channel of the heart, from the aortic arches above (III, IV, and VI, remember) to the bottom (or apex) of the heart itself. Up above, left IV, which will become the aorta, is already beginning to grow larger than left III or right III and IV. In time these latter three arches will become side channels of left IV. Right and left VI are behaving differently. Their root, that is, the point where they separate from the arterial trunk, now begins to nip inwards. The process is a mixture of differential growth and of actual closure; its result is a progressive division of the arterial trunk into an aortic channel which leads primarily to left IV and a pulmonary channel which leads exclusively to the root of VI.

Since this closure passes progressively down the arterial trunk one can think of it as a kind of septum which divides the arterial from the pulmonary outflow. To achieve that division this septum must clearly meet the septum growing up towards the target line and separating the ventricle from the heart bulb. And they must meet in such a way that the pulmonary circulation, which comes out of the *back* of the arterial trunk, is linked to the heart bulb, which lies at the *front* of the heart. In other words, the septum growing down the arterial trunk must spiral clockwise through about 200°.

As soon as the systemic and lung circulations are separated in this way, the heart's own blood supply begins to get tidied up. The two arteries that lead out from the base of the aorta become the main feeder channels – the coronary arteries – which subdivide and further subdivide throughout the heart muscle. The larger parts of them lie on the outside of the heart, where they will not be squeezed by its contractions. A special branch runs from the front coronary to the foremost part of the front atrium – the site of the future pacemaking apparatus of the heart (see chapter 4).

A structural miracle

Let us give these events their true dynamic setting and scale. At day thirty-four the heart is just over 1 mm long; by day forty-eight it still measures only 4 mm or so. Throughout that period it is contracting vigorously at sixty-five beats a minute. During each such minute it puts out something like forty times its own volume of blood. It is also growing and changing its shape. It is also twisting on its axis. And in the midst of this maelstrom these tissue-fine septa are growing inexorably towards each other to meet not a fraction of a millimetre too soon or too late. Even a lifetime's exposure to the more inward mysteries of embryology can never blunt one's sense of wonder at these elementary and well-known sequences.

To look at the other side of the coin, we can imagine all that could go wrong – and sometimes does:

The septa could fail to grow entirely, in which case the foetus rarely survives.

One septum could fail to grow, resulting in a three-chambered heart; survival here, too, is rare.

A septum could grow but fail to grow fully, resulting in a defect in which arterial and venous blood mix. A defect the size of a fine needlehole in a day forty-eight heart could grow, proportionately, to pencil size in the adult. Such a hole in the atrial septum need not be significant: the atria fill and contract simultaneously and at similar pressures, and so little blood may mingle. But a similar defect in the ventricular septum is always serious. The back ventricle normally peaks at 120 mm Hg pressure whereas the front one reaches only 18 mm Hg; so there is a big gradient to push blood through even a small defect. Only surgery can help in such cases. However, because of the peculiarities of the foetal circulation, such a defect may have no effect whatever on the development of the foetus; the trouble comes at birth.

The septum may fail to develop in the arterial trunk, resulting in a completely mixed arterial and pulmonary circulation. Again, this may not become hazardous until birth.

Finally, the septum growing down the arterial trunk may not twist enough, so that the aorta comes to sit over both ventricles. This, too, need not be hazardous until birth, when the lung circulation comes into action for the first time. I will, therefore, postpone discussion of these last three defects until we look at the changes around the hour of birth.

Arteries and veins

Now it is time to see what the rest of the system has been doing during these three crucial weeks. By day twenty-seven, remember, the embryo measures 4 mm and weighs 0·02 gm. By day forty-eight its length is up to 17 mm and it weighs just under 1 gm. This is an almost fiftyfold increase in weight; clearly we can expect enormous changes in the blood supply to all that extra tissue. Earlier figures have shown that the system has a bilateral symmetry (the sequence

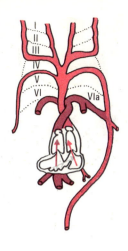

3·10 This diagram of the foetal aortic arches employs the same conventions of layout and colour as figure 3·6. The significance of the flap valve between the two atria is explained on page 64. The arterial duct (VIa) is explained below.

in figure 3·6 reveals it most clearly). Such a system is ideally suited to gill-breathing fish, which could be described as tubes designed to insinuate themselves horizontally forward through a medium that makes them practically weightless. But with massive land-based animals, breathing through puckered up sheets the size of a tennis court deep in their chests, the modifications demanded by both feats make a nonsense of strict bilateral symmetry. If one compares the sequence of diagrams in figure 3·6 with figure 3·10, one can see how the original symmetrical plan is modified for the human embryo.

In particular, note that the left arch VI is preserved, being called the arterial duct. It forms part of the special circulation of the embryo; and its closure at birth marks the changeover to lung-breathing life. As you see, this duct short-circuits the circulation to the lungs. Foetal lungs are collapsed and filled with fluid; the capillary network within them therefore offers a high resistance to the blood flow. At birth, when the lungs expand, this resistance drops dramatically. It would be a most inapt preparation for life if the front ventricle had to pump all its blood through this high resistance; yet its output must be kept fairly high if the pulmonary artery and valve are to form properly. For, in the absence of flow, the genetic blueprint has no medium through which it may act. The

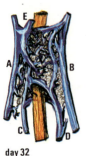

day 32

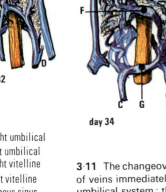

day 34

day 36

A right umbilical
B left umbilical
C right vitelline
D left vitelline
E venous sinus
F cranial anastomosis
G caudal anastomosis
H portal vein
J umbilical vein
K hepatic duct

3·11 The changeover from a symmetrical umbilical/vitelline system of veins immediately below the heart into an asymmetrical portal/umbilical system; the developing liver is in grey, the gut in brown. Key elements in the change are the two labelled anastomoses and, between them, the dorsal anastomosis (unlabelled and partly hidden by the gut). This view obscures the development of the inferior vena cava, which grows from a comparable plexus of veins on the other side of the liver, beginning about day 39. Development of the other big veins is shown in figure 3·12b.

arterial duct is the answer to that problem. It allows the front ventricle to maintain a high output even though the flow through the compressed lung capillaries is reduced to a mere trickle. Now we can see the reason for the opening between the two atria. If it were not there, the back atrium would be reduced to pumping the mere trickle of blood seeping through the compressed lungs. With it, the freshly oxygenated blood from the umbilical veins can pass (with little mingling) across the front atrium, through the hole, and into the back atrium and ventricle.

The veins, too, begin with a bilateral symmetry that, except for the limbs and the head (which are, themselves bilaterally symmetrical) is almost completely lost in the final system. The only veins we have so far studied are the vitellines (from the yolk sac), the umbilicals (from the placenta), and the cardinals, which are the

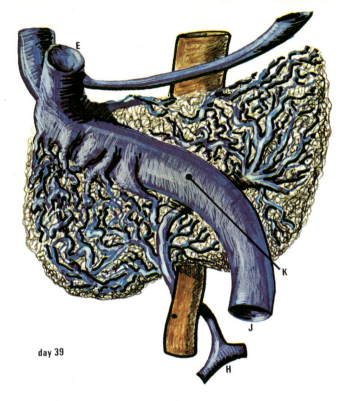

E

K

J

H

day 39

first veins to drain the body cavity itself.

The first of these to lose their symmetry are the food carrying veins – vitellines and umbilicals – which, as one would expect, are greatly involved in the formation of the liver. By day forty-two the liver must be ready to embark on one of its main foetal functions: the formation of new blood. So it is going to need a large network of vessels. These form in the characteristic way by a rich series of branches from the two sets of food veins immediately below the heart. Some of the branches form anastomoses between the main veins. And the blood, obeying the simple laws of fluid dynamics, chooses the easiest path through this labyrinth. As figure 3·11 shows, this simplification comes between days thirty and forty; the two paired veins that drain the placenta and the now rudimentary yolk sac atrophy and combine, forming just two veins – one to drain the newly forming gut, the other to drain the placenta.

As soon as this is complete, the main body-draining veins also begin to lose their symmetry. The cardinal system, which harks back beyond even the most primitive vertebrates, is supplemented by two other systems. One, which in the horizontal plane of most animals lies below the plane of the cardinal system, is known as the subcardinal system. The other, lying above that plane, is the supracardinal system. Both start with a bilateral symmetry which they rapidly lose. Both contribute finally to the main vein of the trunk, the inferior vena cava (ivc hereafter); but otherwise their functions differ.

The subcardinals are chiefly linked with the development of the sex organs and kidneys, allowing them to drain directly back to the heart (the kidney circulation, remember, takes about a quarter of the heart's output). The supracardinals end up supplying a link between the veins below the heart and those above it. They therefore play an important part in balancing the pressures between systems that would otherwise be separate.

Figures 3·12a and 3·12b show how these three cardinal systems converge between days forty and fifty-six. The head and arms (not shown) are, in general, drained by symmetrical remnants of the primitive cardinal system; and the same is true of the legs. But in the trunk, where symmetry is confined to the lungs, kidneys, sex organs, and body wall, drainage is carried out by the almost totally asymmetrical modifications of the less primitive sub- and supracardinals.

In fact, drainage of the lungs is not achieved by any of these systems but by a special set of veins which run directly to the rear of the back atrium. Figure 3·17 shows their development. At day thirty-nine, when the lung circulation is only a few days old, its veins drain into one common vein in the back atrium, just to the left of the primary septum. Throughout foetal life these veins enlarge and become part of the atrial wall; so that the four veins which ultimately enter the back atrium were quite a way up the original venous tree. In the same way parts of the venous sinus enlarge to become part of the front atrium. Other parts become the coronary sinus and the oblique vein, both of which drain the heart itself. The situation at birth is shown in figure 3·17.

To sum up, then: by about the eighth week of life, when the embryo is only 23 mm from crown to rump, the general pattern of the circulation is fully established. It will ramify further – particularly in the still budding arms and legs – and it will grow considerably larger. Its proportions will change, too; but its general pattern is now final. This finality is achieved well in advance of a similar status in other systems, as one would expect, since a good blood supply is essential to their development.

One final circulation diagram (figure 3·13) sums up the foetal situation from month three onwards. We have already studied the cross-circulation achieved by the hole between the atria and the arterial duct. Now, because of it, the most richly oxygenated blood goes once again to the head, that most favoured region. Note too that the front ventricle must be pumping at a higher pressure than the back ventricle, otherwise the blood would flow up instead of down the arterial duct. This pressure difference is achieved partly by making the aorta larger than the pulmonary artery; but it is, nevertheless, the reverse of the situation when the baby is independent. This explains why, in the newborn child, the two ventricles have roughly the same thickness of muscular wall. The enormous development of the back ventricle, until it becomes some five times more powerful than the front ventricle, takes place shortly after birth in response to the greater demand then placed upon it. And although this extra growth is genetically determined, the delay shows, once again, that without the formative element of flow, the

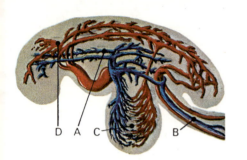

3·12a Plan of the cardinal vein system (A) in relation to the umbilical veins and arteries (B) and vitelline veins and arteries (C) at day 26 (at which time the aortic arches I and II (D) have formed). These cardinals are the veins shown in blue in figure 3·12b.

3·12b The development within the cardinal system (blue) of the subcardinal (red) and supracardinal (yellow) vein systems. Anastomoses between them are shown in green and the hepatic segment of the inferior vena cava is in brown. In the adult, the following veins drain the following regions: head and arms (A), legs (B), suprarenal glands (C), kidneys (D), and sex organs (E). The azygos veins (F) link the lower part of the body with the upper veins and so help balance the venous pressures above and below the heart. The oblique vein (G) lies across the back of the heart and drains its tissues into the front atrium.

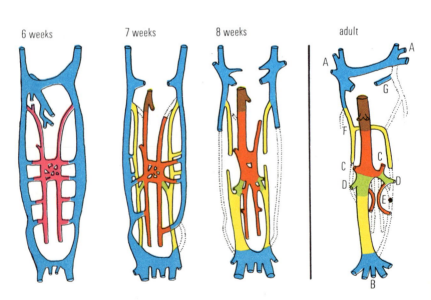

6 weeks   7 weeks   8 weeks   adult

3·13 In this diagram of the foetal circulation the coloration of the blood represents its degree of oxygenation. Note that the most highly oxygenated blood from the umbilical vein passes through the flap valve between the atria (A), to the back of the heart and up the aorta to the head before it is diluted with less well oxygenated blood bypassed through the arterial duct (B). These and other aspects of this arrangement are discussed on p. 67.

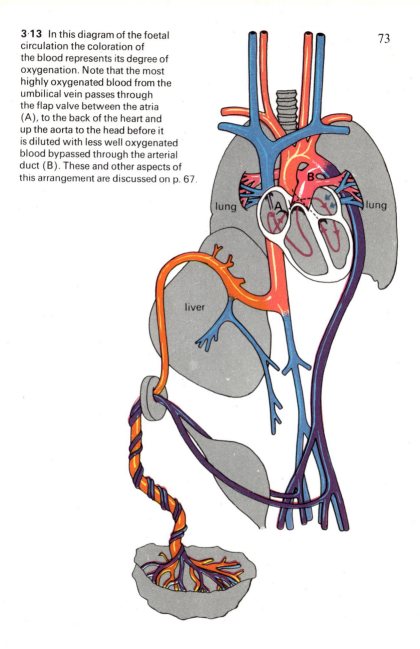

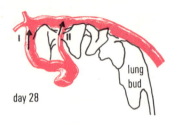

day 28

day 29/30

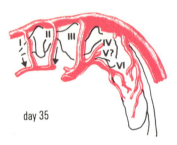

day 35

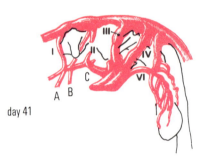

day 41

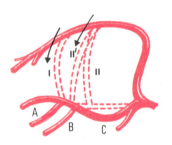

3·14 This sequence illustrates a possible mechanism for the formation of minor arteries – in this case the infraorbital (A) and mandibular (B). If arch I and a brief stapedial variant of II (labelled II^1) persist until day 41 – a few days longer than most embryology texts assume – the flow through them may bias the flow along the external carotid (C) so as to produce the two minor arteries.

3·15 The development of the heart's larger (mitral and tricuspid) valves, highly magnified; the small outline shows the true relative size of the left-hand figure (day 60) compared with the right (day 180).

blueprint could have no *modus operandi*.

While we are on this subject of formative elements let me return briefly to aortic arches I and II. The sequence of diagrams in figure 3·14 clarifies the point I am about to make. Those that show the development between days twenty-eight and thirty-five are to be found in any standard embryology textbook. The one for day forty-one is hypothetical, for I cannot help wondering whether I and II do not persist as rudiments. I was struck with this thought when looking at later developments in this particular region. First, note that the direct connection between the heart and I and II is lost by day thirty-five. This means that the flow through the dwindling I and II must be reversed, as the arrows indicate. Secondly, note that a new anastomosis replaces this lost link and that from it bud two new arteries, the infraorbital and the mandibular. These begin precisely where I and II, still with their reversed flow, impinge. Could it be that this is a fluid biasing device of the kind familiar in fluid switches? In such devices a small flow impinging at the side of a stronger one biases it in the direction of the smaller flow, the principle of which is shown in figure 3·14. If I and II (or its stapedial variant) do persist – even if in a very strangulated form – for a week or so longer than embryologists believe, here then is why: they would bias the stream up the internal carotid so as to hive off the two new arteries. As far as I know no one has yet examined the possibility that this particular biasing mechanism operates in embryos; it might well repay detailed study.

The development of the valves – differential growth again – is shown in figure 3·15. The two larger valves, as one would expect from simple fluid dynamic theory, are designed to pass large volumes at low pressures. Remember, the atria are only topping-up pumps; most of the blood that fills the ventricles is carried there by its onward momentum from the veins of the body and of the lungs. Nevertheless, the valves have to withstand the full force of

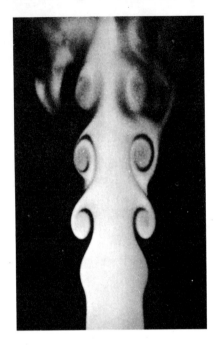

3·16 The flow pattern produced by blowing chemical smoke at the same temperature as the surrounding air through a smooth orifice. The first bulge is powerfully reminiscent of the root of the aorta and indicates the sort of moulding forces at work during the formation of the aorta. (Compare this with figure 6·16 where turbulent out-flow distorts the pulmonary artery.)

the ventricular contraction; hence the tendinous cords, whose function we touched on in chapter 2.

The dynamic moulding of the arterial outflow valves is more interesting. Figure 3·16 shows turbulence in a broad jet of chemical smoke immediately upstream from an orifice. Its resemblance to the shape of the aorta immediately upstream from the root of the aortic valve is more than coincidence, for the forces which produce the turbulence are precisely the same as those that mould the aortic wall. (The same forces, incidentally, also produce widening and deepening in a stream immediately below a waterfall.)

The bulging root of the aorta has a purpose. During outflow the valve leaflets, pushed straight upwards, 'hang' in the space of the bulge. And the very forces that provide lift on an aerofoil – higher flow on the topside than on the bottom – provide a sort of lift here that keeps the leaflets from flattening back against the concavity of the aorta wall. Further, they prevent the outflow from aspirating blood out of the coronary arteries (as in a perfume

3·17 The heart of a day-39 embryo is here contrasted with that of a newborn child to show (1) how parts of the pulmonary veins (orange) are incorporated within the back atrium; (2) how parts of the venous sinus (light blue) become incorporated into the front atrium and coronary sinus; (3) how one branch of the cardinal-vein system (dark blue) becomes the oblique vein of the heart.

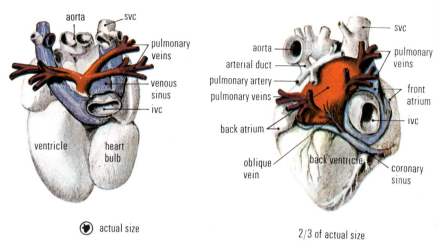

actual size

2/3 of actual size

spray the air, rushing over an orifice, aspirates and entrains the perfume). And finally, as the outflow diminishes towards the end of the heart-beat, the same lift-generating forces cause the leaflets to tilt inward against the dwindling flow so that, as soon as flow ceases altogether, the back pressure from the aorta shuts them instantly. Similar arguments apply to the pulmonary valve (omitting, of course, the bit about the coronaries).

By the end of the third month, then, the heart has reached its definitive form. All the major structural changes that turn the original thickened tube into the twisted four-chambered structure of the mammalian heart have already happened. Of course, there are still big differences between the three-month heart and that of the newborn baby, the hole between the atria and the joined pulmonary and systemic circulations being only two. But the two most important changes in the heart-lung complex between month three and nine can be thought of more as a preparation for independence than as actual development.

Changes that presage birth

From about month six the still collapsed lungs begin to secrete detergents. This may seem an obscure preparation for independence, but without these detergents the baby breathes with great difficulty and invariably dies. Their purpose is to push water molecules farther apart, reducing their attraction for one another and thus diminishing the tension of the watery film which covers the lung surface. This is how they work:

A water molecule consists of a large oxygen atom bound to two smaller hydrogen atoms. The binding force arises from the fact that each hydrogen atom shares its single electron with the oxygen atom. Since an oxygen atom has a nucleus sixteen times heavier than the hydrogen atom, the shared electrons spend more time, on average, around the oxygen nucleus than around the hydrogen nuclei. Thus the molecule has a negative pole near the electron-rich oxygen end and a positive pole near the electron-poor hydrogen end. Such unlike poles have considerable attraction for one another, and the closer they are, the stronger that attraction grows. The effect is most obvious on the surface of water, where the attraction is all one way, downwards and inwards; it is this which gives it a skin. With care one can get cold water to rise over 5 mm above the rim of a tumbler, or float coins, razor blades, and paper clips – all far denser than water – on its surface. But if one adds detergent to the water it will instantly spill over the rim or stop supporting these denser objects. The detergent molecules, insinuating themselves between the water molecules at the surface, diminish the attraction between the unlike poles and so reduce the surface tension.

What makes the detergent molecule behave in this way? Detergent molecules are shaped like matchsticks: their tails are hydrophobic (water fleeing) and their heads hydrophilic (water seeking).

H H
H–C–H H–C–H
⋮ ⋮ **TWO**
H–C–H H–C–H **FATTY**
| | **ACID**
H C H H–C–H **CHAINS**
| |
O=C C=O
| |
O O **GLYCEROL**
| |
H–C————————C———C–H
| | |
H H O
|
PHOSPHATE O=P—O ⊖
|
O
|
H–C–H
|
H–C–H
CHOLINE   H | H
H–C—N—C–H
| | |
H | H
H–C–H
|
H

3·18 The structure of a lecithin molecule, the lung's basic surfactant; two electrically neutral fatty-acid chains (dots represent a dozen or so CH_2 groups, omitted) repel water; phosphate and choline groups, carrying electric charges, attract water. A glycerol group links these two elements.

The tails will seek anything – dirt, grime, fat, oil, dust, fabric, solid surfaces, air – anything that is not water. In the wash tub this accounts for their power to liberate dirt and hold it in suspension: the hydrophobic tails, fleeing water, will surround the dirt and, helped by the agitation of the water, actually start gouging it off the fabric. Once liberated, the fabric will instantly be surrounded, like a rolled up porcupine, by a thicket of detergent molecules. Any two such particles, coming together, will meet detergent-head to detergent-head and mutually repel each other. This hydrophobic/hydrophilic behaviour, as well as the attraction and repulsion, are all aspects of the charge carried on the detergent molecule (see figure 3·18).

This ability to roll up dirt and suspend it is important in the lung of an independent baby; any minute particles of dust or smoke that may penetrate all the way to the alveoli will be trapped and passed up the airways to emerge with coughed-up phlegm. But it is the ability of detergents to diminish surface tension that is of prime importance, both at birth and afterwards. For this reason they are usually known in biology as surfactants (i.e., surface active materials) rather than as detergents, though functionally the two are identical.

The second important change, also in the lungs, comes a month or so before birth. The lungs partly fill with fluid. Whether the baby breathes in a bit of the fluid in which it floats, or whether the fluid is expelled from the now almost complete lung circulation, is not yet clear. In any case, even after this partial filling, the lungs still have only a fraction of the volume they will occupy immediately after the first breath; the rib cage remains cone shaped as compared with the barrel-like shape it will show after birth.

Nevertheless this partial expansion of the lungs allows the capillaries to unbend a little and so increases the flow of blood through them until, just before birth, it is a quarter of the postnatal circulation. Again, an obvious preparation for independent existence, and in more ways than one. For not only does this partial expansion increase the pulmonary blood flow, it also makes the full expansion of the lungs easier at the first breath.

Independent life

Before we look at that first breath of life, consider what a stressful moment this is for a baby. Imagine yourself lying in an emptying bath and you will be able to grasp something of the experience – the chill, and the unwieldy and weak limbs. For the baby this experience comes suddenly, as the warm fluid-filled sac in which it has grown breaks abruptly. Before long a series of peristaltic contractions begins to squeeze him down, and, no longer buoyed up by the amniotic fluid, he begins to *fall*. He has 'fallen' before, of course, every time his mother went downstairs or sank into a chair. But this fall is different. It is infinitely longer, and it ends outside in a new world of unaccountably rich and painful sensations. Even though the adults tending him may be sweating a little with the heat, it seems cold to the wet baby. His world is also filled with light. Until now he has seen nothing but the occasional random pressure on his eyeballs, which his retina and brain have conspired to interpret as light. But here there are lights of fixed and fiery intensity, and they move bewilderingly at random. He has heard his mother's voice and viscera, and the thunder of distant water if she did not turn off the taps before she got into the bath. But these new sounds are undamped and almost explosive – the sounds of sheets, voices, feet on the floor, instruments rattling, traffic, bird-song. His nervous system is a chaos of alarm calls.

We need not look far for the stimulus that starts him breathing. The traditional slap on the bottom, beloved of old-fashioned physicians, could have added very little to the violent new sensations that already assault the baby.

Some babies take their first breath even before their feet appear; most wait between fifteen and forty-five seconds; two minutes is about the limit of normality; and if the baby does not breathe within five minutes it is in bad trouble. Remember that for part, if not all, of that time the placental circulation is still partly intact so that the baby is not absolutely dependent on his lungs. The old technique of clamping a face mask on to the baby and turning on the oxygen is now rarely used, for it carries the risk of inflating the food pipe and stomach rather than the windpipe and lungs – which could actually make the first breath more difficult. The modern technique in these difficult cases is to put a tube down into the windpipe and connect it to a T junction. The oxygen cylinder is connected to the other branch of the T through a gas governor that keeps the pressure within safe limits. The physician then blocks and unblocks the open end of the T with his thumb in a natural breathing rhythm until the baby takes over fully. Often the first cold draught of oxygen on the nose and lips is enough to start

3·19 Relations between pressure and lung volume in a newborn baby: the first three breaths (*at left*); from 2 through 10 and 40 minutes to one week (*at right*). Note that a hefty suck and blow (from over −45 to nearly +30 mm Hg) are needed for the first breath, whereas only 4 or 5 mm Hg of suction are needed after a week. Surfactants, by reducing the surface tension of the lung airways, make this reduction possible. Note also that after the first breath the expanded lungs never fully contract again (a fact often relied on by forensic doctors in determining whether a baby was genuinely stillborn or criminally drowned).

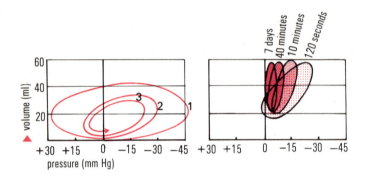

the baby breathing (further confirmation that bottom-smacking doctors have applied the wrong sort of stimulus to the wrong end of the child).

The heroic efforts involved in drawing that first breath unaided are hinted at in figure 3·19. At seven days, as can be seen, a negative pressure (i.e. a sucking in) equivalent to only a few mm Hg is enough to expand the lungs by some 30 ml. (The negative pressure is caused by the muscles which pull the diaphragm between the chest and stomach cavities downward and that hinge the ribs upward and forward.) Only a slight increase in the negative pressure – though this fact is not illustrated in the figure – is enough to draw in a full 150 ml of air, which is the maximum capacity (called the vital capacity) of a week-old baby. Compare this with the huge pressure range – almost 80 mm Hg. from more than −45 to +30 – needed to draw in the first 40 or so ml of air.

A glance at the smaller airways of the lungs (figure 3·20) shows

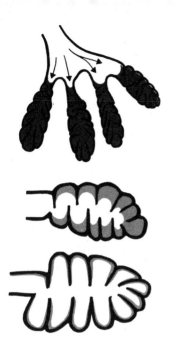

3·20 At birth the alveoli, the terminal airways of the lung, are nearly collapsed and filled with fluid (grey). Surface tension at the rounded fluid-air interface resists incoming air (arrows). Secretion of surfactants reduces the tension and enables the lungs to expand. The two lower figures, which show just one alveolus, reveal the sort of expansion needed to fill out the chest. Over the first few hours the excess fluid drains off through lymphatic vessels, leaving a very fine film over the alveolar surface.

why this huge effort is needed at first. The fluid that fills them is the problem. Surface tension causes the air-fluid interface to round out, and since the tension gets greater as the curvature gets smaller, the baby encounters stronger and stronger resistance as the air reaches deeper and deeper into the ever-narrowing branches of the bronchial tree. It is here that the surfactants play a vital part in lowering surface tension and in easing the course of the first breath.

Surfactants also prevent the collapse of individual alveoli after the first breath. The point here is that the smaller alveoli automatically have a greater surface tension than the larger ones. Thus, these smaller alveoli tend to empty into the larger ones to the point of collapse. The smaller alveoli secrete more surfactants than the larger ones (why we do not know, though the stimulus can only be the greater surface tension itself) and so even out these forces. (Interestingly enough, only mammals have surfactants. Birds, which have more or less rigid lungs through which the air is pumped from large elastic sacs, have none, nor do reptiles and amphibia, whose alveoli are many times larger than those of mammals. The minutely divided lung space of mammals, dictated by their warm-blooded requirements for a huge oxygen supply, would collapse without surfactants.)

From the very first breath the expansion of the lungs stimulates the secretion of surfactants so that, with lower surface tension, breathing becomes easier and easier. Note that the tidal volume (the volume of air involved in quiet breathing at rest) does not greatly change between the second minute and the seventh day of life, but the pressure needed to achieve it drops from over 30 mm Hg to 4 or 5 mm Hg. The surface tension does not of course fall to zero; so the alveoli have a permanent, though reduced, tendency to deflate, like an untied balloon, to their minimum volume. This is why in normal tidal breathing, one does not need to actively expel the air in one's lungs.

The importance of the first breath extends far beyond the fact that it enables the baby to breathe normally. It is also the primary event in a complex sequence that turns the foetal circulation into that of the independent baby. Three major changes must take place: 1. The placental circulation must be handed over to the baby's own systemic circulation, which has hitherto absorbed only a part of the cardiac output; 2. The flap valve between front and back atrium must be shut and sealed; 3. The arterial duct, which shunts 75 per cent of the pulmonary artery output into the aorta, must also be closed and sealed.

The closure of the placental circulation is not related to the first breath. It begins with the contractions of the mother's uterus, which massage the blood in the umbilical cord towards the baby. An extra 50 ml of blood is squeezed into the baby in this way during the first minute. After two or three minutes the pulse vanishes from the cord as the muscles around its blood vessels go into slow spasm, beginning at the placenta and working back toward the baby. In thirty minutes, if the cord is not broken and tied, a further 50 ml of blood can be transfused into the baby from the cord. This fairly massive transfusion stimulates the heart, by mechanisms we shall study in the next chapter, and raises its output. The tied-off cord withers to a dry fibrous stalk, the external part of which drops off naturally in a week or so. The internal part, up to the IVC, also turns fibrous; its remnant, a fine cordlike ligament, remains throughout life.

The other changes are intimately related to the first breath. The expansion of the lungs straightens the pulmonary capillaries, whose resistance thereupon drops to next to nothing. Blood is thus further diverted from the arterial duct through the lungs and into the back atrium, which, until this moment, has taken a mere trickle from the pulmonary veins. Now the mounting flow from that quarter puts up the pressure in the atrium and makes it more difficult for the flap valve to open. The extra pressure and volume in the atrium stretches it more, and this makes it contract more vigorously. This puts up the filling pressure in the back ventricle and makes it, too, contract more vigorously. This, in turn, puts up the pressure in the aorta until it is higher than that in the pulmonary artery. As a result the flow of blood through the arterial duct actually reverses, flowing now *from* the aorta *to* the pulmonary artery. The nature of this blood is all-important. Until this moment the arterial duct has carried only blood low in oxygen. The blood that now flows through it in reverse, having passed through the lungs, is rich in oxygen. The muscular coat of the duct is, it happens, highly sensitive to oxygen and goes at once into spasm, closing the duct temporarily.

This closure accelerates the tendencies that caused it in the first place. All the output of the front ventricle now goes through the lungs, raising the back atrial pressure still further and making it almost impossible for the flap valve to open. Both these closures are temporary; before they can become permanent new endothelium must grow and form a tight seal. (Endothelium is the one-cell-thick lining of the cardiovascular system.) This does not always happen, especially with the flap valve. Why this sealing does not always happen is a mystery—though anyone familiar with living tissues would put it the other way around: why the endothelium of the flap valve or duct should fuse permanently is the true mystery. All over the body there are large areas where membranes and linings are in contact, yet, while some fuse together, others never do so, not in health anyway. What prompts this difference in behaviour between seemingly identical tissues is unknown.

An unsealed atrial septum is of no great consequence; in fact one person in four has such a failure. There is plenty of overlap in the flap and only a surgical probe can pry the flap away from the septum on which it seats, so for all practical purposes it is as good as sealed. But an unclosed duct is serious; for when the muscular spasm that produced the temporary closure relaxes, the duct becomes patent (open) again and remains so. Some of the aortic pressure (and blood) is now transmitted to the pulmonary arteries. This increases the load on the front ventricle, which develops abnormally strengthened muscle to cope (a condition known as ventricular hypertrophy).

Similar arguments apply to a defect in the ventricular septum (VSD). There are, of course, degrees of severity in both cases. Patency may vary from needlehole size to maximum, which in the adult is an inch diameter for a VSD and less than one-third of that for a patent duct. The needlehole defects are immaterial; you could go through life with one and never know it. At the other extreme they are fatal in the sense that they reduce life expectancy by twenty years or more, and diminish the zest even of the years they do not curtail.

It might be expected that as the front ventricle grew in power it would come into balance with the back ventricle and blood would cease to flow either way. In fact, the raised pressure in the pulmonary artery causes irreversible damage to the lung arterioles; their resistance continues to rise and the front ventricle, fighting to keep pace, grows more powerful than the back ventricle and so pushes venous blood into the arterial system. Since the head arteries leave the aorta before the arterial duct, now leaking deoxygenated blood, joins it, the result is less drastic than it might otherwise be. For the lower parts of the body are more tolerant than the head of poorly oxygenated blood. People with this kind of mixing do not even begin to look blue in the legs and body until venous blood accounts for 30 per cent of the mixture. And this state *may* not occur until late middle age, though with most people it comes in their twenties.

The severest of the common defects at birth is the 'blue baby' defect known as the tetralogy (fourfold defect) of Fallot. The basis of this condition, as I mentioned on page 66, is the failure of the septum growing down the arterial trunk to divide the pulmonary and aortic outflows, to meet the ventricular septum properly. As a result the aorta comes to sit over (or ride, we usually say) both ventricles; the pulmonary artery grows skimpily (giving pulmonary stenosis) or not at all (giving pulmonary atresia). In such a case, both ventricles must pump at equal power since most or all of their output must leave via the overriding aorta. Where there is complete or near complete pulmonary atresia the lung's own systemic arteries are the only means of getting blood to the lungs; and they enlarge accordingly. (There is, of course, no arterial duct since there has been no blood flow along the nonexistent pulmonary arches to form such a duct.) The tetralogy, to sum up, is: 1. Overriding aorta; 2. A VSD, a direct and inevitable consequence of the failure of the septa to meet properly; 3. Front ventricular hypertrophy; 4. Pulmonary stenosis or atresia.

The resulting circulation is even less efficient than that of the most primitive fish, since mixed blood flows throughout the entire system – head and all. The comparison is not intended to suggest that a Fallot baby is some kind of evolutionary throwback; but the precarious hold these babies have on life does indicate the huge evolutionary progress that divides us from that primitive ancestor. The complete separation of arterial and venous blood; the consequent development of a low pressure pulmonary and a high pressure arterial system; the stable and highly responsive internal self-regulation that the separation permits – all this and more is denied the Fallot baby. Only the surgeon can restore it to him.

In chapter 7 we shall look at the surgical techniques involved in righting this and other defects of the heart. Here, by way of conclusion, let me say that even the most experienced surgeon must feel a slight thrill of awe when he first opens the chest of any Fallot child. What confronts him has resulted because in the seventh week of embryonic life a membrane growing and spiralling down a minute blood vessel little thicker than a hair came to rest a fraction of a millimetre from its proper place. Every day of foetal life brings numberless chances of a similar mishap and one might be forgiven for wondering that any child is born normal. But millions of years of evolution has produced incredible feats of biological regulation. When Socrates, close to death, dismissed his own flesh as 'vulnerable rubbish' he could not have been more wildly wrong. Compared with other materials flesh is the most tenacious, self-preserving stuff we know.

4 How the heart works

In the first chapter I said, rather airily, that Harvey's discovery of the true circulation made modern physiology possible. In the long perspective of history this is true; but in the immediate perspective of Harvey's own time it is far from so – in fact, many have argued that his discovery, like the work of Newton, so rivetted men's attention on the physical aspects of nature that chemistry was all but forgotten. Newton himself, remember, devoted a good part of his life to fruitless alchemy. For Harvey the difficulty was acute. His triumph lay in showing beyond all doubt that the heart released the body's total complement of blood once every minute and was thus a pump rather than a generator; his problem was to explain this huge flooding of the tissues.

The answer, which lay in physiology, took over 250 years even to draft; in fact, as we saw in chapter 2, many of its details have yet to be worked out. And the more we learn of them the more we discover that the function of the heart and blood vessels is not merely to fetch food and carry waste, to exchange gases between the tissues and the environment, to ferry glandular messages, to fight off invaders, and so on; vital though these functions are, the heart and vessels have evolved the equally vital capacity to perform all these varied roles with the minimum expenditure of energy. In a word: they optimise.

This word optimise is new to medicine, but the idea behind it has a long history. For instance, as far back as the seventeenth century Robert Boyle, refuting the then common belief that animals breathe in order to cool their blood, threw in the argument that it was against the economy of nature to make heat only to throw it away. Nevertheless, the intense interest we are now beginning to take in 'the economy of nature', or optimisation, is entirely novel.

I have to stress this to the reader right at the outset: as he works through this chapter he will meet a number of graphs that seem alien to the intuitive-descriptive spirit of medical practice. Most of the medicine practised on one when one falls sick is based on generations of elaborate and loving description. Some fields are now so intricately mapped that it takes more than half a researcher's lifetime to master one corner of his chosen speciality – and the rest of his life to make just one or two significant contributions. I cannot believe that much progress lies down these cluttered byways. The important advances are now being made by researchers who are looking at the big picture: taking diverse and poorly related bodies of knowledge and out of them composing the first tentative models of biological action as a whole. In this chapter we are going to work towards a very simplified version of one such tentative model.

Beginning with the nature of heart muscle, I have to admit that the temptation is strong to follow the traditional course: to begin with the microscopic appearance of the muscle (as shown in figure 4·1); move on to the atomic level and describe how long molecules of actin, by climbing up long molecules of myosin, produce the contraction characteristic of muscles; and then on to the subatomic level to show how Ca^{++} ions, flooding through the membrane of the muscles, allow ATP to degrade to ADP, releasing energy which allows the actin and myosin to bind temporarily. It would be easy … and unproductive. Anybody who has ever worked in this way from biology to subatomic physics ends up in the realm of metaphysics, knowing more and more about less and less. Instead we shall treat this muscle as something of a black box. The only details that concern us are those that clarify the big picture.

We can draw certain conclusions from the microscopic anatomy of the muscle. It forms, as can be seen in figure 4·1, a kind of elongated mesh of branching fibres, interrupted here and there by intercalated discs. Opinion about the function of these discs is divided. Some say they aid conduction between fibres, ensuring rapid and near-simultaneous contraction of the entire cardiac

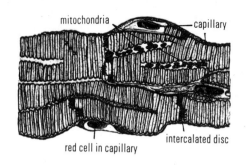

4·1 A 100-micron length of heart-muscle fibre; note the richness of the capillary blood supply and the profusion of mitochondria.

mitochondria

capillary

red cell in capillary

intercalated disc

muscle; others say they offer high resistance to conduction, which prevents the sporadic misfiring of one or two fibres from setting off neighbouring fibres. (That two quite contradictory theories can coexist about the function of a structure which is visible with an ordinary light microscope speaks volumes for the present state of our knowledge of the heart.) What is certain is that, unlike voluntary muscle, the heart has an all-or-nothing response. For example, when a person lifts his arm he can do so at any chosen rate and halt at any point in the movement. The heart cannot possibly contract in such a graded way; when it contracts it does so fully, and then it completely relaxes.

Another difference between the heart and voluntary muscle is the heart's extremely rich blood supply (about one capillary per muscle fibre) and the abundance of mitochondria, the 'power-houses' of living cells. Voluntary muscle, which is used intermittently and usually in short bursts, can metabolise without oxygen. If, for instance, a person runs quickly up one flight of stairs, his muscles will store up unoxidised wastes until the body's slow acting responses (deeper breathing, increased heart rate, extra blood to the working muscle) come into play. He may not feel breathless until ten or fifteen seconds after he has reached the stairhead. In short, voluntary muscle can build up what is called an oxygen debt, most of which is repaid when the slow acting responses bring oxygen to them, the rest being lost through the kidneys or, indeed, being used in the heart itself, which can fully metabolise these halfway products of muscle metabolism. To do so, of course, it needs oxygen; it has no capacity for building up an oxygen debt. Hence the rich capillary network, to bring food, gases, and hormonal stimuli; hence, too, the large numbers of mito-chondria, which quickly oxydise lactate and other products of metabolism, making ATP in the process.

The mesh-like arrangement of cardiac muscle fibres has a kind of counterpart in the heart as a whole. In its embryonic beginnings it was a tube of circular fibres surrounded by longitudinal fibres that ran the length of the tube. The bulging and swelling of this tube at first favoured the longitudinal fibres; but the endless con-traction and relaxation of the developing chambers promoted the growth of a new set of encircling fibres. When one dissects a dead and preserved heart specimen one can (with a bit of goodwill) find evidence that these encircling fibres are arranged in layers each at about 45° to its neighbour. Under the cold white light of surgery, however, such fine details are not even apparent; all that one can see is that the inside of the heart consists mainly of up and down columns of muscle terminating in the papillary muscles, and the outside is composed of a dense belt of encircling fibres, thicker in the more powerful back ventricle than in the front one.

One other feature is common to the microscopic and macro-scopic aspects of the heart; it is also the single most important feature of cardiac muscle. On the microscopic scale it concerns the length of the sarcomere – the basic unit of muscle. The length of the sarcomere defines the degree to which the muscle is stretched, and the degree of stretch is related directly to the power of the subsequent contraction. As figure 4.2 shows, there is an optimum degree of stretch: if the fibre is stretched less or more than this optimum, its power during the subsequent contraction is reduced. The optimum sarcomere length is 2.2 microns (1 micron is a thousandth of a millimetre).

On the macroscopic scale the degree of stretch obviously corre-lates with the filling pressure. As the filling pressure increases, the prestretching of the fibre will also increase. The optimum sarcomere

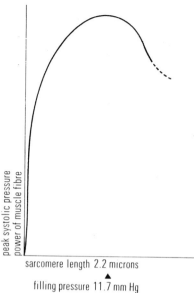

4·2 The graph relates the microscopic properties of heart muscle (the length to which the sarcomere is prestretched before contraction and the subsequent power of the muscle) to the macroscopic properties of the whole heart (filling pressure and peak systolic – or output – pressure). As can be seen, the optimum prestretch to 2·2 microns corresponds to a filling pressure of 11·7 mm of mercury. The curve demonstrates Starling's Law.

sarcomere length 2.2 microns

filling pressure 11.7 mm Hg

length of 2·2 microns corresponds, as one would expect, to the normal ventricular filling pressure of 11·7 mm Hg. Sarcomere length, filling pressure, and ventricular volume at the end of diastole (filling) are all related; so is the power of the muscle and the pressure it exerts at the peak of systole (emptying). All these terms are included in the graph. The version that relates pressure to volume is named Starling's curve (or law) after the great cardiac physiologist Ernest Starling who discovered the relationship in 1914.

Three broadly interdependent quantities govern the activity of the heart. Two we have already met: stroke volume and systolic pressure. The third is a measure of the state of the muscle – specifically its contractility.

We can divide a ventricle's contraction into two phases: the phase before the valve (pulmonary or aortic) opens, and the phase after it does so. Take the back ventricle. The minimum pressure in the aorta is normally 80 mm Hg. The filling pressure of the ventricle is, as we have just seen, 11·7 mm Hg. Since liquids are incompressible one would think that the volume of the ventricle cannot change until the internal pressure of the ventricle reaches 80 mm Hg. This is true only in the sense that the total blood volume in the ventricle does not change; but since it is impossible for a muscle to exert a force without altering its length, something has to give. In the first place the interventricular septum, together with the muscle bands that run around the top of the ventricles and end up in the papillary muscles, contracts before the rest of the heart. In response to this contraction the leaflets of the mitral valve belly upward like a double vaulted ceiling into the recently emptied atrium. And since the muscle at the bottom of the heart is still in its resting phase, there must be a slight increase in tension down there, too. The effect is shown in figure 4·3. So, by changing shape and redistributing blood the heart is able to contract without changing its total volume.

As soon as pressure reaches 80 mm Hg the valve opens, the blood flows upward, and most of the work of the heart-beat is done. The outflow causes a rise in aortic pressure which normally peaks at 120 mm Hg. Between these two pressure levels the muscle is completely free to contract; the velocity at which it does so (its contractility) is clearly an important parameter.

The problem is that the velocity varies both with the initial stretch and with the aortic pressure. Ideally we would like to know the maximal velocity (V_{max}), that is, the velocity at which the muscle would contract if it was optimally prestretched and had no aortic pressure to overcome. Experiments with isolated papillary muscle have helped to provide an answer, which is summed up in the three graphs in figure 4·4. Without going into the experimental details it turns out that V_{max} is fairly steady over the normal range of prestretch (equivalent, remember, to the stroke volume in the intact heart). As zero prestretch is approached, V_{max}, too, quickly approaches zero. The right-hand graph shows how *actual* contraction velocity falls off with increasing aortic pressure. One can see

4·3 The sequence of contraction in the back ventricle is shown in simplified form from immediate presystole (*left*) to end-systole (*right*). The grey arrows show the direction of the electrical impulse that triggers contraction. The red arrows show the direction of movement of the parts. Basically the contraction of the septum and papillary muscles provides temporary rigidity against which the subsequent contraction of the remaining muscle can 'bite'.

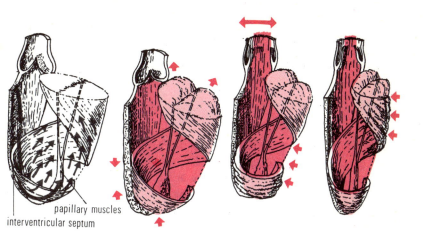

papillary muscles

interventricular septum

4·4 These three graphs relate three parameters of the heart's activity: aortic pressure (the load against which the heart must work); stroke volume (the quantity of blood it must pump); and muscle contractility (V_{max} —see p. 94). The seeming oddity of the points of origin in these graphs is explained in figure 4·5a.

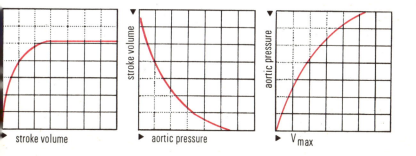

stroke volume

stroke volume

aortic pressure

aortic pressure

V_{max}

4·5a Opposite left The 'action space' of the heart is defined by a three-dimensional combination of the preceding figures. Subsequent figures show the changes in this space under various conditions.
4·5b Opposite right The events of a single heartbeat are related to the 'action space' and are discussed fully below. Power is represented by the shaded area on the vertical plane; work by the shaded area on the horizontal plane.

that only a slight aortic pressure is enough to drop V_{max} quite a bit from its ideal peak; at higher pressure the drop is less drastic. The centre graph relates the stretched length of the fibre to the tension it develops during contraction; looked at another way this also relates ventricular volume to contraction pressure.

The heart's 'action space'

Putting these three graphs together in 3D form, as in figure 4·5a, we now define the space, as it were, within which the heart acts. Choosing these parameters has the advantage that we can use the graph to compare input (or power exerted) with output (or work done). Taking the case of a single heart-beat, as in figure 4·5b, the ventricle has filled at 11·7 mm Hg, prestretching the fibres to their optimum length. The aortic valve is shut, so that in the first milliseconds of systole, there is no aortic pressure to overcome, and the fibres contract at V_{max} (AB). As internal pressure rises to 80 mm Hg. contractile velocity tails off (BC). At that pressure the aortic valve opens and the blood flows out; the fibres contract further, pressure rises to a peak, and the volume of the ventricle begins to drop (CD). The blood continues to flow, the fibres to contract, but the pressure now falls from its peak, until at some intermediate point the valve shuts (DE). The fibres relax until ventricular filling prestretches them again (broken line EFA). Of the two shaded areas the vertical represents power, the horizontal work. (Specialist readers will at once see an objection here, since strictly speaking, changes in volume, dv/dt – the true measure – are not quite colinear with changes in fibre length, or dL/dt, which is the measure I have chosen. However, for the points I am about to make the departure from linearity is small enough to ignore.)

Complicated though it appears, this graph is but the crudest representation of a very subtle phenomenon. For instance, it takes

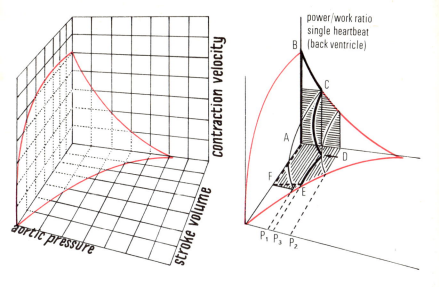

no account of the fact that the contraction is sequential, so that some fibres contract when ventricular pressure is low, others while it is high. Nevertheless, the graph *is* capable of illustrating all the more obvious facts of cardiac behaviour with a fair degree of accuracy, as figures 4·6a to e demonstrate.

The first of this series illustrates the power/work ratios of the two ventricles. The front ventricle is 20 ml larger than the back one, yet, obviously, their output during equilibrium is the same. The front ventricle thus has unused or potential stroke volume. As the graph shows, during equilibrium it does only about one-fifth as much work, and exerts only one-fifth of the power, of the back ventricle. But with exertion the muscles compress the veins (which hold 80 per cent of the blood) and so increase the venous return to the heart. That extra 20 ml now comes into play and, following Starling's law, the output goes up. One heart-beat later this extra output has traversed the lungs and reached the back ventricle, whose output, obeying the same law, also rises. This automatic response to exertion occurs even in hearts that are completely cut off from their nerve supply (a fact of obvious importance to transplantees, whose hearts are to start with completely denervated).

98

4·6a–e Figures 4·6a (*opposite*),
b (*below left*), c (*below right*),
and d and e (*overleaf*) compare the heart's
dynamics in different circumstances.
All are fully discussed on pages 97–8.

In figures 4·6b and 4·6c are contrasted two ways of increasing
the heart's output: by increasing stroke rate, and by increasing
stroke volume. Increased rate is the characteristic response of the
sedentary majority of western man. Heavy manual workers and
athletes, by repeated exertion, cause an adaptive response whereby
their stroke volume increases. As the figures show, the result is far
more efficient.

Figure 4·6d shows the baleful effects of raised aortic pressure:
when for instance, an artery hardens or becomes furred up, or
when arteriolar resistance rises. The ventricle exerts more power,
does slightly more work, but the stroke volume is actually reduced.
Hearts subjected to this kind of load show the response characteristic of athletic training, and the reduced heart rate plus increased
stroke volume helps to improve efficiency. But if the pressure
goes on rising, the new muscle created to cope with it eventually
outstrips the fixed amount of blood capable of passing through
the coronaries; so the adaptation is self-limiting and finally self-
destructive.

Figure 4·6e illustrates the effect of an increase in muscle contractility. Compounds like adrenalin promote such an increase;
and since the sympathetic nerves (see page 104) work by releasing
adrenalin and similar chemicals, stimulation of the sympathetic
nerves has the same effect. The result, as can be seen, is an increase
in the total operational 'space' but with a relatively larger rise on
the power side than on the work/volume side. Since this change
buys greater output at the expense of efficiency it is biologically
acceptable only as a short-term response. The long-term response
of the heart to sustained extra demand is always to increase stroke
volume, so that optimum prestretch and contractility are restored.

Because I have isolated five states in the above series of graphs
it must not be assumed that they are similarly isolated in the real
world. In fact, during a normally active day one's heart probably

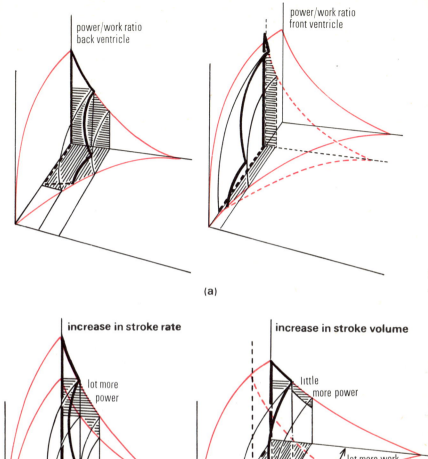

(a)

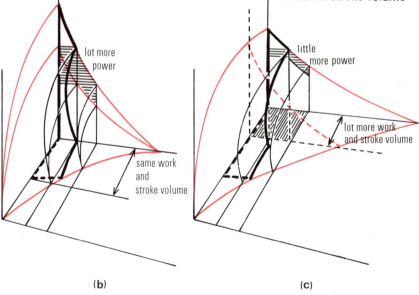

(b)   **(c)**

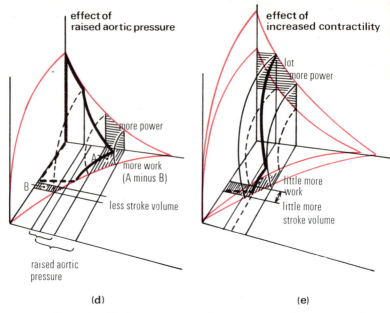

effect of raised aortic pressure

more power

A

more work
(A minus B)

B

less stroke volume

raised aortic
pressure

(d)

effect of increased contractility

lot more power

little more work

little more stroke volume

(e)

passes through all these states and many more in an unending
adaptive sequence. But if these graphs have at least focused the
reader's attention on the general constraints under which the heart
acts, they will have served their purpose.

Constraints are one thing, mechanism is another. It is now time
to look at what triggers the heart-beat with such clocklike regular-
ity, and what accelerates and decelerates it. Even the earliest
embryonic heart has regular peristaltic contractions – showing that
heart muscle has the innate ability to make spontaneous contractions independent of nerve stimuli. In the embryo these contractions start in the atrium and pass forward over the ventricle. The
atrial end continues to dominate in this way throughout life; but
when the two chambers, atrium and ventricle, divide to form four,
the tissues between the two atria and the two ventricles become
fibrous and nonconductive, in this way forming the 'skeleton' of
the heart. As a result the electrical impulses that arise in the atrium
are barred from influencing the ventricle – or rather would be
barred were it not for one small gap in the skeleton that contains
conductive tissue: the atrioventricular (AV) node and bundle in the

front atrium. The bundle, which is in fact modified muscle, called the bundle of His, runs down the ventricular septum, where it soon branches into a front and back bundle, each serving its respective ventricle. Each bundle divides repeatedly, pushing finer and finer threads amongst every part of the muscle. The first parts to be served are the septal wall and papillary muscles, then the apex, and finally the remainder of the ventricles from the apex upwards. This explains why the heart contracts sequentially in the way I described earlier in this chapter (p. 94).

The AV node is not merely an impulse-collecting junction. The conducting fibres that link it to the atrial muscle have a much smaller diameter than the fibres of the node itself; as a result they conduct the impulse much more slowly (0·05 m/sec) than do the AV fibres (1·0 m/sec). This delay means that the atria contract between 0·12 and 0·2 second ahead of the ventricles, allowing them to complete their topping-up before the ventricles begin to contract. Conduction along these very narrow fibres is decremental; that is, the impulse tends to peter out, and the weaker it is, the less chance it has of getting through. This protects the system from any weak random impulses which may arise spontaneously in the atrial muscle.

The pacemaker itself is the sinoatrial (SA) node. It is a pale, narrow area, 3 or 4 mm wide and 20 to 25 mm long, high on the front atrium at its junction with the superior vena cava. To grasp the peculiarities of the cells in the SA node, the electrochemical basis of all nerve and muscle cells must first be understood. Like all living cells in the body they operate a sodium-potassium pump; that is, they actively pump sodium ions out of the cell and potassium ions into the cell until the inside is electronegative compared with the outside; the actual voltage is about -90 mv (thousandths of a volt) for muscle and about -70 mv for nerve, and between -60 and -100 mv for other cells. This negative gradient, or polarisation, counteracts the osmotic attraction of the cell contents for the water outside the cell membrane. It prevents the water from invading the cell, diluting its constituents, and rupturing the membrane. Nerves and muscle cells have the ability to reverse this gradient for very brief periods – minute fractions of a second; during this time the gradient can reverse and reach as high as $+30$ mv on the inside of the membrane. The process is known as depolarisation. According to one widely held hypothesis, small pores in the membrane open very briefly and allow ions to flood into and out of a cell, destroying or even reversing the gradient.

In a nerve fibre this depolarisation begins at one end and travels along at rates between 0·5 and 300 m/sec to the other. The passage of this depolarisation wave *is* the nerve impulse (see figure 4·7). When it arrives at a muscle fibre it brings about changes in the membrane (or sarcolemma) which make it temporarily permeable to ions. Again, we assume that some kind of pore-opening mechanism operates. The sudden change in internal ionic composition allows ATP to change rapidly into ADP; in other words it creates a rapid release of energy, which the muscle consumes in contraction.

A model of excitation and inhibition

In 1964 Sir John Eccles, whose lifelong study of nerve physiology had been honoured with a Nobel laureate the previous year, put forward a hypothesis to explain how nerves excite and inhibit one another. Since nerve to nerve and nerve to muscle effects are similar (both involve the selective passage of ions through a polarised membrane with consequent depolarisation), a generalised form of the Eccles hypothesis can serve as a simplified model of *all* forms of excitation and inhibition (see figure 4·8).

It assumes that the receptor membrane, whether of muscle or nerve, is riddled with pores near the terminal part of the incoming

4·7 The passage of a nerve impulse. In its resting state a nerve membrane (grey) has many more sodium (Na$^+$) ions outside than it has potassium (K$^+$) ions inside. The result is a positive polarity outside, negative inside. Stimulus at the input end of the nerve makes the membrane briefly permeable to ions, which flow in and out as shown. Pumping mechanisms in the membrane soon restore the status quo, but until they do so no further impulse can travel. This nonconducting phase is known as a refractory period.

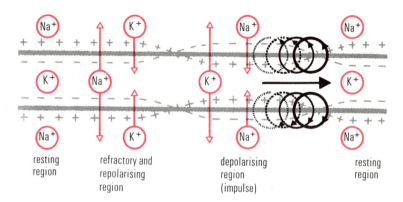

resting
region

refractory and
repolarising
region

depolarising
region
(impulse)

resting
region

nerve (called the end plate in a nerve to muscle junction and the synapse in a nerve to nerve junction). In the resting state the pores are plugged. The end plate or synapse liberates a transmitter substance that lodges in a site near the pore and combines with the plugging molecule in such a way that the plug hinges upward, opening the pore. Ions then flood through the opening. In an excitatory junction the flow constitutes depolarisation, which causes a muscle fibre to twitch or a nerve to fire; in an inhibitory junction different ions flow, keeping the membrane electronegative inside and thus preventing depolarisation. The pores achieve this selection of ions partly by their size and partly by the electrical charge on their walls. Enzymes near the receptor site rapidly destroy the transmitter substance, so that the pore closes again. At some junctions the whole sequence, from the release of the transmitter through depolarisation to repolarisation, can be completed in as little as two milliseconds.

In figure 4·8 the story involving the transmitter substance is greatly simplified. The substance liberated by the incoming nerve may be acetylcholine, adrenalin, or noradrenalin, or it may be

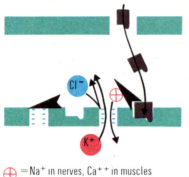

α receptor or excitatory synapse

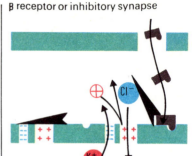

β receptor or inhibitory synapse

⊕ = Na⁺ in nerves, Ca⁺⁺ in muscles

some precursor of these substances. Indeed, there may be a whole chain of reactions, each aided by an enzyme, and each differing at differing types of nerve ending. We know for certain that drugs which 'block' a receptor site (i.e. fill it without unplugging the pore) in an excitatory, or alpha, junction have no effect on an inhibitory, or beta, junction. Moreover, drugs that block, say, an excitatory junction at one level in the nervous system (the nerve-muscle junctions, for instance) have little or no effect at higher levels (nerve-nerve junctions in the spinal cord, for example). There are even differences between neighbouring ganglia in the spinal cord, where substances that will block one ganglion will leave its neighbour open to traffic. Such differences are an obvious security measure – much as a large office building has a different key for each office door.

The end product of all this activity is an all-or-nothing response: the fibre, nerve or muscle, either depolarises or it is prevented from doing so. Throughout the body individual nerve fibres are firing like this all the time, and individual muscle cells are responding by twitching. These haphazard firings and twitchings are far below the level that results in organised movement; they constitute what is known as nerve and muscle tone. It is only when thousands of nerve fibres fire in an organised concert, and thousands of muscle fibres respond simultaneously, that organised movement results.

The peculiarities of cardiac muscle and of the nervelike fibres of

4·8 Possible mechanisms of excitation and inhibitions in nerve to nerve and nerve to muscle junctions. The excitatory junction has a single large pore with negatively charged sides. In its resting state the pore is blocked (black shape). The arrival of an impulse at the end membrane of the incoming nerve (upper green bar) releases a transmitter substance (which may be acetylcholine, adrenalin, noradrenalin, or related compounds – they vary with the site), shown here as a brown shape. This substance combines with the receptor membrane and the block in such a way that the site is opened, allowing positive ions to pass; the negative charge repels negative ions like chloride (Cl^-). The inhibitory junction has a two-pore site. The small pore, being less than $2·9 \times 10·8$ cm in diameter, allows only K^+ ions to pass; the larger Na^+ and Ca^{++} ions are blocked. The large pore, being positively charged, allows only negative ions to pass. This exchange preserves a negative polarity within the nerve or muscle membrane, whose pumping mechanisms must restore the status quo before excitation can occur. Enzymes in the membrane rapidly degrade the transmitter substance; so the opening of the pore is as brief as one millisecond.

the SA node show in the way they de- and repolarise. Figure 4·9 contrasts their pattern of de- and repolarisation with that of typical voluntary muscle and its attendant nerve. Broadly speaking, with voluntary muscle and its nerve the whole thing is over in a flash; they de- and repolarise within 2 milliseconds and are ready to repeat the cycle. Thus a voluntary muscle fibre can contract and relax a couple of hundred times a second. With heart muscle the depolarisation (marked 0 in the figure) is just as rapid, but the repolarisation phase (1) is interrupted by a long refractory period (2–3). In the phase marked 2 no stimulus, however great, can cause a further contraction, but this high threshold drops during 3 until at the end, where 4 begins, it is at the normal resting potential. This is the relative refractory phase – also known as the vulnerable phase because a stimulus during this period can send the entire cardiac muscle into the random and disorganised form of contraction known as fibrillation. This long refractory period means that the heart cannot develop tetany (the rigidity due to repeated and ultra-rapid contraction of voluntary muscle).

The graph of the SA node fibre's depolarisation makes it clear that, in health anyway, such a mistimed stimulus cannot arise from the natural pacemaker, since both it and the muscle reach phase 4 at about the same time. In this phase, however, while the muscle remains at its resting potential of -93 mv, the nodal fibre immediately and spontaneously begins to depolarise, slowly at first, until it gets up to about -40 mv, then rapidly. This rapid depolarisation triggers off another cardiac beat. Until recently the impulse from the SA node was thought to travel generally through the atrial muscle, where it was picked up by the AV node and passed on to the ventricles. However, there is some evidence of a direct connection between the two nodes, for it is possible chemically to inhibit all the atrial muscle from contracting and still get an impulse at the AV node; such evidence is not conclusive, for no special anatomical connection between the nodes has, as far as I know, yet been discovered.

The time base for these events varies from just under 0·3 sec at extremes of emotion or exertion to just over a second during sleep. The spontaneous rhythm of the SA node fibre is around 0·5 sec. In other words, left to itself, the heart would race at about 120 beats a minute. Since its resting rate is only 70/min, the SA node must be under the continual influence of an inhibitor.

The inhibitor is the vagus nerve, which arises near the base of the brain and controls many of the automatic functions of the chest and gut regions. It is generally opposed by a network of nerves that arise from paired ganglia down the spinal cord – the sympathetic nerves. The arrangement for the heart is illustrated in figure 4·10.

Nerves can inhibit or excite other nerves as well as muscle, and the vagus has connections to the sympathetic system which allow it to inhibit sympathetic activity. Between 70 and 120 beats a minute the vagus controls the situation; at 120 the activity of the sympathetic nerves exactly counters the basic tone of the vagus, and the SA node is free to run autonomously; above 120/min the sympathetic nerves are actively exciting the heart's muscle fibres and its whole conducting network in such a way that the refractory period is shortened and the contractility and conductivity is enhanced.

4·9 The peculiar behaviour of an SA node fibre (upper trace) is compared with
the characteristic de- and repolarisation of nerve to voluntary muscle (red,
bottommost trace), which is completed in less than 2 milliseconds. By contrast,
an SA node fibre takes about 150 milliseconds to repolarise and, moreover,
spontaneously begins to depolarise – slowly at first, until it reaches −40 mV,
then almost instantaneously. The 'dot-dash' trace shows the depressor effect of
the vagus nerve, which slows down the slow phase of spontaneous depolarisation. This produces the resting heartbeat of 70 per minute. The red trace shows
the stimulatory effect of sympathetic nerves, which lower the threshold for the
rapid phase of spontaneous depolarisation (broken line). The rate shown here
is 220/minute, close to normal maximum for the heart. The rate for the black
trace is 120/minute, which is normal for a denervated heart. The middle trace
shows the corresponding potentials for a heart muscle fibre (see page 105).

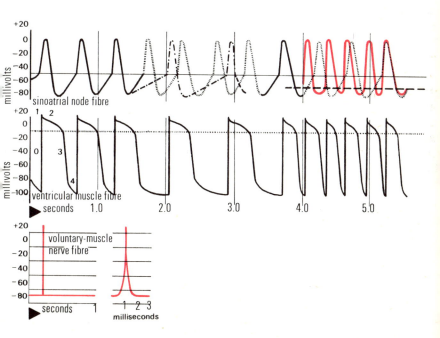

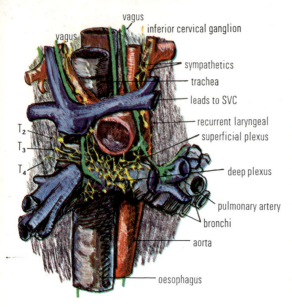

vagus

vagus

inferior cervical ganglion

sympathetics

trachea

leads to SVC

recurrent laryngeal

superficial plexus

T_2

T_3

T_4

deep plexus

pulmonary artery

bronchi

aorta

oesophagus

4·10 The cardiac nerve connections are shown (*left*), in part, in something like their true anatomical complexity (the heart has been cut away) and, in full, schematically (*below*), where sympathetics are in blue and parasympathetics in grey. The pathways shown are efferents (i.e. they carry impulses from the nerve system to the heart). Afferents, which carry impulses from the heart, use some of these channels.

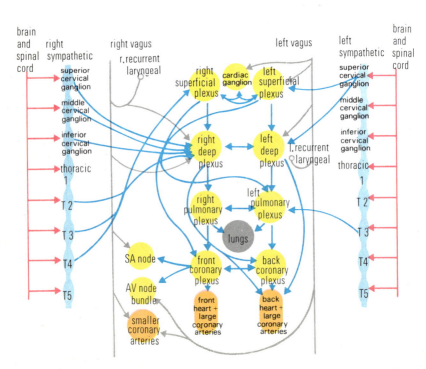

Not surprisingly, then, the cardiac branches of the vagus run mainly to the two nodes: the right vagus mostly to the SA node, the left mostly to the AV node (though there is a considerable overlap). The sympathetic nerves, as one would expect, affect every part of the heart, stimulating the nodes, the conducting tissues, and the muscle fibres. Again there is a difference between the right and left parts of the system: the right sympathetics have the effect of increasing the heart rate, the left ones tend more to increase the contractility of the fibres.

The delicate interplay of this accelerator/brake system compensates for the lack of graded response in the heart muscle, so that although the muscle contracts on an all-or-nothing basis, the autonomic nerve system (sympathetic and parasympathetic combined) makes it do so with varying force and frequency.

The heart's self-control

Figure 4·11 shows the system in outline. The heavy black lines denote control paths in the classical sense of 'orders from above'. The red lines denote feedback paths of the kind that we are learning to interpret as the real controllers of the system. Through these pathways the various parts of the system monitor its total activity and adjust themselves accordingly. The reader will observe that it is an essentially self-regulating system: a heart, above which stands a hierarchy of two further self-regulating systems, the autonomic and central nerves. To complete the picture, all the feedback loops of these three systems are united. In the higher centres of the brain some of the loops are actually feedforward rather than feedback; that is, they modify the system in anticipation of demands it is about to face. The sudden rise in rate, pressure, and output that accompanies fright but that precedes the actual demands of flight or fight is an example. Stage fright, which makes the actor and interviewee more alert and the athlete more athletic, is another.

If one thinks back to the three parameters that determine efficiency – contractility, stroke volume, and pressure – one will see that the system includes ways of monitoring all three. Contractility is determined directly by the sympathetic nerves. Volume is equivalent to prestretch, which is monitored by sympathetic stretch receptors. And pressure is monitored directly.

Like all good adaptive systems this one has short-, medium-, and long-term arrangements. No diagram can reveal them since they operate through common pathways. The short-term arrangements cope with instantaneous fluctuations in demand or in such external factors as temperature and oxygen depletion at altitude. The medium-term arrangements cover changes during sleep, illness, or prolonged exertion of a moderate kind: for instance, they help a distance runner to get his second wind. The long-term arrangements cause adaptive changes to chronic demands; athletic training, prolonged illness, and defects within the system itself.

For most of man's early history as a species these long-term adaptations were beneficial. Today they are not always so. Consider what happens when the blood pressure rises – a common condition due to general constriction of the arterioles. The pressure receptors in the carotid and aortic arteries command the vagus to step up its depressor activity. If, as a result, the cardiac output falls, the deficiency will soon show in an accumulation of wastes and CO_2 in the bloodstream. Sensing these, the system will raise output regardless of the effect on pressure. Over the weeks the pressure and chemical receptors will fight it out. The system is so designed that the pressure receptors will fatigue first and will reset themselves to a new zero at the elevated pressure. Very helpful to a wild animal. But what happens when the doctor gives drugs or performs surgery to restore the pressure to its original level? The pressure receptors now fight hard to preserve their new zero line!

An enormous amount of research remains to be done on the

4·11 The control system of the heart abstracted into block-diagram form. All the pathways shown belong to the sympathetic and parasympathetic nervous system, the two most important parts of which — the vagus and spinal respectively — are singled out in the centre block. Factors external to this system are listed on the right. A + sign identifies those that stimulate cardiac activity; a − sign those that depress it.

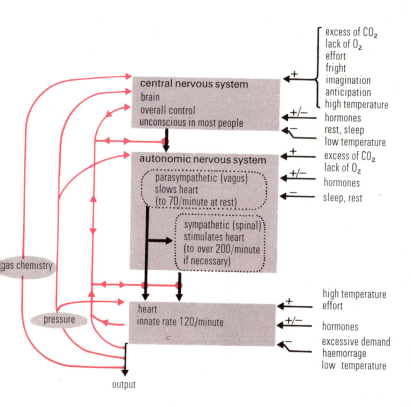

excess of CO_2
lack of O_2
effort
fright
imagination
anticipation
high temperature

central nervous system
brain
overall control
unconscious in most people

+
+/− hormones
− rest, sleep
low temperature

autonomic nervous system

parasympathetic (vagus)
slows heart
(to 70/minute at rest)

sympathetic (spinal)
stimulates heart
(to over 200/minute
if necessary)

+ excess of CO_2
lack of O_2
+/− hormones
− sleep, rest

gas chemistry

pressure

heart
innate rate 120/minute

high temperature
+ effort
+/− hormones
− excessive demand
haemorrage
low temperature

output

mechanics of this system. The physiological effort is already well deployed but it needs the support of mathematical and statistical insight. In the relatively simpler field of respiration, statistical techniques have already revealed a few surprises. By sampling the depth and rate of breathing in different situations and then applying statistical techniques to smooth out transitory effects, Dr Ian Priban

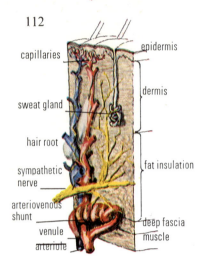

capillaries

epidermis

dermis

sweat gland

hair root

sympathetic
nerve

fat insulation

arteriovenous
shunt

venule

arteriole

deep fascia

muscle

4·12 The outer millimetre of the human skin, partly schematised to show the blood (red and blue) and the sympathetic nerve supply (yellow). Sympathetics consist entirely of constrictor pathways (except in blush-prone areas). They can constrict either the vessels and precapillary sphincters (thus forcing blood through the shunt), or the shunt (thus forcing blood through the capillaries), or both (stage 2 of the strategic shutdown — see figure 4·15a). Active sweat glands liberate substances that dilate vessels when the body is hot. The fat layer insulates the blood in shunt.

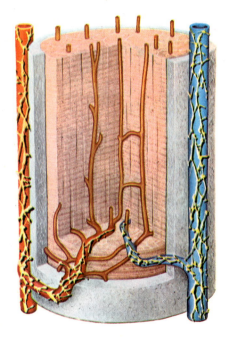

4·13 A small section of voluntary muscle fibre (about 1/25 millimetre in length and breadth), with attendant venule (blue), arteriole (red), capillaries (orange), and sympathetic nerves (yellow), illustrated semidiagrammatically. Each cubic millimetre of muscle contains about 6 metres of capillary (compared with about 11 metres for the heart). The sympathetics can both dilate and constrict the vessels, which can also be controlled by local reflexes in response to the buildup of metabolic waste products.

and co-workers at London's National Physical Laboratory have revealed several innate periodicities that underlie breathing. These rhythms, they postulate, correspond to the delay times built into the controlling mechanisms. The shorter-term ones are dominant during exercise, when the body needs to be alert to sudden change; the longer-term ones are dominant during sleep, when sudden change is less likely. They have also shown that the effect of these controls is to optimise the balance between blood CO_2, blood pH, and the rate at which the lungs exchange CO_2 for O_2. This exchange rate is determined by the rate and depth of breathing. The point is that among the wide choice of rate/depth combinations the system selects the one in which efficiency is greatest. It performs this selection most rapidly when the body is active, least rapidly when the body is inert. And therein lies the supreme subtlety of the control system: all monitoring and control devices consume energy; if the energy to be conserved is small (as it would be in a minor change during sleep) and if a rapidly responding device would consume a high proportion of that energy, then such a device is abandoned in favour of a nominally less effective device that consumes a smaller proportion of whatever it may conserve.

If a relatively simple activity like breathing has evolved such a richness of alternative and interacting control circuits, think, then, of the complexities we have yet to discover around the heart. In Priban's field, physiologists could have worked for decades before they found even a trace of the evidence that his statistical techniques revealed at once. Cardiac research greatly needs the benefit of this sort of approach.

A blueprint, or basis, for such research is offered in figure 4·14. It is, in fact, a more detailed version of the block diagram we have already looked at (figure 4·11), so I shall comment only on certain of its features:

1. What figure 4·11 simply labelled 'hormones' is here spelled

out at length. The adrenal medulla (a gland which lies immediately above the kidneys) secretes adrenalin and noradrenalin into the bloodstream. The sympathetic nerves, as we have already seen, liberate the same two hormones at their endplates or synapses, so that the appearance of these hormones in the bloodstream reinforces the activity of the sympathetic system, stimulating the heart, reducing the circulation to the skin and dilating that to the muscles. The hormones from the adrenal cortex (the outer part of the same gland) are steroids like cortisol; their general effect is to increase output, though whether by acting on the sympathetic nerves, or the heart, or the thyroid gland, is not clear. The thyroid hormone, thyroxin, stimulates the sympathetic nerves and diminishes skin vessel resistance.

2. The sympathetic nerves have direct connection with the microvessels of the muscles and skin. They shut down the circulation to the skin and open up that to the muscles – an obvious preparation for flight or fright. The same nerves can also constrict the veins, reducing their volume. Since the veins hold 80 per cent of the circulating blood, a 5 per cent reduction in their volume is equivalent to raising the blood volume by fully 4 per cent, or about 210 ml – a fair sized transfusion.

3. The kidney has its own defence. When arterial pressure falls the kidney secretes renin, which activates a substance in the bloodstream known as angiotensin. This constricts both muscular and skin microvessels, thereby shunting more blood through the kidney.

4. None of these general constrictors operates on the vessels of the brain or of the heart itself; they have their own specialised arrangements.

From these last three points we can generalise a sort of overall strategy for the management of the circulation (figure 4·15). When demand rises above what the heart can supply, the strategy is to cut down successively on the various circulations shown: first the skin and gut; then the muscles; then, in deep crisis, the kidney, followed by the brain; and terminally the heart-lung circuit itself.

Let us round off this account by looking briefly at the two special circulations which have figured so prominently in both the previous figures: muscle and skin.

The skin circuit is shown in figure 4·12. It consists of an arteriole and a venule. Above the fat layer they are joined by capillaries; below it by a shunt. Control of these vessels is via the sympathetic nerves, which can constrict either the arteriole, or the shunt, or both together. The chief regular influence on the system is local temperature. Cold, acting directly on the skin and via temperature receptors in the brain, will constrict the arterioles but not the shunt, thus keeping the blood below the insulating layer of the fat. The skin is now starved of nutrients, but since it is also cold its metabolism is much slower, so the starvation is not as serious as it would be in an internal tissue. However, this effect will diminish with time; outdoor workers, adapted to cold, will show cheerful ruddy skin compared with indoor workers, who have to exercise hard before they begin to glow.

Heat causes the shunt to constrict. There is no dilator nerve to the skin (except in the parts where one blushes), but the sweat glands produce a substance called bradykinin, which causes the arterioles to dilate – creating the flush of the sweating man. When the blood is needed elsewhere (shut down 2 of the strategic management) the sympathetic system constricts both the arteriole and the shunt, creating a resistance that drives the blood elsewhere.

The muscle circuit (figure 4·13), is easier to comprehend. The site of action is the sphincter muscle which stands between each arteriole and the capillaries it feeds. Both constrictor and dilator sympathetic nerves reach these sphincters, unlike the skin arterioles, which have only constrictors. Local metabolism also influences

4·14 This block diagram, an elaboration of figure 4·11, identifies the principal channels and reflexes in the heart's control system. Only the less obvious features are discussed in the text (p. 114). The + and − signs relate to an increase in the originating 'box'. Thus increased peripheral resistance has two effects: increased arterial pressure and diminished venous return.

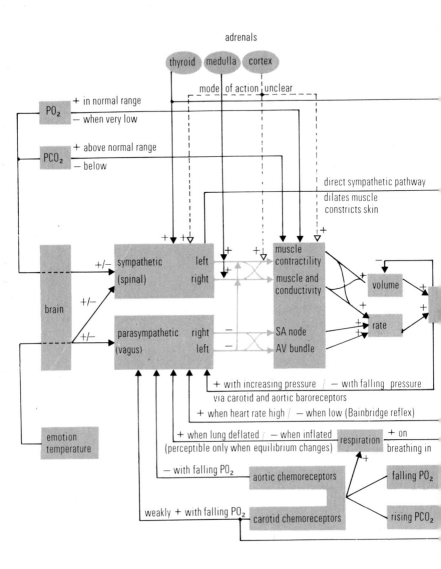

In each case the converse is also true. Thus at any given level of (normal)
activity, the entire system is self-stabilising ; and so rich are the
interconnections that this stability persists even when damage or disease
has reduced the effectiveness of many of the pathways. The glands (thyroid
and adrenals) are under the overall control of the nervous system.

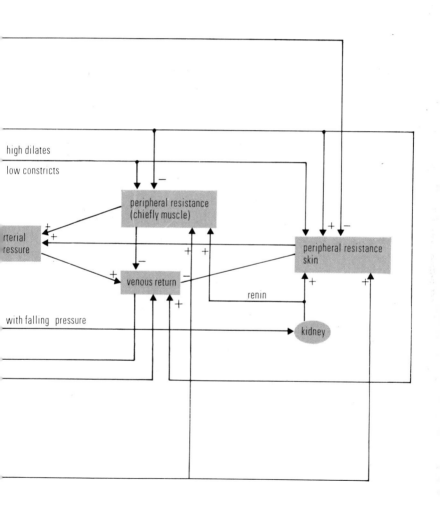

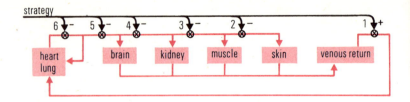

strategy

6 − 5 − 4 − 3 − 2 − 1 +

heart lung   brain   kidney   muscle   skin   venous return

4·15a The figure above outlines the strategy for restoring equilibrium when the blood is inadequate to meet demand – in haemorrhage, for instance, or during shock. The first action, when the inadequacy is mild, is to constrict the major veins, which hold 80 per cent of the circulating blood (the subject has a sinking feeling in his stomach). If this fails, the strategy is to shut down successively on the circulations to the skin (the subject blanches), muscle (the subject feels weak), kidney, brain (the subject passes out), and terminally the heart-lung itself (the subject dies). The graph (*opposite*) shows a different strategy in a nonpathological situation: the transition from rest (A) through moderate (B) and hard (C) to maximal (D) exertion. The situation being temporary, circulations that would otherwise be protected, like the kidney's, can be reduced without harm. To dissipate heat, the skin circulation rises almost fourfold during hard exertion ; but for the supreme effort (by its nature brief) this, too, can be cut. The brain circulation is unaffected by any of these changes – a fact that comes out clearly in the second graph (*far right*), which shows the same quantities as percentages of the consumption at rest. Even clearer is the fact that the heart's own rise in consumption exactly matches the total rise. Both features underline the supremely 'tailor-made' nature of the heart's controls, as well as their speed and efficiency.

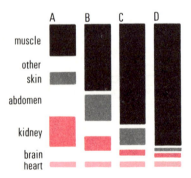

A   B   C   D

muscle

other
skin

abdomen

kidney

brain
heart

4·15b The histogram (*left*) shows the proportion of total output consumed by tissues at each stage. When read in conjunction with the other graphs it shows vividly where the squeeze comes when blood is temporarily needed elsewhere.

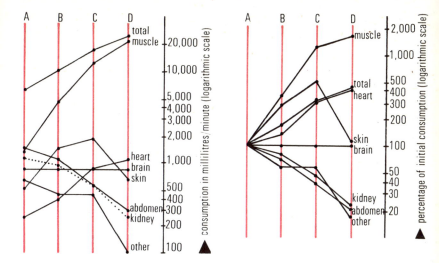

these sphincters, opening them up if wastes are beginning to accumulate in the nearby muscle. (This particular effect, I should add, is not confined to muscle but is common to many arterioles throughout the body). The very fact that a muscle is being exercised also aids local circulation, for exercise squeezes the venules and veins, expelling blood from them towards the heart.

The control systems and mechanisms that I have outlined in this chapter are, we can be sure, only the most obvious ones. To a modern biologist their existence is evidence that far subtler systems have yet to be discovered. Some are tied to the circadian (24-hour) 'clocks' we all carry within us; others are deeply entwined with our neurotic and psychic conditions; yet others are governed by those elusive systems that regulate all tissue growth, maintenance and repair throughout the body. To unravel these systems we must lift our sights far beyond the confined range of the cardiovascular circuit, to the vast and richly complex information network that we call 'life'.

It is a task to daunt the stoutest-hearted researcher for it will require the coordinated effort of every bioscientist whose work in any way impinges on this field. Yet the most rewarding consequences lie along that path of discovery – as the next three chapters reveal.

In them we are going to look at how the cardiovascular system can go wrong; how we can measure the damage; and what we can do about it. It is no great catalogue of wonders but the story of our bewildered and ignorant incursion into an area whose complexities we can only just glimpse.

A century from now – perhaps less if we can organise better – all the material in this book, and especially that of the next three chapters, will be classifiable as a summary of barbarian and primitive bioscience. To repeat this qualification in every chapter would soon become tedious; but I hope the reader will remember it and apply it to every 'achievement' recorded in these pages. The day in which books choked with optimism about 'miracles of modern medicine' could appear has long vanished.

5 The heart's vulnerability

Diseases of the heart and blood vessels are the biggest single killers in the developed world. Recent figures for Britain and the United States (see figure 5·1) make the comparison: cardiovascular disease kills more people than cancer, accidents, pneumonia, influenza, and diabetes combined. It used to be commonplace to shrug off this uncomfortable fact with the statement that people have to die of something, and now that communicable diseases as major causes of death are eliminated, only the degenerative diseases are left. And because more people are living into old age more people are succumbing to the diseases of age. But as the chart shows, more *under*-sixty-fives also die of cardiovascular disease than of cancer, accidents, pneumonia, and influenza combined. This is the crux of the problem, and it helps to define the questions we must answer in the rest of this book: What does 'cardiovascular disease' mean? This chapter provides the broad answers, and the last two chapters describe the recognition and treatment respectively of cardiovascular disease.

There is an element of hubris in any attempt to cover cardio-vascular disease in one short chapter. Whole libraries – not to mention careers – have been built around minute aspects of the subject. We could not hope to explore more than the smallest fraction of this specialist world; and we shall not try. (The reader who is hoping to hear the latest on that rare ejection click which sometimes accompanies left ventricular myopathy in breast-fed mongol children – or any of the other delights that galvanise so many cardiovascular meetings into frenzied somnolence – has strayed here into the wrong book.) Instead we shall seek to gain a satellite's-eye-view of that world, note its major areas, and see what chiefly preoccupies those who specialise in each one.

The name 'cardiovascular' suggests at once the easiest way to divide the diseases so named: those that affect the heart primarily; those that mainly affect the vascular system; and those that (how-

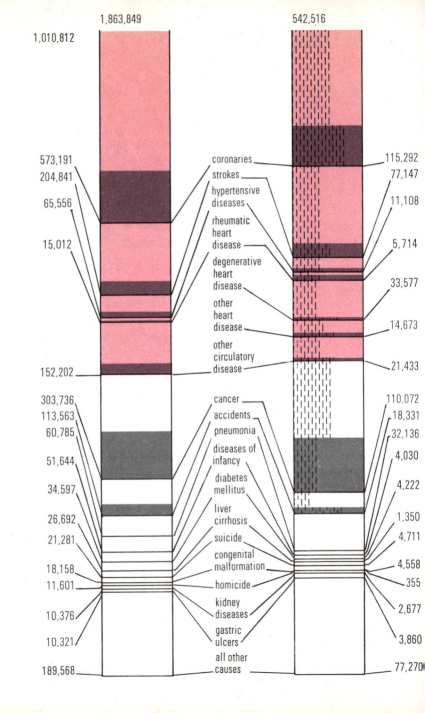

1,863,849

1,010,812

542,516

573,191
204,841
65,556
15,012

coronaries
strokes
hypertensive diseases
rheumatic heart disease
degenerative heart disease
other heart disease
other circulatory disease

115,292
77,147
11,108
5,714
33,577
14,673
21,433

152,202

303,736
113,563
60,785
51,644
34,597
26,692
21,281
18,158
11,601
10,376
10,321
189,568

cancer
accidents
pneumonia
diseases of infancy
diabetes mellitus
liver cirrhosis
suicide
congenital malformation
homicide
kidney diseases
gastric ulcers
all other causes

110,072
18,331
32,136
4,030
4,222
1,350
4,711
4,558
355
2,677
3,860
77,270

5·1 Opposite The charts compare cardiovascular (pink tint) and other major causes of death in the United States (*left*) and England and Wales (*right*)—figures for 1966 and 1967 respectively; both are drawn to the same height to facilitate comparison. For certain causes the proportions of under-65s who die is shaded grey. The figures for England and Wales are broken down in slightly greater detail they distinguish, for instance, between certain heart diseases that the American figures included under 'other circulatory disease'; and they distinguish male (stippled texture) from female deaths in certain causes. The short-comings of the classification used here is discussed further in the appendix.

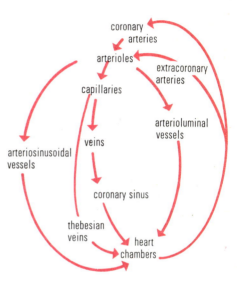

5·2 Schematic diagram of the heart's own circulation. The main circuit is down the centre line (capillaries — veins — coronary sinus). The other circuits can be seen anatomically but their role in the living heart is obscure.

ever they arise) affect both with about equal force.

There are four basic reasons why a heart gets into trouble: 1. Its blood supply fails; 2. Its architecture is faulty; 3. Its muscle is inadequate; 4. Its conductivity fails. The first two are far commoner than the third and fourth. (See appendix for a full list of cardiovascular diseases.)

Coronaries

In 1966, coronary attacks killed 115,292 Britons. There are a further 390,000 left incapacitated after an attack, as well as 2·2 million with an inadequate blood supply to their hearts. Corresponding United

States figures are 570,000, 3·5 million, and 20 million. What is worse, the disease is highly selective, taking its victims from among the most responsible and dynamic members of society. It is to our century what plague was to the Middle Ages.

Figure 5·2 shows in schematic form the heart's own blood supply. The system is actually much less complicated than it looks, for although the channels shown can be demonstrated anatomically in dead hearts, there is scant evidence that they are all of importance in life and health. Virtually all the blood that nourishes the heart comes via the coronary arteries. It used to be taught, and many textbooks still maintain, that only about 60 per cent of this blood finds its way back through the coronary sinus, which opens into the lowest-pressure chamber of the heart; the remaining 40 per cent, according to this belief, finds its way back through the thebesian veins, small vessels (about the diameter of a pin) which connect the coronary venules and veins with the cavities of the heart. Those of us who performed the earliest open-heart experiments were therefore surprised to find that once the heart chambers were emptied of blood and swabbed dry they did not at once begin to ooze with thebesian-venous blood. During some operations we do not maintain the coronary circulation but allow the resting heart to become anoxic; when, towards the end, coronary circulation is restored the arteries become maximally dilated, and the flow through them must be at least a litre a minute; yet even with this flow, which is four times the resting flow, the atrial and ventricular walls remain dry after swabbing.

Although the surgically opened heart is in a highly abnormal state, it is difficult to escape the conclusion that the human heart is supplied and drained entirely by the coronary system, and that if the other vessels (the extracoronary anastomoses, the arterioluminal and arteriosinusoidal vessels, and the thebesian veins) play any part, it is only at the extremes of exertion or as an occasional adaptation to slow changes in the coronary supply. It is equally difficult to accept such a conclusion, for, as I pointed out in chapter 3 (p. 52), blood vessels in the embryo grow with use, vanish with disuse. Rich plexuses like the thebesian and arterio-sinusoidal systems do not persist unless they are constantly used. The fact is that although we know a great deal of the anatomy of the heart's circulation we know almost nothing of its dynamics in an intact human being going about his daily business.

The coronary attack is a blocking of this system at some point in the arterial end. Such blocking is associated with arteriosclerosis, a universal degenerative condition in which arteries become invaded with fat, or calcification, or the acellular material known as atheroma. The lumen of the coronary vessels grows smaller and smaller until a tiny thrombus of clotted blood is enough to seal it, or until sudden exertion steps up the coronary blood flow and leads to turbulence at the narrow point, turbulence that forms clots *in situ*.

Those bits of muscle and the conductive tissues fed by vessels downstream from the blockage may then grow anoxic and, since the heart has little capacity to build up oxygen debt, die. If the arteriosclerosis has built up slowly, the vessels may have had time to adapt and produce an alternative flowpath less menaced by blockage. The chief hazard with coronary thrombosis is not the actual death of tissue. It surprises many people to learn that if they are over thirty they could already be carrying a few dead areas around in their heart, or at least the fibrous scars of them. By the age of forty a person will probably have had several minor coronary blockages already, though most would have been minute, even the severest probably mistaken for indigestion.

Yet the coronary that kills is not necessarily large. Most deaths after a coronary are due to rhythm disturbances. The dying patch of muscle, downstream from the blockage, acts as an irritant focus, emitting false triggering pulses at random times, or recycling the natural pulse through an unnatural path. If the resultant stimulus, in either case, arrives during the relatively refractory period (see figure 5·3) it can trigger ventricular fibrillation, which, unless the heart is defibrillated within minutes, is fatal, for no blood is pumped from a fibrillating heart.

This explains why one can find post-mortem hearts with almost totally blocked coronaries and muscle riddled with dead patches whose owners in life never once complained of chest pain, intolerance to exercise, faintness, or any other symptom of coronary blockage. Such people had had time to adapt other channels (perhaps the extracoronary anastomoses around the great veins, which provide a possible 'back door' for arterial blood to reach the heart muscle) and had, by some good fortune, avoided dangerous arrhythmias. Other post-mortem hearts from coronary victims may show an almost perfect heart with just one dead or dying patch of muscle; its owner had the bad luck to get an arrhythmic triggering pulse from this patch – or, to be precise, from the irritated interface between this patch and the surrounding healthy muscle – and was not near a cardiac resuscitation unit.

The coronaries can also be blocked in people with syphilis, a disease whose effects are still common wherever antibiotics are scarce. Typically the root of the aorta grows lumps of fibrous tissue, which may slowly invade the coronary openings and block them.

One of the most frightening of all symptoms, angina pectoris, or chest pain, is also due to the lack of coronary blood. If all the arteries, normal or back door, are narrowed, the heart may be unable to face exertion or the generalised vasoconstriction that follows eating or any emotional episode, such as an argument. The lack of oxygen in the heart muscle causes a pain, which may be mild but may also be crushing and gripping, radiating as far as the

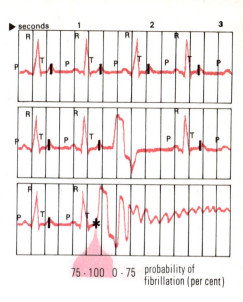

5·3 The vulnerable period in the heart's electrical activity centres on the T wave, which represents the repolarisation of the ventricles (see also page 105).

If an extra triggering pulse – perhaps from dying muscle nearby – arrives during the 0·01 second immediately before the T peak, there is a 75 to 100 per cent probability of triggering ventricular fibrillation (wavy trace at end of recording) and death. In the 0·01 second before this phase and the 0·02 second after it the probability is between 0 and 75 per cent.

left arm. The severity of the pain has no necessary relationship to the severity of the attack that produces it. The victim often feels convinced that death is near. In fact, the condition, unlike that of total coronary blockage, is manageable by using certain drugs.

Failures of architecture

We have already looked at many of the defects under the headings of patent arterial ducts, Fallot tetralogies, and so on. The others are identical in principle: ventricles that failed to grow; septa that grew misaligned so that one ventricle is small, the other large; babies with missing pulmonary arteries, whose gas-exchange circulation is fed by branches from the arteries which normally supply the lung tissues themselves. Many born with such defects do not long survive infancy.

Some valve defects, however, may cause no trouble until middle age. An aortic valve with two semicircular leaflets, instead of the usual three triangular ones, usually takes a long time to deteriorate. Such a valve cannot open fully, so that when the heart's output is high the outflow is turbulent. Over many years the turbulence causes the leaflets to become progressively calcified, until they solidify as a single hard membrane with a small lens-shaped hole at its centre. Only surgical replacement can cope with such a defect. Indeed, surgery provides the only effective remedy to all architectural faults, though it is by no means a panacea. The surgeon cannot recreate missing chambers, for instance, or enlarge tiny ones; but he can patch leaks and implant new channels.

Muscle troubles

It is rare, though by no means unknown, for babies to be born with too much heart muscle. Many cases cannot be explained though sometimes the trouble has been traced to stenotic valves and, more rarely, to raised blood pressure, coronary artery anomalies, infection, or rare storage diseases (in which substances such as fat or glycogen are stored in abnormal quantities in the heart, liver, or other tissues). There can be so much muscle that some has to be cut away before the blood can flow out properly. The same is true of a myxoma (a growth in the cavity of the heart), which can grow so big that it almost fills the cavity.

Most heart-muscle problems crop up later in life. The greatest threat is rheumatic fever. Though this disease, whose peak incidence is among nine to eleven year-olds, was described as long ago as 1760, its origin is still in doubt. We believe it is an auto-aggressive disease, due perhaps to a recessive gene, for there is a marked hereditary tendency to it. To complicate matters it is almost always accompanied by streptococcus invasions that produce sore throats, aching joints, and so on. The streptococci alone are not the cause of the disease. Many people who have 'strep throats' do not get rheumatic fever; and we can control the streptococci with drugs to the extent that there is no fever, no ache, no microscopic inflamed nodules, and still not mitigate the later effects of the disease itself.

Everyone who has rheumatic fever suffers some heart damage, though it is serious in only one-quarter of all victims. The nodules, called Aschoff bodies, form fibrous scars in the heart muscle and, more especially, the valves. The weakened muscle has to fight against stenosed or regurgitating valves, and ultimately one of the ventricles, usually the back one, gives up. Replacing the valves early can help to prolong the life of the muscle, but its performance will always fail to match that of a healthy heart. Scarlet fever and St Vitus's dance can have similar effects to rheumatic fever.

Indeed, any really serious debilitating disease can cause the heart muscle to waste away. Starvation in its very late stages has the same effect.

In all cases the results are similar to those of rheumatic fever: the back ventricle, unequal to the task of maintaining an average 90 or more mm Hg in the big arteries, puts out less blood than the front ventricle puts into the lungs. The blood dams back in the lungs, which become congested; and then the front ventricle begins to fail, following which the whole vascular system becomes passively engorged with fluid. Low output heart failure, as this is called, can be controlled for a time by drugs, diet, and regime; but the only permanent remedy for a failed heart is a new one.

Conduction failure

The effects of conduction failure were noticed by doctors long before they could be explained. The German physician Marcus Gerbezius, who died in 1718, wrote of a patient with 'a pulse so slow, that before a subsequent pulse followed the preceding one, three pulsations would certainly have passed in a healthy person'. Over the next 150 years all the other phenomena associated with faulty conduction were reported: dropped beats, extra beats, irregular beats, and fibrillation. But no explanation was possible until, early in this century, anatomists found the conduction pathways and the ECG enthusiasts showed how those pathways were used.

Heart block, the slow pulse noted by Gerbezius, arises from a failure of the AV node or bundle to conduct the pulse from the atria to the ventricles. The ventricles then contract at their own slow rate – 20 to 45 per minute. The failure, in turn, may be due to the absence of fibres – a congenital defect – or to a failure in blood supply. In rare cases it can be traced to parasites, heart tumours, and faulty surgery. The commonest cause, defective blood supply, is due to coronary blockage.

If the blood supply to the AV node and bundle is curtailed, the whole ventricular system is isolated. If the supply to conductive fibres lower down the tree is affected, conduction leaks through, so to speak, from nearby healthy tissue. In any case the finer fibres of the system are so intimately meshed with the muscle that it becomes pointless to distinguish between dead conductive and dead muscle tissue.

Conduction fails in a different way when the atria begin to flutter (beat around 150 times a minute) and fibrillate. Fibrillating muscle depolarises again as soon as it reaches the relative refractory period, as explained on page 127. In atrial muscle this takes about 200 microseconds; so any given muscle fibre in a fibrillating atrium is twitching some 5 times a second, or 300 times a minute. When the AV node receives stimuli at this rate from the nearby atrial fibres it finds itself unable to pass them along; instead, it seems, one (or two or three) ineffective stimuli can make the node more susceptible to every second (or third or fourth) stimulus. The result is a ratio block, 2-to-1, 3-to-1, or 4-to-1. With an atrial-fibrillation pulse of 300, a 2-to-1 block gives a ventricular rate of 150; the other-order blocks give ventricular rates of 100 (3-to-1) and 75 (4-to-1). Sometimes the AV node may give up, as it were, trying to follow these rapid atrial pulses and settle down to become the main pacemaker, mostly providing its own pace but sometimes responding in a mixture of 2-to-1- or 3-to-1-block modes.

The AV node can become the pacemaker in a variety of other circumstances; whenever, in fact, the SA node or conduction from it is defective. The result, nodal rhythm as it is called, is not as serious as might be thought for the AV node is every bit as responsive as the SA node to the control centres which dominate the heart. Nevertheless, the topping-up function of the atria is lost in nodal rhythm, so that the total system loses about 5 per cent in efficiency.

Sometimes the bundle appears to fatigue (the Wenckebach phenomenon) so that successive impulses take longer and longer to get through; ultimately one impulse fails altogether. The next one is normal in timing, followed by progressively increasing delays until another atrial pulse fails to get through ... and so on in an endless cycle.

In some hearts there are anomalous pathways between the atria and the ventricles (usually to the front ventricle) which conduct faster than the rather slow AV node. As a result the ventricle contracts prematurely and the topping-up from its atrium is lost (called the Wolff-Parkinson-White syndrome). There is a peculiar situation, closely related to this syndrome, in which a normal atrial impulse, having passed down the bundle as far as the front and back branches, passes on in the normal way to the two ventricles, but also appears to pass back up the bundle to the AV node and retrigger it. The result is an autonomous, cyclic triggering of the ventricles whose rate depends solely on the velocity of conduction in the bundle.

We have reached the area in which the subtler distinctions between various kinds of conductive disturbance (there are at least a dozen more) are of interest only to the specialist. To sum up: there are straightforward conductive failures, such as heart block, permanent or temporary, total or partial, and there are more complex failures, which produce various rhythmic or cyclic disturbances. All of them reduce the efficiency of the heart and of its owner, severely in complete heart block, for instance, barely in nodal rhythm. In each case the mechanism of impairment is the same: effort goes up, output down; and because output is reduced, so is venous return. In those conditions where the ventricles beat fast the coronary supply is reduced (most coronary flow, you will remember, is during diastole), so that the heart, in effect, adds to its own existing burden. This is a further example of low output failure. In general, heart block is treated by fitting some kind of pacemaker; rhythm disturbances are treated by drugs and diet.

To pass now to the system outside the heart, there are circumstances in which it may demand so much that, even though the heart may be in perfect condition, it cannot meet these excessive demands. The result is a high-output failure. There are two general causes: excessive pressure in the system, and excessive demand for circulatory volume.

High blood pressure

There are several causes of high blood pressure, or hypertension, as it is called, though the commonest form, unhelpfully known as 'essential' hypertension, cannot yet be explained. I cannot quote exact figures for the pressures that define hypertension since the normal pressure varies markedly with age, body type, and ethnic group; but one can say that a sustained increase of 15 per cent or more in any individual is enough to label him hypertensive. Pressures can commonly go as high as 200/90 mm Hg, rarely higher than 220/140. The most obvious-seeming cause, a general hardening of the arteries, can be ruled out; there are people with arteries like clay pipe stems but with completely normal pressures; and many people become hypertensive while their arteries are still pliable – though, it is true, prolonged high pressure does promote hardening of the arteries.

Known causes of hypertension include kidney disorders, narrowing of one or both renal arteries, coarctation (hereditary narrowing) of the aorta, tumours and other diseases of the glands that secrete hormones involved in blood-pressure control (shown in figure 4·14) – chiefly the adrenal cortex and medulla – excessive production of red cells (polycythemia) and pulseless disease, due to narrowing of the arteries at the neck, armpit, and groin.

In all these conditions, except pulseless disease, hypertension may be the only physical sign; so it is important to pursue any hypertension diagnosis to the point where these other conditions can be eliminated or confirmed. The importance is heightened by the fact that these conditions are frequently curable, apart from the kidney conditions (curable, *in extremis*, by transplantation), polycythemia, and pulseless disease. If the disease is allowed to persist, the arteries may become irreversibly damaged. Some resetting of the pressure receptors described in chapter 4 is almost certainly involved in the unexplained type of hypertension, for one can surgically destroy practically all sympathetic nerve activity and produce a pressure normalisation which may last as long as six months; but then the pressure begins its inexorable rise once more. However, the resetting lags behind the onset of hypertension, so it is an effect, not a cause.

The two most favoured explanations for 'essential' hypertension are: 1. A generalised constriction of the arterioles, perhaps due to an abnormal sensitisation of the constrictor muscles to stimuli; 2. A complex failure in the homeostatic autoregulation of the system: for example, if the blood electrolyte balance began to drift there could be a slow increase in plasma volume; and if the system adjusted so as to keep *flow* constant, *pressure* would inevitably rise. It is difficult to decide between these possible causes, for each could have the other as an effect.

Whatever its cause, the results of hypertension are clear. The heart responds at first as if to athletic training, its stretched fibres contracting vigorously, enabling it to put out more volume without putting up the rate. But there is a world of difference between the periodic effort needed to meet training and the sustained effort to meet high blood pressure. The muscle continues to develop far beyond normal until it is between two and three times its proper thickness. This hypertrophy (figure 5·4) takes place partly at the expense of ventricular volume, so that output per stroke now goes down. Though the oxygen consumption per unit of muscle is unaltered, there is so much more muscle that the total oxygen demand of the heart is greatly increased. The coronary arteries, however, remain essentially the same. As a result the heart is increasingly vulnerable to coronary attacks. A degree of narrowing which would not imperil a normal heart can cause a coronary in a hypertrophied one. Also, for some reason, hypertensives are more susceptible than others to haemorrhage and thrombosis in the vessels of the brain.

Hypertension of any kind can suddenly enter an accelerated phase of deterioration (called malignant hypertension) marked by arteriolar damage, congestion of the retina, brain lesions, and progressive kidney failure. Unless treated it is fatal, usually within two years of its onset. Deterioration in all kinds of hypertension can be halted, or at least decelerated, by drugs and, in some cases, by surgery.

High volume demand

An abnormal channel linking the arterial and venous systems can short-circuit the blood and leave the body tissues relatively low in oxygen and nutrients. The body's autoregulatory systems then start flogging the heart to make good the deficiency. Such channels can be congenital. They can also come with disease: for example, Paget's disease, a painful distortion and thickening of the bones (chiefly the skull, spine, pelvis, and femur) through which abnormal arterio-venous circuits develop. Today such channels can be man-made; the Scribner shunt, for example, the metal-and-plastics tubes which people on kidney machines wear permanently implanted into an artery and a vein in the wrist or groin. Between sessions on the machine the ends of these tubes are joined. This prevents the blood from stagnating and clotting, but it also creates a short-circuit for the blood. The doctor who fits a Scribner shunt must keep a close watch for untoward cardiovascular effects.

Excessive thyroid gland secretion, by leading to a great increase in the metabolic rate, can also lead to a demand for blood greater than the heart can supply.

The effects of excessive volume-demand on the heart may closely resemble those of hypertension, even when pressures remain normal. But, though the ventricles dilate, the walls do not necessarily become as musclebound as in hypertension. The first response is athletic, putting up the volume but not the rate. In time, however, the muscle is strained and the rate must also rise. With sustained high pulse rate the diastolic period (the time when the heart drinks) is reduced and the heart becomes relatively starved.

Unless the basic cause is treated (by surgically closing the short circuits, for instance, or by removing the overactive thyroid) the heart will fail.

Finally we come to those conditions which involve the whole

5·4 In this transverse section of a hypertrophied back ventricle (*below*) the expected outlines of a normal heart are superimposed – showing the hypertrophied muscle to be two to three times its normal thickness and the cavity to be about half its natural volume. *Opposite:* a longitudinal section of a normal back ventricle. The glass rod shows the axis of the chamber and passes out through the aortic valve. The scissors handle encircles one of the coronary arteries near the aortic root.

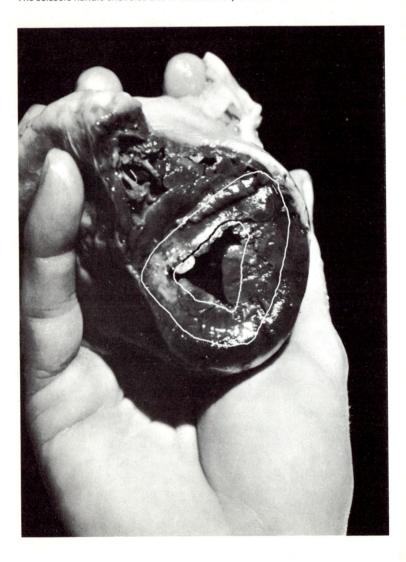

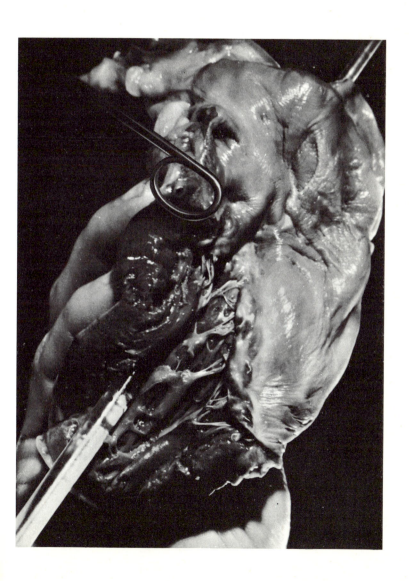

system. The cause may lie in the heart or in the vascular system, or it may be some external agency; but when the crisis comes it is the whole system that responds. The response is called *shock*.

Shock

When the heart fails acutely to put out enough blood, its owner develops a condition known as shock; it may be worsened by whatever caused the acute failure, and it can be fatal.

Shock has three possible causes, none mutually exclusive: 1. The heart fails for any of the acute reasons we have already looked at, such as coronary blockage; this is called cardiogenic shock; 2. The blood volume changes acutely because of bleeding or burns; this is low-volume shock; 3. The resistance of the blood vessels drops acutely in response to infection, allergic reaction, metabolic disorder, or organic malfunction; this is low-resistance shock.

For cardiogenic shock there are almost as many treatments as doctors. Even in the same hospital we can find shock patients in a surgical recovery ward receiving quite different treatment from shock patients in a next-door coronary intensive care ward. In the recovery ward the surgeons and anaesthetists, influenced by their experience of acute (i.e. sudden) events during open heart operations, are likely to emphasise the importance of raising the venous pressure (typically from zero to the more normal 4 to 6 mm Hg) so as to increase the return to the heart and raise its output by the Starling mechanism described on page 93. Simultaneously they give drugs to stimulate heart action, raising V_{max} at the expense of efficiency. Such therapy is in tune with the acute sort of world in which surgeons move.

Physicians, by contrast, tend to live in a chronic sort of world. Their traditions, in this particular field, go back over a hundred years to Hilton's classic book *Rest and Pain*, in which the author preached that organs in trouble should be rested, not worked. In the intensive coronary unit the physicians are likely to sedate the patient and keep a close watch for rhythm disturbances that presage an impending cardiac arrest. By treating the heart only when such disturbances appear, they can almost eliminate arrests without straying far from the Hilton tradition.

The two approaches are not, in fact, contradictory. The surgeon's therapy is suited to the critical state of shock, but the longer it is continued the more damaging it can be. The physician's therapy is the best avoidance strategy currently available, and recovery patients should be so treated as soon as the crisis is over. One wishes the two were combined in this way more often than they are.

Low-volume shock (which is often marked by cold, clammy skin, quick breathing, and intense thirst) can be due to burns, in which plasma is lost, or to bleeding, either internal or external. In both cases the strategic shutdown described on page 118 operates in an attempt to reroute the remaining blood through the essential organs. There is also an increase in hormone secretion and auto-nomic nerve activity, all of which constricts the veins (to return more blood to the heart), puts up the heart rate, puts up the breathing rate (the extra-thoracic pumping also helps draw blood into the great veins), draws tissue fluid into the capillaries (hence the thirst) and, in the longer term, raises plasma protein and red cell levels. These responses can last for days even though the crisis is usually over within hours.

Low-resistance shock is most commonly caused by bacterial poisons. One meets it, too, in people massively stung by bees or wasps. There are also a number of metabolic disorders that dilate the total blood channel; to make matters worse, they may also reduce the amount of circulating blood. In all these cases it is massive vasodilation that precipitates the crisis. Often fever, by opening up all the skin capillaries, and the accompanying sweating (the fluid for which can only come from the blood) is a severe complication. Low resistance leads to low arterial pressures, which, in turn, mean low coronary blood flow – a further hazard.

In low-resistance shock many of the normal responses to inadequate circulation (strategic shutdown, vasoconstriction, venous constriction, and so on) are unable to operate because the dilating forces are more powerful. Indeed, as we shall see in a moment, venous constriction may combine with vasodilation in special circumstances that lead to a fatal kind of shock.

Both low-volume and low-resistance shock are dealt with in ways whose importance is underlined by the natural response itself: first bring back the filling pressure in the great veins near the heart so as to activate the Starling mechanism. This increase can be achieved by raising the patient's feet and giving massive transfusions, preferably of blood, but in an emergency any sterile physiologically compatible fluid is better than nothing. Plasma is often used since it does not have to be matched for blood group; so is saline solution; even gum arabic has worked, though like any concentrated fluid it achieves its effect partly by leaching water from the tissues, contraindicated in a patient already dehydrated. In the slightly longer term, warm drinks are a good way to raise the fluid volume – anything except alcohol, which dilates the vessels and so opposes the natural mechanisms.

If when the venous pressure is restored the arterial pressure remains low, it must be restored by vasoconstricting drugs, even at the expense of the general circulation, so as to give the heart a good high-pressure drink. (One difficulty here is that if the patient is a hypertensive, a mean arterial pressure as high as 85 mm Hg could signify severe shock.)

In passing, it is interesting to note that getting a person out of shock is very like bringing a patient off a heart-lung machine. Surgery inevitably puts him into shock, so that he needs more blood after the operation than he had at its start. We have no way of calculating how much, because of inadequate data and a dynamic situation. The heart-lung driver has to 'feel for' the right quantity by putting in the blood in measured amounts (100 ml to begin with, 50 ml later) and watching the arterial pressure rise in response to the Starling mechanism. He stops when he goes over the top, so to speak, of the Starling curve; when, that is, a further rise in venous pressure produces a slight fall in arterial pressure.

Not all people recover from shock. Badly burned victims (say 75 per cent of the body surface covered with third degree burns) hardly ever recover, even if one temporarily manages to get their pressures and outputs up around normal. It is not difficult to understand such a failure: the scale of the wound is so massive that the body's self-righting mechanisms are irreversibly damaged and quite unable to respond to normalisation and sustain it. It is more difficult to understand why the therapy that revives a larger number of shock victims should, in the odd case, completely fail.

In such cases, it seems, there is a prolonged shutdown of the capillaries at both ends (that is, constriction of the precapillary sphincters and of the venules). In most people this responds to a restoration of venous pressure and, if necessary, of arterial pressure; but in a few cases the constriction (the shock) persists. Lack of oxygen damages the tissues. Ultimately the capillary sphincters relax, but not the venules. Blood enters the capillaries and stagnates, and the pressure rises. Fluid leaves the capillaries, whose starved walls degenerate and rupture, allowing massive bleeding. This kind of shock is difficult to recognise before tissue damage occurs and is impossible to reverse once that state is reached. Fortunately it is very rare.

Another factor is the state of the heart muscle. If the coronary blood flow is reduced, both by rapid heart-beats and low arterial pressure, the muscle may be damaged beyond its ability to recover quickly when better circulation is restored. In such cases it is useless expecting the unaided heart to restore normal output. For these patients, above all, we urgently need a heart-lung machine that can take over the circulation for days rather than hours; more will be said about this in chapter 7.

6 Measuring the damage

Practically all heart surgery and surgery of the great vessels inside the rib cage involves cutting right down the breastbone and opening up the cavity. It is major surgery and (emergencies apart) a surgeon cannot undertake it unless he knows exactly what he will find and has already decided his major corrective strategy. In almost a decade of open heart surgery I can recall only one non-emergency case where preliminary tests were of little help, and that was in a man whose chest anatomy was so grossly anomalous that one simply could not interpret the results of the tests. In other words, we have developed machinery to tell us practically everything we need to know about the heart without opening the chest and looking at it.

The defects we chiefly look for are those we can do something positive about: holes in septa, stenosed or incompetent valves, faulty conductivity, defects in the great vessels and, to a limited extent, impoverished coronary supply. Short of surgery a lot can be done by drugs or changes in diet and habit; before starting such therapy the doctor needs just as much detail as the surgeon.

In one way cardiologists are lucky. The heart is so physically active that it is fairly liberal with clues about its performance. We can hear it working, and feel it; and the depolarisation wave which spreads around the heart before each contraction emits an electrical signal at least one hundred times stronger than those from the brain. By listening to the sounds, with a stethoscope or a phono-cardiograph, by recording the reaction of the body, either at specific points (as in pressure and pulse taking) or the whole-body reaction (with a ballistocardiograph), and by measuring the heart's electrical activity with an electrocardiograph, we can diagnose practically every heart condition and even make a fair estimate of its severity. If we need to tighten the diagnosis there are a number of more refined techniques that will make possible the most precise quantitative assessment.

The sounds of the heart

The pounding of one's heart at moments of stress, or the fluttering and delayed beats that often accompany, say, a head cold, are such obvious features of cardiac performance that you might think doctors had used them from the earliest days. Astonishingly enough it was not until 1816 that a French doctor, René Laënnec, introduced the technique to medicine. Until then the custom had been to feel the heart pulse much as one still feels the pulse at the wrist; if it was faint, the doctor put his ear to the chest, but only to note the rhythm, not the detailed heart sounds. Laënnec tells us that the technique 'could embarrass both parties if the patient were young, female, modest, and physically well endowed'. And it was during such an encounter that he hit upon the idea of rolling up a quire of paper into a tube, applying his ear to one end and the other end to the girl's chest. The device augmented the sound so well that Laënnec became the first to hear 'the language of pathology . . . Lesions within the thorax that for centuries had been inaudible now announced their presence.' The modern stethoscope is, in principle, no different from that simple quire of rolled up paper. Most of the sounds one hears with it can, in fact, be heard better with the naked ear to the bare chest, but there are circumstances, as Laënnec pointed out, where a little distance helps to keep the heart-beat normal. The stethoscope is also useful in spot (that is, noncontinuous) measurements of blood pressure with the sphyg-momanometer. This simple gadget, which did not enter clinical medicine until the first decade of this century (one hundred years after the invention of the stethoscope), consists of an air-inflatable cuff attached to a column of mercury. The doctor puts the cuff around the upper arm and pumps it up until the pulse sounds in the brachial artery vanish. On releasing the air in the cuff, he notes the pressure at which the pulse sounds reappear. Normal is

120 mm Hg for the aortic valve opening sound and 80 mm Hg for the closing sound. These are equivalent to the maximum and minimum pressures in the aorta at systole and diastole. By themselves they offer little guidance to the state of the heart; abnormal pressures are associated with so many organs or systems. Nevertheless, the pressures are a guide to whatever the heart may be having to cope with.

The heart sounds are most easily discussed in connection with the phonocardiograph (PCG). This machine (see figure 6·1) consists of a microphone, amplifier, a frequency filter, and a writing device. Usually it has extra channels for a simultaneous record of the electrocardiogram and either the venous (jugular) or arterial (carotid) pulse. These help to locate each sound in its exact place within the cardiac cycle.

The sounds recorded in the PCG arise out of the flowing of the blood. That deliberately vague sentence steps around a lively but sterile controversy about whether the heart sounds arise as the valves close or as the blood thrusts outward through the vessels. There is, however, no controversy about their meaning. Figure 6·2 shows the main sounds (which are never as perfect as diagrams can make them) and explains their sequence. Sound 1 is associated with the closing of the mitral and tricuspid valves which, a twentieth of a second later, merges with the opening of the pulmonary and aortic valves, either in that order or simultaneously. Sound 2 is associated with the closing of the aortic and pulmonary valves, usually in that order. So between 1 and 2 the ventricles are emptying, and between 2 and the next 1 they are filling. If the outlet valves (pulmonary and aortic) are stenosed, we should hear the resulting turbulence between 1 and 2. But we should also hear turbulent sounds if the inlet valves (tricuspid and mitral) were incompetent and allowing blood to regurgitate. Fortunately the two sounds are different in character, as figure 6·3 shows. Simi-

6·1 Photograph of a patient connected to a phonocardiograph (PCG) machine. Its microphones are held by suction to his chest near his heart. Clamps round the arms and legs are electrodes for simultaneous ECG recording. The collar round the neck can record either the carotid (arterial) or jugular (venous) pulse wave. The tube in the nose records breathing – which can influence the heart's performance.

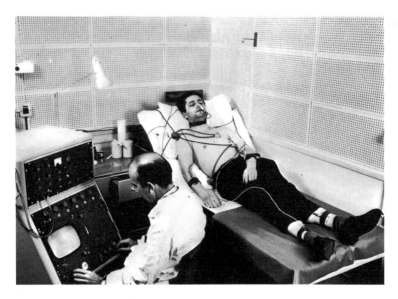

larly, incompetent outlet valves play a different tune from stenosed inlet valves. But from the sounds alone it may be difficult to tell which of the inlet or outlet valves is defective; here we need the arterial or venous pressure traces (or x-rays and other tests) to reveal the culprit.

The only real difficulty with PCG interpretation comes in telling a ventricular septal defect from an incompetent mitral. (An atrial septal defect causes no sound, except for a murmur in the pulmonary artery caused by the extra volume of blood cycled through the defect.) Only experience can help the cardiologist here, for apart from slight variations in the volume when the microphone is moved, the sounds are not logically separable.

To sum up: the PCG reveals defects in the valves and septa; and if the microphone is moved over the great arteries, it can reveal

6·2 Idealised traces of the major processes usually monitored on a PCG machine. The PCG trace is the audible record of the heart. Sounds 1 and 2 are discussed on p. 145; sounds 3 and 4 (related to ventricular filling and atrial topping-up) are not always present. 'OS' is the opening snap (so-called) of the mitral and tricuspid valves. Two major events, atrial and ventricular contraction, are shaded grey and related to the jugular and carotid pulses; the slope indicates the time lag. The jugular pulse helps in investigating the front, or venous, side of the heart; the carotid pulse in investigating the back, arterial, side of the heart.

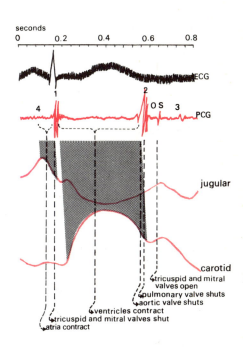

6·3 Below Idealised drawings of PCG traces associated with various valve defects. The sounds are those labelled in figure 6·2.

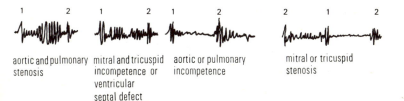

aortic and pulmonary stenosis

mitral and tricuspid incompetence or ventricular septal defect

aortic or pulmonary incompetence

mitral or tricuspid stenosis

defects in them, too. It can also give a slight indication of the state of the heart muscle. On the other hand, it cannot reveal the precise nature of the defects and it allows only the crudest estimate of their severity. Its great advantage from the patient's point of view is that it involves no insult; that is, no knives, needles, or radiation.

The electrical activity of the heart

The depolarisation wave which precedes and triggers the heart's contraction is a fairly massive movement of ions that reverberates throughout the body – so much so that we can detect it at the fingertips quite as easily as at the shoulder.

The crude way to measure this activity would be to pepper the surface of the heart with electrodes, gather masses of data for each beat, and then, after several hours of computer-time, we might emerge with a guide to what had happened during the recording. In fact we choose the electrode positions so that they do a lot of the processing for us. The general direction of the depolarisation wave is from the upper right front corner of the heart obliquely downward and leftward to its apex, and then halfway back up this axis (see figure 6·4). Any two electrodes, anywhere on the body, will pick up some component of this general movement, but the most effective positions lie on the same plane as this electrical axis. It so happens that the shoulders and hips lie in this plane; further-more, since the arms and legs are (electrically speaking) conductive extensions of the shoulders and the navel (which is between the hips), the lower arms and legs provide sites that are both convenient and informative. Let me make this point quite clear: as long as the patient's skin is dry it does not matter whether he puts his arm above his head, behind his back, stretches it before him, or hangs it by his side; any electrode on it effectively measures the activity from the heart towards or away from the shoulder.

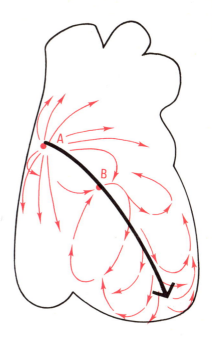

6·4 A schematic diagram of the passage of the depolarisation wave (coloured arrows) from the SA node (A) to the AV node (B) and down through the ventricles. The black arrow shows the major resultant (the heart's electrical axis) of these currents. It is *general* movement that the electrocardiograph (ECG) measures.

Thus the three standard positions for the ECG electrodes measure not the total activity of the heart but its electrical activity towards or away from three points: the right shoulder, the left shoulder, and the navel. The triangle thus formed (see figure 6·5) is named Einthoven's triangle, in honour of Willem Einthoven, the great German cardiologist and father of the ECG as we know it. By convention the circuitry is arranged so that a movement down the axis in a normal heart gives an upward deflection in the record from all three standard leads, as in figure 6·5 ('normal' diagram). On the same figure, the other diagrams show the changes that come with a shift of the axis to the left or to the right.

Such a shift can mean an actual displacement of the heart. In a fat man, for instance, the stomach can push the heart more horizontal to give a left axis deviation; and in a thin man the reverse can happen. But a deviant axis more often means that part of the heart muscle is dead, that its conductivity is distorted, or that one or other of the ventricles is fighting some resistance and has grown larger in response.

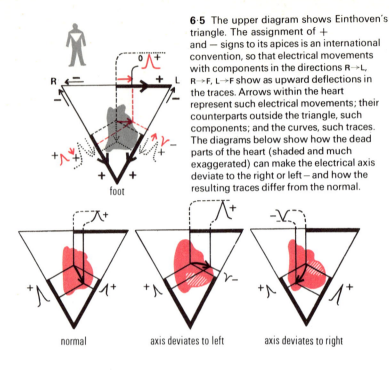

6·5 The upper diagram shows Einthoven's triangle. The assignment of + and − signs to its apices is an international convention, so that electrical movements with components in the directions R→L, R→F, L→F show as upward deflections in the traces. Arrows within the heart represent such electrical movements; their counterparts outside the triangle, such components; and the curves, such traces. The diagrams below show how the dead parts of the heart (shaded and much exaggerated) can make the electrical axis deviate to the right or left — and how the resulting traces differ from the normal.

normal   axis deviates to left   axis deviates to right

ECG traces (see figure 6·6) are usually written with a hot-wire stylus on heat-sensitive graph paper travelling at 25 mm/sec; each fine line is 0·04 sec apart, making the interval between the thicker lines 0·2 sec. Precalibration ensures that a 1 mv potential deflects the stylus 1 cm. As figure 6·6 shows, the trace has three main deflections, labelled P, QRS, and T. The P is the depolarisation of the atria; the QRS is the depolarisation of the ventricles; and the T is the repolarisation of the ventricles. The 'atrial T wave' representing the repolarisation of the atria is usually masked by the QRS complex. In patients with heart block the QRS, being a ventricular event, is quite divorced from the P, which is an atrial event. In tracings from such patients one can often see the atrial T wave (see the tracing in figure 6·7).

The same tracings also show how other defects can be revealed by the ECG. The usual ECG record has twelve traces: the three

6·6 These tracings (again idealised) show normal ECG readings from (upper line) leads I, II, III, aVR, aVL, aVF, and (lower line) v1 to v6; the positions of these electrodes is given in figure 6·8. The convention of v leads is that current toward an electrode gives an upward deflection – thus the v leads show a general movement away from v1 and v2 (nearest the SA node) toward v5 and v6 (near the heart's apex). The letters P, Q, R, S, and T (repeated as stars in the other traces) are explained on page 150.

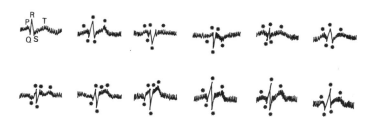

standard leads (I, II, and III), the three av (augmented voltage) leads (aVR, aVL, and aVF), and the six v (for voltage) leads (v1 to v6). Figure 6·8 shows the electrode combinations which produce these leads. The standard leads reveal most of what we want to know about the heart; the av leads are useful for exploring its detailed electrical behaviour and for evaluating the deflections produced by the standard leads; the v leads are useful for locating dead or dying patches of muscle, for it is quite possible to get a patient with, say, a normal v1, abnormal v2, normal v3, abnormal v4, and normal v5 and v6 traces. Leads that can discriminate so finely between areas so close have proved invaluable in detailed diagnosis.

To sum up, the ECG tells us about the electrical activity of the heart, not its physical activity; one can get a perfectly normal ECG from a heart that is not pumping at all, though the resultant lack of oxygen soon, of course, begins to distort the traces. The rhythms it records tell us of the health of the conductive and muscular tissue, the position of the heart in the chest, its responsiveness to various stimuli and drugs, the degree of oxygenation of the muscle, where dead areas are located, and any abnormal muscular development. It is less revealing about such things as valve and septal defects and anomalies of the great vessels, except insofar as these have produced changes in the muscle.

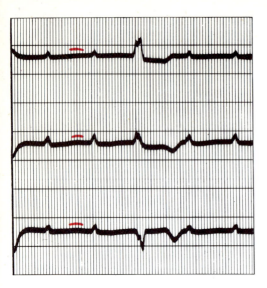

6·7 Actual ECG traces from a patient with total heart block. Tilt the page and look along them and you will see a clear 'atrial-T' wave below the coloured marks. Their significance is explained on page 150.

6·8 Below The electrode positions for the twelve standard (international) ECG leads. Leads I, II, and III are the three sides of Einthoven's triangle. The av leads are achieved by matching two sides of the triangle (through a resistor) against the third. The v leads match all three sides of the triangle (again through a resistor) against each of six carefully placed electrodes. Twelve-channel machines are too cumbersome for clinical use; recordings are usually made in sequence on a single-channel machine.

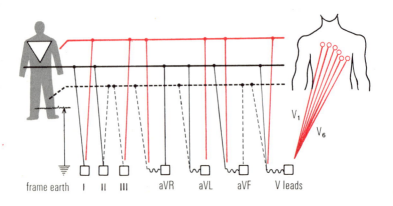

frame earth   I   II   III   aVR   aVL   aVF   V leads

V_1 V_6

6·9 These tracings (redrawn for clarity) show various defects revealed by ECG recordings.

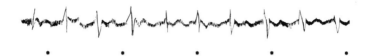

The stars mark 1-second intervals. The pattern is normal but, at 120 beats/minute, fast; the result of emotional disturbance, fever, and some kinds of poisoning and drug overdose.

Inverted P waves (P) reveal an irritable focus in the atrium giving out SA-node-type stimuli and triggering early ventricular contraction. The rest of the conducting system is normal so the QRST complex is normal, too. Treatment: drugs to 'damp down' the irritable focus.

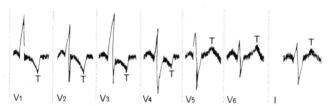

Tall R waves and inverted T waves in V1 and V4 and distorted QRS in lead I reveal hypertrophy of the front ventricle. Treatment: surgical unblocking of the outflow from the ventricle or of the mitral valve.

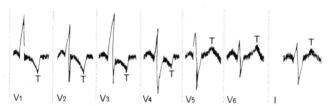

Gross ST elevation in leads II and III and V2 to V5 shows that coronary thrombosis has killed part of the front of the heart. Treatment: rapid surgical repair or replacement of the coronary or transplantation.

The ballistocardiogram

The BCG has had a long and unhappy history. For almost a century people have been trying to measure the impulse imparted to the body by the blood ejected from the heart. The basic science goes back to Newton's third law: to every action (such as the ejection of blood) there is an equal and opposite reaction (such as the contrary movement of the body).

The equipment could hardly be simpler. There are two standard BCG machines. One consists of a table hung on wires from the ceiling; it incorporates a magnet that, moving within a coil, translates the patient's motion into a varying current. The second is a table held on tough springs incorporating strain gauges which record the patient's motion. The natural oscillation of the suspended table is much slower than the heart-beat; that of the sprung table is much faster. With both there is thus no confusion between motion due to the patient and motion due to the natural oscillation of the table.

The difficulty of distinguishing between these two motions hampered all early attempts to establish the clinical value of BCGs. The results, too, did not accord with established cardiological findings: a patient with a poor BCG, for instance, might show no other abnormal signs and feel no symptoms at all. And when such a patient died – of causes not connected with a heart condition – necropsies showed an apparently normal heart. For these reasons BCGs fell into disfavour; only a few pioneers like Dr Isaac Starr, former Professor of Therapeutics at the University of Pennsylvania, persisted. What cardiologists failed to realise, and what is only now becoming apparent, is that the BCGs were giving entirely new information about the heart, information that ECGs, PCGs, pulse, and pressure readings cannot by their very nature provide.

Put simply: a heart can deliver normal quantities of blood, at a normal rate, show normal electrical and sound patterns, and still be abnormal. Figure 6·10 explains this apparent paradox in terms of physics. The medical background is more complex. In a normal, youthful heart the contraction of all the ventricular muscle fibres is strong and closely coordinated. Starr discovered how strong it is in the early 1950s when he pushed syringe pumps with dual outlets into the aortic and pulmonary roots of cadavers and tried to match the ejecting action of a young heart. He could match the output all right, but the acceleration was quite beyond him – and it is the acceleration which is the true measure of the heart's strength. His utmost efforts matched those of a middle-aged heart.

How do we explain this important difference between normal young hearts and normal old ones? What seems to happen with age is that the muscle is progressively invaded and weakened by fat and fibrous deposits, and it acts less and less in concert. In a patient with angina, for instance, the muscle lacks coordination, which shows in a tremulous BCG. In the ultimate stage, ventricular fibrillation, incoherence is complete.

It is not difficult to equate a shaky BCG with angina or some other cardiac event. Much more surprising was the discovery that many apparently healthy people also had tremulous BCGs; this was what made cardiologists tend to sniff at the whole technique. Then in 1967 Dr Benjamin Baker and his colleagues at Johns Hopkins University announced the results of a nine-year study of old and young people with normal and abnormal BCGs. It was, and is, the strongest vindication of ballistocardiography. Briefly, they found:

The older the age group, the greater the incidence of BCG abnormality, whether or not there were clinical signs of a heart condition.

Those who had abnormal BCGs at the start of the study (whether outwardly healthy or not) were six times more likely to have some kind of heart attack than those whose BCGs were normal. Elaborating this in terms of age: The abnormal under-fifties were twelve times more likely to suffer than the

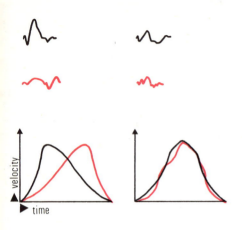

6·10 The small traces represent idealised BCG readings. The upper trace shows that though both hearts put out below it, one from a weaker heart. The graph below, derived from these traces, shows that though both hearts put out the same volume (areas below curves) in the same time, the stronger heart has the greater initial acceleration (slope of curve). The black curve is typical of a young healthy heart; the red curve of an old healthy heart. The right-hand sequence shows the difference between a firm and a tremulous BCG. The shaky nature of the coloured curve here indicates a vulnerable heart with poor coordination.

normal under-fifties; among the over-fifties the likelihood was over three times as great.

Not all victims of heart attack had abnormal BCGs, but those who did were twice as likely to suffer a second attack, within the nine years of the study, as those who did not. More surprisingly, this likelihood was quite independent of the patient's age.

This third finding alone guarantees the BCG a place in cardiology. Victims of a heart attack naturally want to know desperately what chances they stand of getting a second attack. The BCG can take some of the guesswork out of the cardiologist's answer.

With the characteristic fervour of the committed, Starr said in 1967: 'The conventional cardiology of today detects only the last stage of cardial weakness – if it detects it at all!' (a view shared, let me say, by many of the uncommitted, too). In a quieter moment he pointed out that BCGs would complement, not supplant, conventional heart investigations; for the BCG shows

abnormalities ... not recognised by conventional techniques ... abnormalities ... related to the later development of disease and to diminished longevity. One sees new facts about familiar diseases ... one sees the effects of cardiac therapy demonstrated in striking fashion; so one becomes better able to adapt therapy to the needs of the patient. And let us not forget that this new knowledge can be gained without disturbing the patient in any way, without subjecting him to either discomfort or danger and with little trouble or expense.

If I may interject a personal note: I have no clinical experience of BCG machines, but a colleague of mine, Dr Denis Deuchar of Guys Hospital, London (one of the few British cardiologists to see the importance of BCGs) has been getting excellent results with a home-made table in his department. Nevertheless it took him more than a year of patient experiment with various damping systems to get a reliable record. Now that the clinical value of the BCG is generally established it is surely time for research institutions to start spending more heavily on a production line model. I cannot believe that strain gauges and magnetos are the best transducers that the technology of 1970 can supply. It seems to me that inertial guidance devices, or laser interferometers, or mekometers could step up the signal-to-noise ratio several times over, and so help to rid the record of random vibration, an important source of error in large cities.

Ultrasound analysis

A few years back it looked as if the ultrasound cardiogram (UCG) might quickly gain a place alongside the traditional machines of cardiology. The technique is to bounce high frequency sound waves, between 15 kHz and 1·5 MHz (1 Hz = 1 cycle per second), radar-like, from the various surfaces of the moving heart and to display the echoes on an oscilloscope. Just as an oceanographer maps the ocean bed, its sediments and its invisible rock base, from reflected sound waves that can penetrate mud and ooze, so the cardiologist could actually watch the heart in action. The same technique, of course, could also be applied to any other organ that reflects ultrasound. Recently, however, a number of workers have begun to doubt that these high frequency waves are as harmless as we once thought.

Waves of this wavelength can, if their intensity is high enough, completely disrupt and homogenise the contents of a cell. At

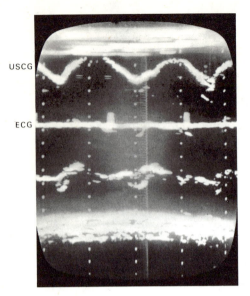

6·11 An ultrasound record of the pumping heart surrounded by pericardinal effusion (see below) compared with (*above*) a normal trace. The 'blips' in the ECG trace are QRS complexes. Other traces are not relevant here. The photograph is a time exposure of a cathode ray tube display.

USCG

ECG

moderate levels they can interfere with cell division and nerve conduction. And even at low levels they can damage certain cell components: DNA, mitochondria, and proteins. Against this it must be said that at the very low intensity levels used in ultrasound diagnosis – and only for brief periods at that – no damage or after-effect of any kind has ever been demonstrated. At these low levels, ultrasound is probably safer than x-rays, and even x-rays are pretty safe these days.

As far as the heart is concerned, ultrasound is still a minor technique because it is not yet good enough to reveal as much as we can get from x-ray cine and angiograms. At the moment there is only one condition in which ultrasound can confirm a diagnosis that is otherwise difficult to make. This is pericardial effusion, a condition in which fluid fills and enlarges the pericardial sac. It can be difficult to tell whether the whole heart is enlarged or just the sac; ultrasound, as figure 6·11 shows, can easily separate the surface of the sac from that of the heart proper.

With greatly improved signal-to-noise ratio and more graphic display, perhaps even computer enhanced, ultrasound may become an important tool in all kinds of internal examination. Already experimental ultrasound holograms of the liver have been made, revealing damage that only the surgeon's knife could otherwise have shown. Potentially the technique offers the chance of watching the heart – and other parts of the body – at work. And with Doppler-shift measurements (discussed on pp. 169-70) it would be possible to superimpose a picture of the flow lines on to this view of the heart. No other technique can match that sort of potential.

The final group of standard cardiological tests involve some degree of insult or risk to the patient.

X-ray examination

The risks with x-rays were always slight, except in the very earliest days of the technique. (An interesting sidelight on those days is provided by the fact that the Victorians were far more worried by what the prurient radiologists might photograph through ladies' clothing than by the unknown hazards of radiation, which could have been guessed at.) Today, with electronic image intensifiers, which make it possible to reduce the dosage without loss of image, it is safer than ever. The reduction in dosage, in turn, allows us to expose the patient continuously for as much as forty minutes, though in normal work this figure is rarely approached. And by rotating the patient we can actually see his heart in action from every angle; in addition we can record the exposure on movie film or video tape and rerun the sequence at leisure and as often as we need without further exposing the patient.

Because of these twin advances, cardiac radiography is now the single most revealing test we can make of the heart and great vessels. Even two or three carefully chosen still pictures can tell a skilled interpreter all he needs to know for qualitative diagnosis. This is one of those skills more easily demonstrated than talked about, as figures 6·12a and 6·12b show.

6·12a This chest x-ray reveals: (1) ribs too horizontal, lung field too large (diagnosis: emphysema); (2) enlarged back ventricle, producing classic 'boot-shaped' heart, with dilatation of aorta (probable diagnosis: aortic valve disease).

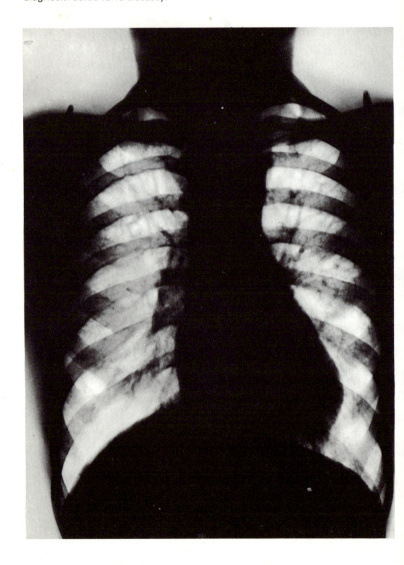

6·12b The heart shape here is virtually normal, the back ventricle *slightly* enlarged. The real interest here is in the ribs, many of whose lower margins are 'notched'. This is a sign of coarctation of the aorta (see also figure 6·18). Blood is rerouted through other arteries which swell and press on the ribs — hence the notches.

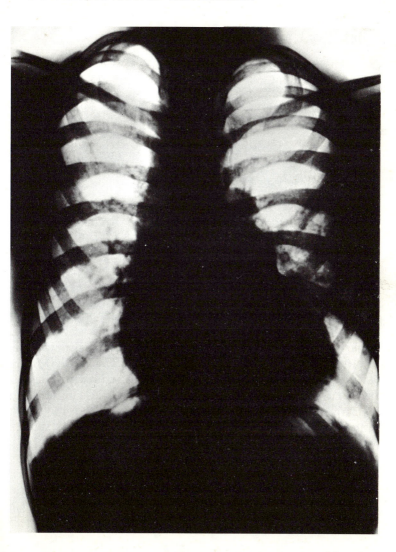

6·13 The layout of a catheter room during an investigation of a 5-year-old child. The doctor, gowned and masked, is working a catheter (coiled over the child's abdomen) through a vein in his right elbow, downstream toward the front chambers of the heart. The x-ray camera (source above bed, receiver below it) provides a picture on the TV screen whenever the doctor presses the foot pedal. Both the doctor and assistant wear lead-shield aprons to guard against x-rays.

Catheterisation

Straightforward radiography can reveal the existence of a defect, but it can only hint at its severity. What *is* the pressure differential across this patient's defect? How badly stenosed is that one's valve? How much blood is mingling through a patent duct? Has this patient's mitral regurgitation got significantly worse during the last four months?

To answer questions like these we have to get a measuring instrument into the heart itself while it is actually working. That instrument, the catheter, is a long, fine, flexible, hollow tube whose tip is slightly bent. To get it into the front of the heart we bare a vein in the arm, groin or neck and cut its wall enough to work the catheter in. To prevent the blood from clotting we inject heparin. Using low power x-rays and image intensifiers we steer the catheter downstream toward the superior vena cava; by rotating it we can point the bent tip in different forward directions so as to select the route and avoid pushing the catheter into other veins. We can thus work the catheter into the front atrium and, by choosing a moment when the tricuspid valve is open, into the front ventricle. The catheter is fine and flexible enough to still allow the valves to close. We can withdraw samples of blood at any point and analyse them. We can connect the catheter to a manometer and record instantaneous pressures in any part of the system. We can also inject harmless dyes that are opaque to x-rays and record the resulting flow pattern; this will reveal defects in septa and valves as well as abnormal great veins and arteries.

The technique for entering the back of the heart is basically similar, except that we enter via an artery in the arm. This is much more difficult, for we are working at higher pressures and against the stream as well as against the action of the aortic valve when we enter the back ventricle.

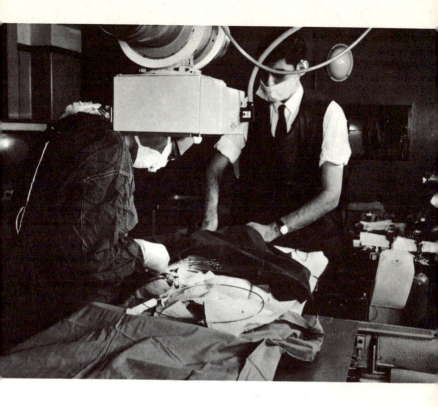

In general the whole business of catheterisation calls for the greatest skill. One needs only to misread the situation slightly in order to push the catheter through a valve leaflet, or a septum, or a vessel wall, even the wall of the heart itself. And in turbulent flow, often found in cardiovascular disease, the catheter can knot itself; the only remedy then being to open the chest on the operating table and remove the knotted part. Nevertheless in skilled hands the risks are small enough and the results of the tests valuable enough to make the technique one of the most valuable open to the cardiologist.

Figures 6·15 to 6·19 explain the basic details of cardiac catheterisation.

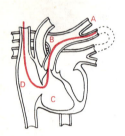

normal | patent ductus arteriosus | atrial septal defect | ventricular septal defect

(normal) 68, 68, 65, 68, 68, 68, 69

(patent ductus arteriosus) 79, 79, 81

(atrial septal defect) 76, 76, 76, 76, 76

(ventricular septal defect) 75, 75, 75, 68, 75

A, B, C, D

6·14 Left This schematic view of the heart shows four points at which pressures or blood samples can be obtained by catheter: A, pulmonary-wedge pressure (gives back atrial pressure); B, pulmonary artery; C, front ventricle; D, front atrium. The figures above show blood-oxygenation readings (in mm Hg, partial pressure) associated with various defects. (*Ductus arteriosus* is the arterial duct.)

6·15 Below Catheter pressure readings at the four points labelled in figure 6·14. Left pair: normal range is shown grey, readings in the vertically striped zone indicate mitral stenosis. Right pair: the coarse-textured zone is the range found with pulmonary stenosis; the fine-textured zone is the range found with tricuspid stenosis.

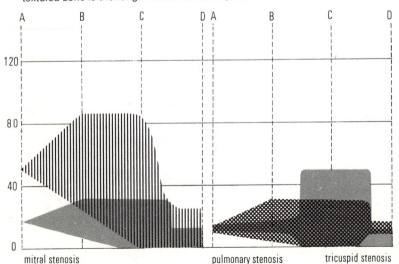

A B C D A B C D

120

80

40

0

▲ mm Hg

mitral stenosis   pulmonary stenosis   tricuspid stenosis

6·16 The angiogram reveals pulmonary stenosis; the expected shape is outlined in colour alongside. Arrows indicate turbulent outflow, which has distended the artery; long bar is expected orifice, short bar actual orifice of stenosed valve. 'U' shape brackets the catheter tip.

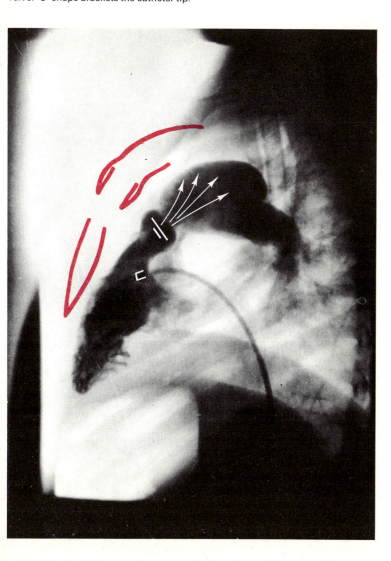

6·17 The angiogram shows a block in one coronary artery (A) which should continue down the front of the heart.
A normal artery is at B and a site of partial coronary blockage at C.
The catheter tip is again bracketed white.

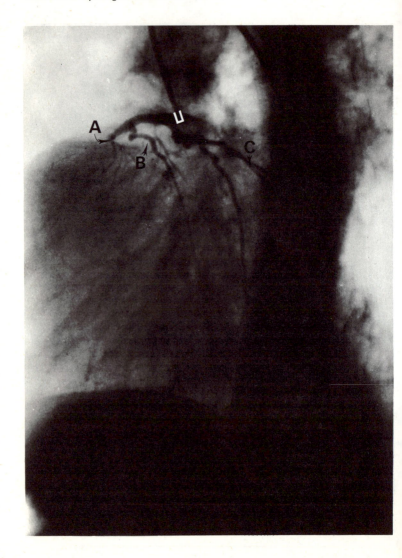

6·18 The angiogram shows how coarctation (narrowing) of the aorta (at F) vastly distends the aorta on the upstream side (E). Blood finds its way through alternate, anomalous arteries (G), normally minute and untwisted. At D you can see the coronary arteries. There are further notes on coarctation in the appendix (page 247).

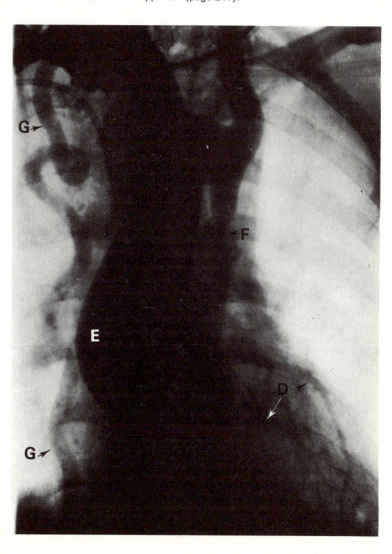

6·19 This postoperative angiogram shows the sutures
(L to L) and 'dent' (K) where the aorta was opened
and closed to replace the aortic valve. Now
the mitral valve does not close properly
(the bar at H shows the size of the opening),
permitting reflux of blood J. Again, the
white 'U' brackets the catheter tip.

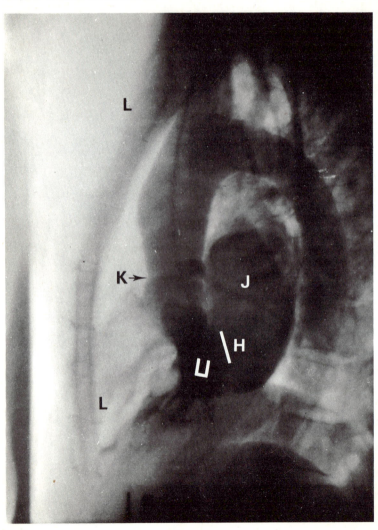

6·20 The principle of the Doppler shift measurement. A transmitted sound wave (black) strikes a moving object and is reflected (colour). Since the object is moving away from the source, the wavelength (λ) is longer and its pitch lower. If the object's direction were reversed the coloured wave would represent transmitted sound, the black wave reflected sound and the pitch would be higher.

Doppler shift measurements

Doppler shift is the change in frequency that happens when a source of waves (for example, of sound or light) changes its speed relative to an observer. Any city dweller has heard it in the falling tone of an ambulance siren as it passes by. The shift occurs whether the source is originating the waves, as the ambulance does, or is merely reflecting them, though it usually needs sensitive instruments to pick up the reflected waves.

When small ultrasound-emitting crystals and the systems for detecting ultrasound became cheaply available in the mid-1960s a number of medical physicists and doctors saw the enormous potential of this new kind of energy in diagnosis and research. We looked at sonar-type applications earlier in this chapter (p. 157). The Doppler shift phenomenon enables us to use the same waves to measure flows and movements. The method, known as Doppler rheography, is diagrammed and explained in figure 6·20.

Doppler shift measurements of average blood velocity in, for example, the aorta are a good guide to the state of the heart muscle. As we saw with the BCG, if the velocity peaks early, the muscle is more healthy and vigorous than if the peak comes late. In short, the Doppler rheograph and the BCG, neither of which insult the patient in any way, together provide the strongest possible evidence of the state of the heart muscle, surely the most important single fact, and something that until now we have had to infer by indirect means from other measurements. The work of Henry Light of the Medical Research Council brings the Doppler shift measurement of acceleration of blood up the aorta within reach of the clinicians.

Ultrasound harmonics

It may also be possible to use ultrasound harmonics to yield information about the state of a person's arteries. Dr Ray Gosling of Guy's Hospital, London, who is studying this possibility, points out that, just as middle C on a piano differs from middle C on a violin only in the matter of harmonics – and that those harmonics are determined by the nature of the string, the way it is set vibrating, and its environment – so a healthy artery and an unhealthy one (having different natures, responding differently to vibration, and providing different environments for sound waves) may alter the harmonics of an ultrasound input in characteristic ways. At present our main way of discovering the state of an artery and the precise site of a blockage is to inject an x-ray opaque dye upstream and photograph its passage with an x-ray camera. The ultrasound technique may reveal information about arterial conditions long before blockage occurs.

Throughout this chapter I have stressed that this or that technique involves no insult to the patient. This is not simply a humanitarian point, important though it is to cause as little pain and do as little damage as possible. As research tools those techniques that involve insult and danger have one great drawback: a doctor cannot conscientiously expose someone who is not ill and not a knowledgeable volunteer to any hazardous technique. Thus it is impossible for him to study random samples of normals; even healthy volunteers, being self-selected, are not random. Techniques that offer neither insult nor hazard will enable a doctor to study truly random samples. He will also know that the results are not distorted by the effects of discomfort, pain, or anaesthesia.

Such studies are an important prelude to unravelling the true nature of the heart. The machines and techniques we have looked at in this chapter focus a doctor's attention so strongly on the heart itself that, in clinical situations, he can easily overlook the general dynamics of the system of which the heart is only one member. And in any case, a specialist who examines a hundred ill people to one healthy one is not at all well placed to study those dynamics. We must look to research departments and foundations to provide the lead here. If we are to use even our existing machinery to the fullest advantage, we need to know vastly more about the *normal* heart and how it meshes with the *normal* system. The machines that offer no insult to the patient give us an ethical route toward this vitally needed information. We must spare no effort or reasonable expense in developing their fullest potential.

7 Treatment and repair

Whenever I feel downcast at the seemingly slow progress of medical science I find it helpful to glance through historical medical dictionaries, or even the clinical textbooks of a decade ago. They underline how much we have learned in that short while. (They also make clear the frighteningly brief shelf life of any textbook!) In the field of cardiology our gains have not simply been in matters of technique but in basic understanding of the dynamics and control mechanisms in the cardiovascular system as a whole. As understanding has grown, our therapy has become increasingly aggressive, both on the surgical side and, though it is less well known, on the medical side, too. Certain aspects of these widespread gains form the substance of this final chapter, which broadly answers the question: What can we do when things go wrong?

Let us start with what *you*, the owner of the system, can do. The best advice, I am afraid, is also the least practical. It is to pick your parents and nearer ancestors with care. Heredity outweighs all other factors among the causes of cardiovascular disease. If your parents, grandparents, and elder siblings have early cardiac histories, it would be deceitful for any doctor to pretend that you can greatly improve your chances of avoiding trouble (though it would be neglectful of him to do nothing for you, of course). If there is no early history in your family, you are very probably safe.

In passing, it is logically trivial to point out that everybody dies of something, but an important corollary is that that 'something' almost certainly has a strong hereditary element; even 'accidents' possibly come into this category. So cardiac disease is not peculiar in this respect.

Nevertheless the customary advice is still sound. The next most important step, after picking your parents, is to spend a lean and active childhood. The heart is partly a learning system; certainly it is adaptive. If you stress it the wrong way in childhood, with a fat or starchy diet and a lazy approach to exertion, you are storing up

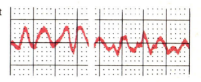

7·1 BCG traces show how smoking can affect a vulnerable heart. The left trace, already shaky, is from a patient with occasional angina pectoris. The right trace shows the same patient after smoking one cigarette; the heart muscle is obviously very ill coordinated. It took 15 minutes for the trace to return to this patient's 'normal'.

trouble early. The advice applies throughout life, of course, but it is particularly important when you are young.

Next avoid damp, temperate climates. The connection with cardiac disease is not clear, but Europeans in the tropics have significantly less trouble than they do in Europe, especially in its damp, cool, maritime fringes. If you have to live in a bad climate, pick a dry, centrally heated home and work-place.

In mature life you should avoid syphilis, a major scourge of the cardiovascular system. It causes degenerative changes in the heart and large arteries, often leading to aneurism (gross swelling) of the aorta. Aortic infection can cause the aortic valve to become incompetent; the ventricle then hypertrophies and, ultimately, fails.

Syphilis can also produce coronary damage, as does smoking, especially if you are from a cardiac family. In this context cigars and pipes are no 'safer' than cigarettes. Nicotine products in the bloodstream are powerful vasoconstrictors which also put up the heart rate. Angina attacks can be brought about by as little as one puff from a cigarette. A BCG taken during one such attack (see figure 7·1) shows how raggedly the muscle was coordinated once the nicotine clamped down the coronaries.

The advice 'don't get fat' needs a little caution. Some people come from fat families or are fat through glandular or psychological disorders; they should take specialist advice, not treat themselves by dieting. But if you are from a normally weighted family and your shadow has been growing by a dozen or so square inches a year over the last decade, it helps the heart if you eat less, or less often.

Regular moderate exercise also helps keep the muscle in a fit, adaptive state. The desk-bound businessman's worst enemy could be the considerate wife who takes him to and meets him from the station and who drags deckchairs and carries sandwiches into the garden every sunny weekend. If such advice falls on deaf ears – if, that is, you are incurably lazy and have no intention of gardening, or sailing, or cycling to the station – then at least be consistent: do not develop a once-a-year itch to split logs; when it comes to moving grand pianos, hire someone; if you are late, resign yourself to the fact. I know of a patient whose angina has practically stopped since he took his doctor's advice to 'put a radio in your car and to hell with it if you're late. Just relax.'

Failed ambition, intense grief, long, grudging hours at a badly motivated job, these have all been found to correlate with cardiac trouble; but it is difficult to frame practical advice around such findings.

The one-time bogeyman, cholesterol, has been the basis of a lot of controversial advice. In the public mind cholesterol has come to seem a kind of poison; in fact cholesterol and its derivatives play many vital roles in metabolism: it is essential, for instance, in activating the enzymes that help amino acids to form into proteins. Nevertheless, there is a significant relationship between arteriosclerosis and high serum-lipid levels, particularly serum cholesterol. Cutting down on lipid-rich diets (chiefly those with cooked animal fats) certainly reduces the level; but for a long time there was no firm evidence that it reduced arteriosclerosis and coronary heart disease. The difficulty in proving this vital link arose because cholesterol is one factor in a multifactorial situation. Now that it has been proved, doctors can confidently advise a person that he can cut his chances of a coronary by reducing his cholesterol. It will be interesting to see what effects the new cholesterol reducing drugs (shown in figure 7·2) have when used on large enough groups to produce meaningful statistics.

Figure 7·2 also gives all the major drug groups used in cardio-vascular medicine. The two final columns show how we think they work and how they are used. In the text, then, I shall merely add a few clarifying remarks and general comments.

A wag once said that cardiologists live by four Ds: digitalis, diuretics, dindivan, and death. He was a surgeon, of course, not a physician. Nevertheless, the joke emphasises two features worth closer study. The first three Ds neatly mark out two major areas in which drugs have proved markedly successful: in stimulating the heart (digitalis) and in reducing congestion in low output failure (diuretics); and one area where success is more controversial (dindivan, an anticlotting drug). The final D, in every sense of the word, reminds us that despite all our success, most cardiovascular disease is degenerative and, in the very nature of things, we are unlikely to find a chemical to *reverse* such disease, or even to completely halt it. Our only hope of doing that is to modify the genetic components of our cells so that we can reverse the changes believed to be responsible for degeneration and ageing in general. Present-day drugs, of course, have no designed effect upon the genes; they work by changing the metabolism or by interfering with large-scale control systems. So when I point out, for instance, that diuretics can at best turn an acute and dangerous degeneration into a very slow degeneration and can even stabilise the system for moderate spells, it is with no sense of criticism; indeed, with the subtle and pervasive power of the degenerative mechanism pitted against them it is really rather wonderful that simple chemicals can do so much.

Hypertensives: drugs to raise blood pressure

Type	Examples	Mechanism	Notes
Sympathetico-mimetics	Adrenaline (US: Epinephrine)	Raises blood pressure by direct cardiac action, increasing contractility and rate. Some peripheral action	Mainly used in emergency resuscitation; distributes bloodflow to essential organs; constricts some blood vessels and dilates others. Caution: it decreases renal blood flow
	Noradrenaline (US: Norepinephrine)	Constricts nearly all peripheral blood vessels; less direct cardiac action	Given by infusion to maintain blood pressure, but tissue perfusion (including renal) is poor
	Isoprenaline	Peripheral dilator but raises heart rate to more than counteract	Useful short-term drug; usually given by infusion
	Methoxamine	Acts almost entirely by vasoconstriction	Used by single injection or infusion to raise blood pressure in acute hypotensive states; becoming outmoded as they cut blood flow to vital organs
	Mephentermine Metaraminol	Mixed cardiac and peripheral action	

Anticoagulants: drugs to combat clotting

Type	Examples	Mechanism	Notes
Naturally occurring compounds	Heparin	Electronegative charge interferes with clotting enzymes	Immediately effective short-term drug; has to be injected or infused. So named because it was first extracted from liver - now from animal lung tissue
Coumarin derivatives	Dicoumarol Phenindione Warfarin Sinthone	Interfere with liver's production of clotting enzymes, especially factor VII (antihaemophiliac factor); thus not strictly an anticoagulant	Can be given orally but take 2 or 3 days to operate; dangerous in hepatic disease; need close and regular control; used as rat poison, too
Thrombolytic agents	Streptokinase	Dissolves already formed clot	Protein, derived from bacteria - thus may produce allergic reactions; useful for treating pulmonary emboli via a pulmonary artery drip
	Urokinase		Derived from human protein - less chance of allergic reaction
Snake venom	Arvin	Inactivates fibrin, an essential element of clot	May be used prophylactically but potentially very dangerous; requires careful and expert control

Type	Examples	Mechanism	Notes
Oestrogens	Oestradiol	Uncertain; probably metabolic	Effective doses feminise males; little used
	Stilboestrol	Same; synthetic	
	Ethinyloestradiol		Same; synthetic; potent
Thyroid hormone derivatives	Dextrothyroxine	Uncertain	Less metabolic effect than the natural thyroid hormone, laevothyroxine; usually an escape (return to pre-drug status) occurs after a few months
Nicotinic compounds	Nicotinic acid	Uncertain	Lowers cholesterol in some patients - but necessary large doses have unpleasant sideeffects
Antibiotics	Neomycin	Probably inhibits absorption	Not very effective; causes diarrhoea
Ion-exchange resin	Cholestyramine	Causes sequestration of bile acids	Bile acids, products of cholesterol breakdown, are normally reabsorbed and reused; causes an increase in faecal excretion of bile acids
Others	Clofibrate	Increases secretion of neutral sterols	Lowers cholesterol and triglycerides in some patient groups
	numbered compounds (no names)	Probably effect liver metabolism	Effective in some patient groups

Since the metabolism has many alternate pathways, antilipaemics, which generally act on one pathway, may initially be effective. But effectiveness tails off as alternate pathways open up

Cardiac glycosides: drugs to stimulate the heart

Digitalis preparations	Digitalis folia	Direct stimulation of myocardium with increase in contractility and excitability, depression of conductive tissue; vagal activity increased	Impure but long-used decoction from foxglove leaf
	Digoxin		Most widely used form; takes 24 to 36 hours to become effective; fixed by cardiac muscle and takes long to excrete
	Digitoxin		More quickly acting
Others	Lantocide C		Less nausea side effect
	Cedelanid		Quick acting and quick excretion
	Strophanthin Ovabain		Very quick acting forms - but injection only

The absolute indication for cardiac glycosides is atrial fibrillation. Some heart surgeons used to wean patients from digitalis before surgery - both to protect the heart from it and to use it as a postoperative weapon. Now Isoprenaline (see Hypertensives) and Procainamide (see Antidysrrhythmics) are preferred to combat digitalis-induced rhythm disturbances

Diuretics: drugs to reduce oedema

Type	Examples	Mechanism	Notes
Xanthine compounds	Aminophylline Theobromine Theophylline Caffeine Proxyphylline	See under coronary vasodilators	Weak action, variably effective; not much used as diuretics
Pyrimidine derivatives	Aminometramide Amisometradine	Uncertain	Very weak action; not much used since thiazides were introduced
Thiazides	Cyclopenthiazide Bendrofluazide Chlorothiazide Polythiazide Hydrochlorothiazide	Inhibit distal tubule reabsorption of Na	Very useful and widely used; these forms differ only in potency; cause K depletion, so K supplements must be used
	Frusemide	Similar effect to thiazides but on greater length of tubule	Very potent and potentially very dangerous; very useful in acute ventricular failure; causes greater K loss and so requires bigger K supplements
	Ethacrynic acid	Similar action on distal and proximal tubules	Extremely potent; may produce torrential flow of urine, useful in emergency but must have close supervision; K supplement essential
Carbonic anhydrase inhibitors	Acetazolamine	Inhibit carbonic anhydrase, enzyme needed by kidney in recovery of HCO_3, Na, and K (and H_2O)	Main use in combination with mercurials to produce acidosis
Organic mercurials	Mercurophylline Mercaptomerin Mersalyl	Inhibits proximal tubule enzymes needed for Na reabsorption	Intramuscular only; may cause renal damage; of declining importance since introduction of more modern drugs
Aldosterone antagonists	Spironolactone	Aldosterone increases Na reabsorption and K depletion; this is reversed	Causes K retention by itself but is a weak diuretic; most effective in combination with thiazides, where it combats thiazide-induced K depletion
	Triamterine	Does not block|aldosterone but|achieves same effect by direct action on tubule	
Osmotic diuretics	Urea Dextrose Sucrose Mannitol	Probably raise the renal blood flow; may also have osmotic effect in tubule	Sucrose is used where a quick-acting diuretic is needed — e.g. with head injuries. Mannitol, being metabolically inert, is the drug of choice in other cases; it has made urea and dextrose obsolete

Antidysrrhythmics drugs to combat rhythm disturbances

Type	Examples	Mechanism	Notes
Opiates	Morphine	Relaxes plain muscle and, to lesser extent, cardiac muscle	Sometimes relaxes outflow tract of heart and so restores normal rhythm
Local anaesthetics	Quinidine	Depresses all myocardial activity, both of muscle and conductive tissue, by affecting the electrical activity of the cell membrane	Mainly used against abnormal atrial rhythms
	Procaineamide		More effective in ventricular rhythm disturbances
	Lignocaine	Unknown	Frequently used; drug of choice against ventricular rhythm disturbances. Most hold it safe but some have doubts
Beta-sympathetic blockers	Pronethalol	Block both intrinsic and extrinsic beta-symphathetic activity in heart, thus reducing its excitability	Not now used; toxic effects shown in animals
	Propranolol		Widely used but suppresses myocardial activity and may precipitate heart failure
	Practolol		Very useful for atrial rhythm disturbances; little effect on contractility

Introduction of these drugs was based on a theory of cardiac activity involving complex alpha- and beta- blocking mechanisms. In fact, their action failed to support that theory and so has advanced our understanding of the heart's control mechanisms

Type	Examples	Mechanism	Notes
Cardiac glycosides	Digitalis	See section on cardiac glycosides	Depresses conducting tissues and so slows ventricular rate when atrial rhythm is fast.But overdose, by increasing myocardial irritability, can cause a wide variety of rhythm disturbances
Vagal blockers	Atropine	Blocks the decelerating effect of the vagus nerve.Essential premedication for anal operations and abortions	Mildly unpleasant side effects - dry mouth
	Propantheline		Less unpleasant but not always effective
Barbiturates	Phenetoin Mesentoin	Has prime effect on central nervous system - used against epilepsy	All are useful for ventricular rhythm disturbances
Vagomimetics	Neostigmine	Inhibit enzyme that destroys acetylcholine and so simulates vagal decelerating action. Main use is against myasthenia gravis	Relatively short-acting; may have unpleasant side effects
	Physostigmine		Longer acting
	Edrophonium		Very short-acting and thus useful for preliminary tests

Antidysrrhythmics (continued):

Type	Examples	Mechanism	Notes
Others	Antihistamines	Unknown	Useful for ventricular rhythm disturbances
	D-Propanolol	Unknown - but not a beta-blocker like propanolol	

Antihypertensives: drugs to reduce blood pressure

Type	Examples	Mechanism	Notes
Vegetable alkaloids	Veratrum Veriloid	Raise vagal tone thus reducing heart rate and blood pressure	Experimentally interesting - may elucidate mechanism for resetting cardiovascular control; not used clinically - therapeutic dose close to toxic dose
Rauwolfia extracts	Reserpine Alseroxylon	Deplete natural supply of noradrenaline at sympathetic nerve endings	Useful in mild hypertension but high dose may cause depression - possibly due to depletion of brain noradrenaline
Ganglion blockers	Pempidine Mecamylamine Pentolinium	Block sympathetic ganglia and so lower blood pressure but also block parasympathetic ganglia	Now outmoded for general use - but still very useful in acute hypertensive crises
	Trimetaphan Arfonad		Used for lowering blood pressure in surgery; frequently in coarctation operations
Sympathetic blockers	Bretylium	Deplete natural supply of noradrenaline at nerve endings and also inhibit its release	Outmoded; toxic
	Guanethidine		Takes several days to act; may cause side effects, especially postural hypotension
	Bethanidine		Quicker acting
	Debrisoquine Guanoxan		Recent drugs with supposedly fewer side effects
	Methyldopa	Blocks noradrenaline receptor sites by formation of methyl-noradrenaline	Less effective but fewer side effects, especially with postural hypotension; good for mild hypertension; may induce haemolytic anaemia
	All these drugs are efficient and are widely used		
Alpha-sympathetic blocking agents	Phenoxybenzamine Phentolamine Tolazoline Thymoxamine	Blocks noradrenaline sites in peripheral vessels, thus producing peripheral vasodilation	Can be used to reduce blood pressure associated with phaeochromocytoma (noradrenaline-producing adrenal tumour); slightly effective at producing vasodilation in peripheral vascular disease. Used to raise peripheral blood flow in low-output failure - in combination with plasma expanders

Type	Examples	Mechanism	Notes
Beta-sympathetic blocking agents	Propanolol	Probably act by direct effect on heart - reducing blood pressure by reducing output	Variable effectiveness - avoids postural side effects but dangerous in cases of incipient cardiac failure

Coronary vasodilators: drugs to increase the blood supply to the heart

Type	Examples	Mechanism	Notes
Nitro-compounds	Glyceryl trinitrate	May directly dilate coronaries, or may peripherally dilate thus reducing blood pressure and cardiac work	One of cardiology's most useful drugs; a form of the explosive TNT; therapeutic effects long known; absorbed under tongue; oral only
	Pentaerythrityl tetranitrate Erythrityl tetranitrate		Longer acting but much less effective
Xanthine compounds	Aminophylline Theobromine Theophylline Caffeine Proxyphylline	Peripheral and coronary vasodilation; increase heart muscle contractility; diuretic effect; stimulate central nervous system	In cardiology are mainly used in acute ventricular failure; usually given intravenously; also by suppository and, less effectively, by mouth
Pyrimidine derivatives	Dipyridamole	Possibly enhances heart muscles' ability to use O_2	In healthy dogs the effect is dramatic: coronary sinus blood goes bright red and pressure is nearly arterial (so perhaps it opens arteriovenous shunts?). In diseased human coronaries results are disappointing
Sympathetico-mimetics	Adrenaline (US; Epinephrine)	See under hypertensives	

7·2 The chart on this and the preceding five pages lists the major categories of cardiovascular drugs. The text between pages 182 and 187 comments extensively on them. Low blood pressure (hypotension) is no longer recognised as a disease, though in some European countries (particularly, for some reason, Germany) it is still diagnosed and treated.

Digitalis

This drug was introduced into general medicine in the 1770s by the English physician William Withering. He came across a 'receipt' for a folk remedy for dropsy, which he used experimentally on his charity patients. (Reputation-building by using someone else's work on naive 'volunteers' is, you see, well hallowed!) It was clear to him that the active ingredient was an infusion of the leaves of the foxglove, *Digitalis purpurea*, and he prescribed it for dropsy – the oedema, or waterlogging of the tissues, that accompanies low output failure. At first he gave doses large enough to produce vomiting, thinking that this and the following intestinal purge caused the diuresis (reduction in oedema). However, he soon realised that it had a diuretic effect in much smaller doses. And that is his real contribution to medicine.

For about 150 years digitalis was our only effective cardiac drug. During that time it was tried, whether suitable or not, in every conceivable cardiovascular disease and it has collected more literature than any similar drug (a lot of it, as one might expect, 'I have done this, too' papers). In structure, digitalis is a cardiac glycoside, a mixture of a complex sugar and an aglycone; the aglycone contains a steroid nucleus similar to that of the adrenal cortex hormones. Neither part of this mixture, given separately, has any cardiac effect. Combined in one molecule they become one of the most potent of all cardiac drugs. It achieves its effect in two ways: it reduces the conductivity of the heart; and it stimulates the muscle, putting up V_{max}, so that the heart contracts more strongly.

These features make it useful in a heart with atrial fibrillation. By reducing conductivity they make it less likely for the atrial disturbance to trigger arrhythmic ventricular beats. They also explain its diuretic action: The stronger heart-beat raises the arterial pressure and makes the kidneys function more efficiently.

There are patients in whom this diuresis is inadequate and they must be given other diuretics that directly affect the kidneys (we shall look at these other drugs in a moment). This produces one of the major complications of diuretic therapy. Prolonged diuresis upsets the Na/K pumps in the body's cells; they begin to retain more sodium than normal and to excrete potassium. This happens even with modern diuretics designed specifically to promote potassium retention; they merely slow down the depletion. A system low in potassium is abnormally sensitive to digitalis, which then produces spontaneous arrhythmias in the ventricular muscle. The only effective treatment is to put such patients on a low-sodium diet with potassium supplements and use an artificial kidney machine both to get the excess fluid out of the tissues and (by adjusting the make-up of the dialysing fluid in the machine) to remove sodium and put back potassium.

We now have two kinds of digitalis, one which stays in the body for a fairly long time, and one that is quickly removed. The long-stay variety is used for day-in, day-out therapy. The short-stay variety is useful in emergencies. Suppose, for instance, an unconscious patient is brought to hospital in heart failure. If he is fully digitalised, a further dose may cause digitalis poisoning, with vomiting and arrhythmias. If he is not digitalised, a full dose could save him. In these circumstances the advantages of a short-stay compound are obvious.

Another big problem with digitalis is that the toxic threshold is very close to the effective dose. And because the drug accumulates in different people in different ways, its use needs constant supervision by the doctor.

184

Diuretics

We have already seen the main use of diuretics: to reduce the oedema which both signifies ,and accelerates low output failure. The earliest kinds, now obsolescent, were organomercurial compounds that reduce the efficiency of the kidney tubules and prevent them from reabsorbing much. Of course, a lot of useful blood constituents (shown in figure 2·9) are lost, too, and have to be made up in the diet.

More recent diuretics work on the tubules more selectively. Some inhibit the enzymes which are part of the chain of events that lead to water reabsorption in the distal tubules and collecting ducts; thus they leave the proximal tubule free to absorb wanted foodstuffs. The proximal tubule also passively reabsorbs some water, so these diuretics are unsuitable for rapid diuresis in emergencies. Unfortunately the distal tubule also plays a major part in adjusting the Na/K balance, so that the patient still needs a low-sodium diet and potassium supplements.

Other diuretics contain substances like the synthetic sugar mannitol, which the kidney passes but cannot (as it can with other sugars) reabsorb. The mannitol therefore remains on the downstream side of the membrane, where its high osmotic action draws water out of the bloodstream.

Anticoagulants

One of the problems with atrial fibrillation is the tendency of the blood to stagnate in parts of the atria, especially the atrial appendages, and so to clot. A fibrillating atrium is thus a continuously reloading gun ready to fire a steady stream of clots into the arterial tree. A possible remedy was suggested when, in 1934, cows on a farm in Wisconsin began to bleed uncontrollably, even from slight cuts. The farmer took a dead cow and a pail of still-liquid blood to the university, where Dr Karl Paul Link became interested. Link and his colleagues eventually traced the trouble to bishydroxy-coumarin (or dicoumarol), a substance in spoiled clover closely related to coumarin, which gives new-mown grass its attractive smell. Dicoumarol works by upsetting the liver's synthesis of pro-thrombin, a precursor of one element in a clot.

(One wonders, incidentally, how far a similarly affected farmer would have got if his nearest university had been Harvard or Yale, or Oxford or Cambridge. How many Cambridge college porters could have told him where to take a pail of abnormal blood and a dead cow? This Wisconsin farmer won through because he turned up after normal hours and found Link still at work – a good way to select the right man for many a project.)

Dicoumarol derivatives became the basis for a number of anti-coagulants now in widespread use to prevent clotting (dindivan being one of them). The problem is that the doctor effectively turns his patient into a haemophiliac. If he does not, then the therapy is wasted, for clotting is an all-or-nothing affair. If the patient does not clot, he is then a haemophiliac; if he clots only slightly, he clots enough to risk thrombosis. This produces an out-of-the-frying-pan-into-the-fire situation that leaves no one happy.

Nor is that all. There is a possible rebound phenomenon when, for any reason, anticoagulants are stopped. The blood of the patient may then become abnormally prone to clot. In any case, anticoagulants complicate the surgeon's work because, of course, he cannot attempt major surgery of the heart and vessels with an effective haemophiliac. Long-term anticoagulants must be stopped before an operation (though the patient may be given a short-term anticoagulant just for the duration of the operation). The technique is to accelerate the whole process. We give vitamin K_1 oxide to stimulate the liver into producing prothrombin and then, just before the operation we give heparin, another anticlotting agent, but one that can be reversed within minutes by injections of protamine; heparin also, incidentally, works on another part of the clotting mechanism, so it does not compete with dicoumarol derivatives. The clotting mechanism must be suspended during the actual operation because, if the patient is put on a heart-lung machine, his blood would clot the moment it met the foreign surfaces of the tubes, pumps, oxygenators, and so on. We use heparin because it can be reversed so quickly after the operation, when, of course, clotting is an essential part of healing and recovery. Heparin is difficult to use routinely, for it has to be injected. Dicoumarol compounds can be taken orally. They are also cheap, whereas heparin, which has to be extracted from animal tissues, is very costly.

Most surgeons are sceptical about anticoagulants, for during mitral valve operations they have often removed large soft masses of clot from the back atria of patients on anticoagulant drugs; these soft masses are quite different from the hard, organised lumps one gets in patients not on anticoagulants. A surgeon with a patient on these drugs learns to handle the atria as little and as gingerly as possible until he has made an incision and removed all traces of soft clot – taking care to constrict the arteries to the head while he does so, in case any clot should escape into the aorta.

Drugs against arrhythmias

Anticoagulant therapy accepts AF (atrial fibrillation) and seeks to mitigate its effect. The alternative strategy is to return the atria to normal sinus rhythm. This is a tall order, for the conditions that produce AF (such as stretched atrial muscle due to valve disorder, or the aftermath of rheumatic heart disease) are not reversible. The fibrillation is, the reader will remember, due to circular depolarising currents in the damaged muscle, each fibre depolarising on an impulse from its neighbours as soon as it gets into the relative refractory period.

One technique is to give antidysrrhythmic drugs such as quinidine, whose effective dose, like that of digitalis, is very close to its toxic dose. The other is to defibrillate the heart electrically with a 400 joule DC discharge that rises in a controlled way over about 0·15 sec to a peak 6,000 volts. This controlled rise is important in keeping tissue damage to a minimum.

The effect of the discharge is to depolarise all the fibres. The natural pacemaking pulse from the SA node then restarts the heart in sinus rhythm. Usually, alas, the diseased muscle slips back into AF within minutes or hours but sometimes normal sinus rhythm is sustained. Of course, the patient must be anaesthetised to withstand such a shock, and that in itself has a depressing effect on cardiac function. In addition, the shock temporarily lowers V_{max}, so there is a further loss in efficiency. Nevertheless, defibrillation can halt arrhythmias. When it fails, we use drugs.

Heart surgery

Mention of defibrillation has brought us to the transition between medical and surgical aspects of cardiac therapy. The earliest operations on the heart were performed as long ago as 1925, when Sir Henry Souttar of the London Hospital operated on mitral valve defects by putting a 'purse-string' suture into the heart muscle (see figure 7·3), cutting inside it through the muscle, and then inserting a finger through the hole while drawing the purse-string tight so as to minimise blood loss. By moving the finger around he opened and relieved stenosis of the valve. Alas, the cardiology of the 1920s had not learned to distinguish between stenosis and regurgitation, so that he sometimes made regurgitation worse instead of stenosis better. Also, no one then knew enough about the post-operative management of patients who had had ribs removed and whose lung cavities had been opened. They had no ventilators, for instance, to help the patient breathe, and were not aware that pulmonary vascular resistance can greatly increase post-operatively. The disappointing results of Souttar's brave pioneer work led to a general retrenchment for almost two decades.

Then in the late 1940s the American surgeon Al Blalock devised a technique for increasing pulmonary circulation in tetralogy of Fallot. He either joined a minor chest artery directly into the pulmonary artery or he removed a short length of vein and used it to cross-connect the aorta and pulmonary artery, depending on circumstances. By using a special clamp he was able to work on these arteries while they were carrying blood, without either spilling blood or stopping the flow.

Shortly afterwards, Russel Brock (now Lord Brock) in Britain and Charles P. Bailey in the United States revived Souttar's operation, taking advantage of the great improvements in surgery, drugs, diagnosis, and post-operative therapy which the intervening years had brought. Both independently improved Souttar's technique by devising small knives and guillotines to fit over the end of the exploring finger.

Straightforward finger dilation of a stenosed mitral valve was useless where the tendinous cords had shortened and fused (see figure 7·4). Widening the valve merely made a wider mouth to the hardened funnel formed by the cords. The transventricular dilator, pioneered by Andrew Logan in Edinburgh and also shown in figure 7·4, enabled surgeons, again working through a purse-string suture, to both widen the valve and loosen the tendinous cords. The technique is still sometimes preferred to open-heart surgery, since it involves much less insult to the patient; but open-heart facilities ought to be held on standby so that if the surgeon

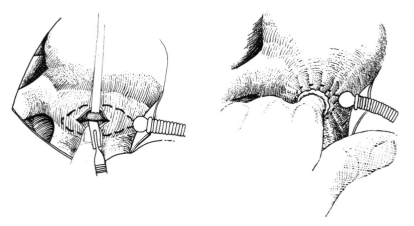

7.4 Right Logan's historic transventricular dilator. It could be passed through a purse-string suture and worked among fused valve leaflets and cords, where it was dilated so as to free them (*inset*).

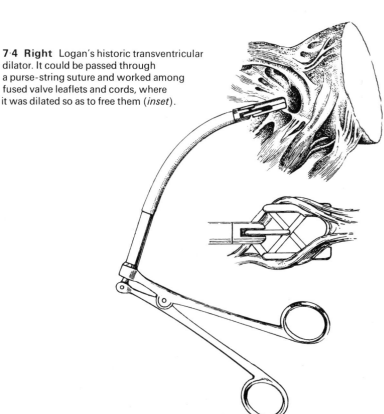

recognises that regurgitation dominates over the stenosis, he can open up and reduce the valve orifice or replace the valve.

There was a widespread outcry of 'bandwagon' following Christiaan Barnard's first heart transplant, an operation which was duplicated in four other continents. It is therefore satisfying to recall how, on the same day in 1953, Russel Brock at Guy's Hospital and Thomas Holmes Sellors at the Middlesex Hospital, less than three miles away, each did an operation for widening the pulmonary valve. Brock worked on the underside of the valve via a purse-string in the front ventricular wall, Holmes-Sellors on the upper side through the wall of the left pulmonary artery. Neither knew that the other had prepared to do this particular operation; within months, other surgeons around the world, using their own techniques, for which they, too, had prepared, did similar operations. There are tides in medicine and surgery that are barely dependent on individual physicians and surgeons.

It is chastening to realise that until Blalock, Bailey, Brock and company adopted these aggressive tactics toward ailments of the heart, cardiologists had never actually seen a human heart beating in a human chest (except back in Leonardo's time, when they often cut open prisoners condemned to death). Surgery like this created an urgent need for much more detailed knowledge about the heart. It also made the surgeons most closely involved a good deal more venturesome. Having at last breached the citadel of the heart it was galling for them not to be able to see what they were doing. I myself entered surgery at this time and remember well the frustration of feeling defects I would never see (or so we thought); and I never closed a purse-string suture without wondering if I had done too much – or not enough.

The next step was to take advantage of the fact that, with competent atrial valves, pressure in the atria usually rises by only a few millimetres of mercury, equivalent to a blood column a few

centimetres high. Thus a wide-mouthed funnel, twenty or so centimetres high (called an atrial well), temporarily sutured to an
incision in an atrium, would quarter fill with blood and allow the
surgeon's hand access to the atrium. This allowed him to close an
atrial septal defect; but he could not work on the valve for fear
that the much higher ventricular pressures would fill and overflow
the well.

Open-heart surgery

Still we could not see the defects we were working on. To do that
we had to open the heart. And before we could do that we had
either to make it safe to stop the circulation or to provide an
alternative pump and, perhaps, an oxygenator.

One alternative pump, tried and abandoned, was another human
of the same blood group. His or her circulation was cross-connected
to the patient's and the healthy heart took on the task of maintaining both while the ailing heart was repaired. The risks were so high
that, in practice, the technique was limited to mother-baby type
relationships. And with the advent of other techniques, cross-
circulation passed into the limbo of history.

The first of these other techniques is hypothermia, in which the
anaesthetised patient is cooled from the normal 38°C to around
30°C. At this temperature the heart continues to beat, though
slowly. The reasoning behind this technique is chemical. The metabolism, like all chemical systems, is temperature dependent; and,
since the rate of reaction in general doubles for every 10°C rise, a
fall of 8°C should, in theory, stretch reaction time by 80 per cent.
The longest time we can safely stop the circulation at normal
temperature is three minutes – not long enough even to open and
close an incision and leave a margin of safety. Hypothermia to
30°C should, in theory, stretch this to about five and one-half

minutes; in fact, because of the oddities of living chemistry, the safe time at 30°C is up to eight minutes.

This is long enough to close an atrial septal defect and to reopen a stenosed pulmonary valve. A very skilled surgeon could also cope with a small ventricular septal defect but that would be the limit. We who had grumbled for years about our inability to see what we were doing now, felt, if anything, even more disgruntled. As precious seconds ticked away we saw horrors it would take perhaps an hour to correct; and we could do nothing but sew the patient up again, knowingly leaving them with valves like lumps of coke and septal defects as big as a thumb.

The next step was obvious: profound hypothermia. At 10°C the circulation can be stopped for up to an hour without too much damage. The problem is to get the patient cooled that deeply. In mild hypothermia (above 30°C) the heart continues to beat. We can thus give the patient a vasodilating drug to open his skin capillaries and simply lay him in cold water at about 10°C. His heart will keep pumping and the circulating blood will cool him all over. But at 29°C the heart begins to fibrillate, so that to get a patient down to 10°C we have to pump his blood through a heat exchanger. In fact, as figure 7·4 shows, we need two pumps because we use the lungs as a gas exchanger; one pump takes over the front ventricle's function, the other that of the back ventricle. These pumps are brought into action as soon as the heart begins to fibrillate.

Many surgeons are against the idea of cooling patients in this way. The fundamental objection is physiological: the metabolism is not evenly decelerated by cooling; in fact, some enzymes even work faster at 10°C than they do at 38°C. There is thus a fair degree of distortion for the patient's system to straighten out after rewarming. There are also practical objections. When the heart is beating normally (even though it is empty of blood) the surgeon can see when he is getting dangerously near the AV node and bundle; the resulting rhythm disturbance in the ECG or the heart itself warns him. The profoundly hypothermic heart can give no such warning. Hypothermia is also a long haul for the patient, for although the surgeon has at most an hour with the heart open, the patient could be unconscious from breakfast till teatime while they cool him, connect and disconnect all the pipes, and rewarm him. And, finally, the knowledge that in sixty minutes or less, come what may, his patient will die unless rewarmed, is an almost intolerable strain on a surgeon. What, for instance, if when every suture in a new valve is neatly in place, both in the valve and in the heart (see figure 7·6), he or his assistant drops it, so that it turns over and tangles? All the sutures would then have to be cut and reinserted and the patient would not stand a chance. The imagination can conjure up a dozen similar disasters without effort. A good surgeon tries to anticipate what might go wrong, but must even so be ready to meet unexpected disasters.

Nevertheless, a few surgeons who really took the trouble to master the technique achieved excellent results and went on doing so until very recently, despite (I believe) and not because of profound hypothermia. Nowadays I know of nowhere where the technique is routinely employed by preference.

The method now universally used is cardiopulmonary bypass with a heart-lung machine. The 'bypass' refers to the lungs as well as the heart, for this machine performs all gas-exchange functions, unlike those used for hypothermia (see figure 7·7). There is thus a great simplification of the connections between patient and machine; one line to drain the great veins into the machine and one line from the machine back to a large artery, either the aorta or the femoral artery at the top of the thigh. If for any reason the aorta is clamped, two small extra lines lead from the machine to the coronary arteries.

7·5 Blood-pumping system for inducing profound hypothermia consists of two synchronised circuits. The one to the left draws blood from the venae cavae, passes it through a cooler, and discharges it at low pressure into the pulmonary artery. After gas exchange in the lungs the blood passes into the second circuit, where it is further cooled and pumped at higher pressure into the aorta. One major drawback is the clutter of tubes this introduces into the surgeon's field.

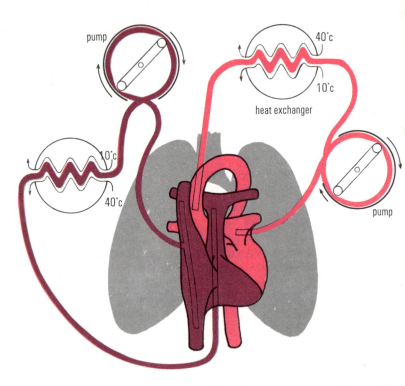

The machine oxygenates the blood, warms or cools it as the surgeon wants, removes all traces of air, and returns it under pressure to the body. In fact, in those rare cases where we still need profound hypothermia, we can induce it with the standard heart-lung machine. Figure 7·8 identifies the parts of one type of heart-lung machine.

The first prototype of the heart-lung machine was used in 1937; it was employed on cats, who survived almost thirty minutes on bypass. Sixteen years later came the successful closure of a human

7·6 An aortic homograft valve with sutures between its root, and the base of the aorta. The two tubes (right centre) are the coronary cannulae. When tied the sutures must withstand full arterial pressure. The text conjures up the nightmare of dropping or tangling these threads in a hypothermic patient who will have to be rewarmed within 10 to 15 minutes of this stage.

atrial septal defect, with the patient on bypass also for nearly thirty minutes. A modified version of the machine went into regular use from 1955. The great advance that all such machines represent is that they offer the surgeon a chance to work, for several hours if necessary, on an open, dry heart chamber at normal body temperatures, and with the muscle contracting normally. In short, the surgeons now had the great gift of time.

At this point the reader will perhaps have begun to notice a pattern: leap-frogging of determination on the one hand and

7·7 Schematic circuit of a heart-lung bypass. Blood is drawn from the venae cavae, oxygenated, rewarmed to body temperature (or, if the surgeon wishes, cooled), passed through a filter designed to remove air and other emboli, and pumped back into the aorta and coronary arteries at arterial pressure. Anaesthetics, drugs, transfusions, and isotonic fluids can be added to the circuit.

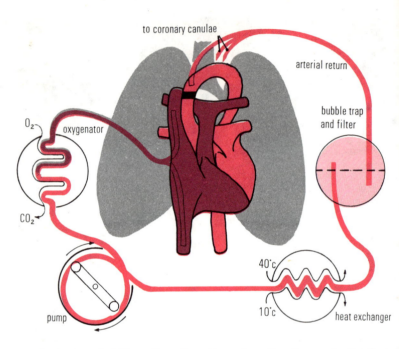

equipment and skill on the other. Ever since Souttar made the first move into the forbidden territory of the heart there had been a steady escalation in our estimates of where the limit of the possible lay. Next we wanted to *see* the structure we were working on, which led to mild hypothermia. Then, aghast at some of the things we saw, we wanted more time to put them right, which led to profound hypothermia. Next we wanted even more time – for a safety margin, for young surgeons to gain experience without hazard to the patient, and for difficult and complex repairs. We also wanted normal temperatures and a contractile heart so that we could monitor the patient's performance and keep his physiology within recognisable limits. That led to cardiopulmonary bypass.

And when it came it inevitably produced its own escalation. We had time in hand, we did not lack for techniques or tools; all we needed was a good repair kit, particularly valves and patching materials. Plastics technologists soon gave us adequate patching materials: Dacron, Teflon, Mylar, Ivalon sponge, polyurethanes, and Stafoam have all been used satisfactorily. They soon become covered with new endothelial cells, which (to the blood and its clotting factors) make them indistinguishable from natural wall lining. The valves have proved more difficult.

Replacements for heart valves

Innumerable designs have been tried. The most successful have not sought to copy the design of the natural valve in any way. The natural valve, because it is self-renewing and adaptive, can withstand 80 million flexions a year; no plastic could do that. The prosthetic valve has no flexing part. It consists of a hollow stainless steel ball trapped in a fine metal cage and capable of seating on a ring that can be sewn into a valve orifice (see figure 7·9).

The main disadvantages are that the blood flow beyond the valve is turbulent; the ball can crush blood as it sits in its ring; and the metal can never become incorporated into the body. In earlier valves, where the ball was of silicone rubber, it could swell and create an incompetent valve; or it sometimes shrank and fired off into the bloodstream, though both mishaps were very rare. The modern valve has advantages, too. Its strength can compensate for weakness and disease in the natural valve roots and it can be kept on the shelf until it is needed.

Dissatisfaction with these valves in their early days led my colleague Donald Ross, in England, Barrat Boys in New Zealand, and others, to try valve transplants. A healthy valve, they reasoned, has no blood vessels, is chiefly of fibre, invested with a few fibre-making cells and covered with endothelium, and could easily be dehydrated. There is also no danger of rejection with these transplants, since little donor protein is carried over into the recipient.

One technique is to dissect the valves from healthy autopsy hearts and, after sterilising them, freeze-dry them in low vacuum. The dried sterile valves are stored in sealed glass tubes until needed (see figures 7·10 to 7·12). The aortic and pulmonary valves are taken with a collar of artery around them: the mitral valve (shown in figures 7·11 and 7·12) has its papillary muscles replaced by little Dacron 'socks' and a Dacron ring is sewn around its root. We cannot, of course, get both the aortic and mitral valves out of the same heart since one leaflet of the aortic is continuous with one leaflet of the mitral. The tricuspid is too difficult to handle as a homograft. It is replaced by a prosthetic valve.

Our early high hopes of these natural valves have not entirely been borne out by experience. In some cases the processes that destroyed the original valves have gone on to destroy the replacement. In others, the fibrous part of the leaflets has reorganised in strange, almost random ways instead of in organised response to the stresses on them. These problems, together with steady improvement in prosthetic valves, has diminished the great advantages that they once, in my view, had.

It is possible that the problems are not fundamental but that they are associated with the particular method of presentation: freeze-drying. At the National Heart Hospital we are now experimenting with many different preservation techniques: gamma-ray sterilisation, flash freezing in CO_2 snow, hyperbaric oxygen, and so on.

Despite many improvements, the modern heart-lung machine is still fairly damaging to blood. The pumps tend to crush red cells; and, even worse, the direct presentation of blood to dry gaseous oxygen rapidly denatures the protein. There are problems associated

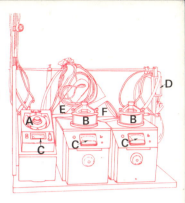

A: Arterial pump with large stroke volume; the pressure gauge is on the column above, near the top of the picture.

B: Suction pumps for sucking leaked blood in the surgeon's field.

C: Rev counters (tachometers) from which pumped volumes can be derived.

D: Box of spare sterile connectors for emergency tube replacement.

E: Sterile tubing for connection to patient, tripple-wrapped in sterile plastic bags. The oxygenator cylinder is partly visible behind and through these bags.

F: Part of heat exchanger.

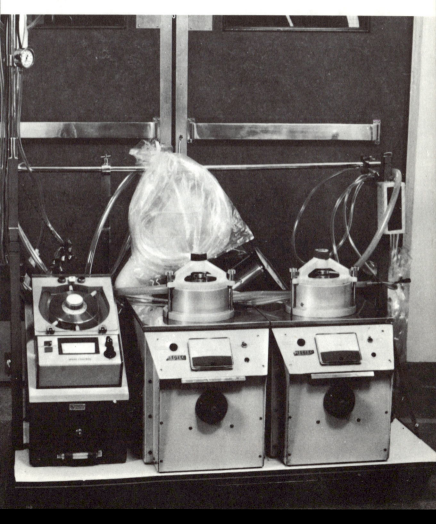

7·9 A prosthetic ball-in-cage-type valve for replacing a faulty mitral or tricuspid valve (aortic and pulmonary replacements are about 20 per cent smaller and have a different ring). Except for the ball its stainless steel surfaces are enclosed in woven Dacron mesh on which new endothelium quickly grows — making a blood-compatible surface. The ball is hollow to give it a similar density to that of blood and reduce its inertia.

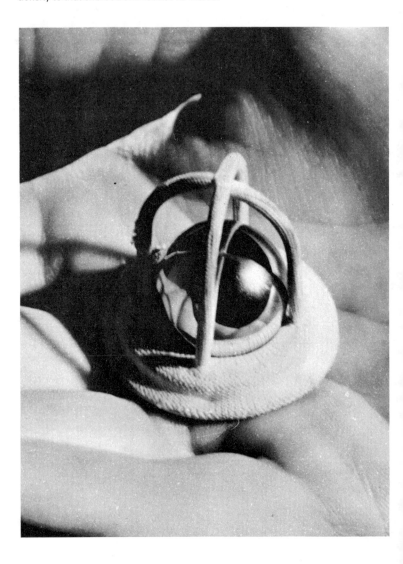

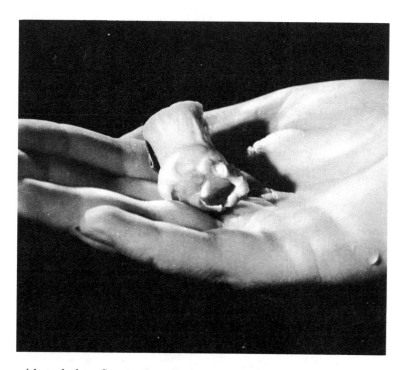

7·10 An aortic homograft valve reconstituted from its freeze-dried state (see figure 7·12) by immersion in normal saline solution. Its bulging root (nearest) is clearly visible. The lower and upper ends are tailored by the surgeon before suturing into the patient (see figure 7·6). The tag has the valve's serial number.

with turbulent flow and cavitation, too. Clearly we are unlikely to overcome such radical problems, touching, as they do, every part of the machine, by simply adding 'improvements' here and there. We need a radical solution.

Two of my colleagues, Dennis Melrose and Norah Burns, of the Hammersmith Hospital, may have the basis of such a solution. Early in 1969 they announced an achievement that plastics technologists around the world had long sought for: the continuous production of thin membranes of silicone rubber. The Melrose-Burns membrane is a mere twelve microns thick, yet it is far

7·11 A mitral homograft valve reconstituted (see figure 7·10). Its root is not strong enough to take sutures and so has been strengthened with a Dacron-mesh ring. The tendinous cords, too, have been sutured to Dacron 'socks', which are sewn into the patient's papillary muscles.

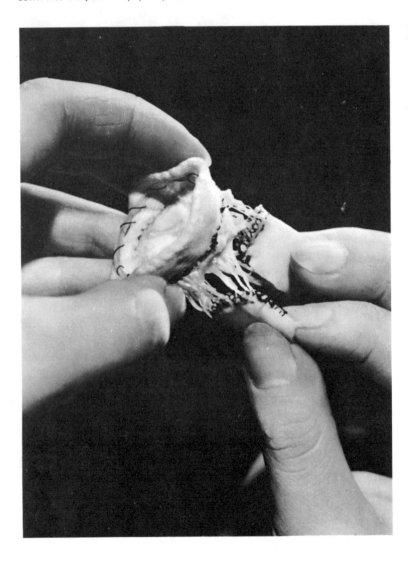

7.12 The two valves shown in figures 7.10 and 7.11 are here seen in their freeze-dried state before reconstitution. The valves are removed from autopsy hearts, tested for strength and disease, meticulously sterilised, and freeze-dried before being put into these sterile containers. The aortic homograft (*lower*) is accompanied by a few spare bits of aorta from the same autopsy to allow destruction tests for strength without damaging the homograft. The technique is becoming obsolescent.

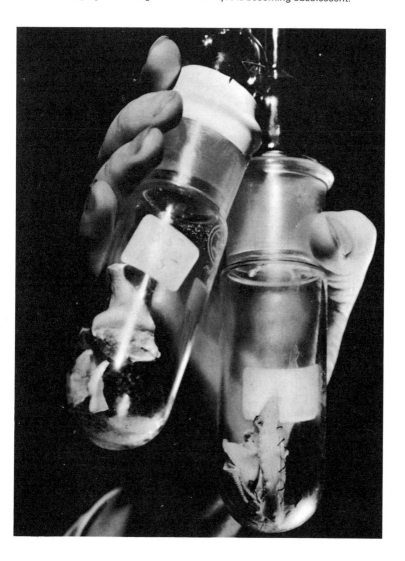

MUSCLE
none dead   all de

	angina	moderate disablement	severe disablement	almost total disablement	terminal state
ECG	possible changes	definite changes			
BCG	possible predictive changes				
other	rhythm disturbances ————————————————————→ repeated crises				
THERAPY					
physician	coronary and peripheral dilators antidysrrhythmics	heart stimulants anticoagulants for atrial fibrillation		diuretics antihypotensives	
surgeon	coronary repair, replacement, or bypass	revascularisation graft		transplantation	

stronger than any previous silicone membrane; it is also easily handled and completely free of pores. The great virtue of silicone rubber is that it allows oxygen and CO_2 to dissolve in it and pass through at least sixty times faster than any other plastic. It is the ideal material for a membrane oxygenator (a device that displays blood to oxygen through a membrane, thus avoiding the denaturing of its protein). Other workers have achieved equally thin silicone membrane but only by curing the polymer in such a way that its ability to 'breathe' oxygen and CO_2 was drastically impaired.

By pulsing the oxygen between the layers of membrane it should be possible to propel the blood forward and so eliminate the blood-crushing pumps from the bypass circuit. In fact, the membrane pump, which now exists in several prototype forms, is perhaps the long-awaited heart assister (a machine that can take over cardiac function for a day or more while an ailing heart recovers strength).

At the moment there is little we can do for such a heart, though here, too, aggressive surgical therapy can achieve far more than the passive-acceptance therapy which is all the physician can offer. Here we must distinguish between hearts in which small patches of muscle are affected and those in which the damaged area is large.

7·13 The figure relates the degrees of damage in the heart muscle with signs and symptoms (ECG, BCG, etc.), physician's therapy, and surgical therapy. In general, the surgeon aims to replace or reopen damaged channels; the physician has to accept damage and confine his therapy to reducing its effects.

Restoring coronary blood supply

Figure 7·13 shows the degrees of damage possible in heart muscle. Where the physician notes ECG changes and anginal pain, and prescribes drugs to suppress signs and alleviate symptoms, the surgeon sees chances to restore blood supply. The chief centre in the world for this aggressive surgery is the Cleveland Clinic, where Donald Effler and his colleagues have operated on over two thousand patients with insufficient coronary supply to their heart muscle. The basis of this therapy was the coronary angiogram technique developed by F. Mason Sones Jnr at the Cleveland. By injecting radio-opaque dye into the coronary openings and the ventricles he was able to make the diagnosis of coronary disease and ventricular abnormality a matter of photographic record. Before that it had been a matter of skilled inference from ECG traces. (He showed, incidentally, that up to 35 per cent of patients diagnosed as coronary cases from their ECGs actually had normal coronary arteries; a rather smaller proportion of true coronary patients had normal ECGs.)

The form of therapy is closely geared to the kind of coronary obstruction and the degree of subsequent damage. Partial blockage high up in the coronaries, near the aorta, will leave most of the muscle relatively starved. The technique here is to cut out the obstructed section (with the patient on bypass, of course) and replace it by a graft of vein tissue cut from the patient's groin (see figure 7·14 which also shows the other techniques). The same technique can be used for single blockages at any point in the larger coronary arteries.

If the blockage is more generalised, it is impossible to cut out dozens of little bits and replace each by a tiny vein graft. Instead, the surgeon uses a technique pioneered in 1946 by Arthur M. Vineberg of McGill University Medical Faculty. Figure 7·14 (which

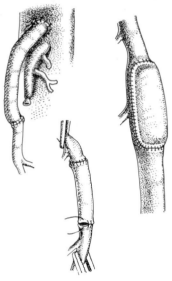

7·14 Techniques for repairing or replacing blocked coronary arteries. Upper left shows a coronary blocked near its root replaced by a new length of artery (the blocked end is tied off). Upper centre shows a blocked section removed and replaced by a new section. In upper right a narrowed section is widened by incorporating a large patch into the existing artery. The modified Vineberg technique, discussed on page 207, is shown in the two diagrams below. In the second diagram (*right*) the heart has been slightly rotated to reveal the undamaged coronaries.

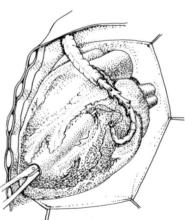

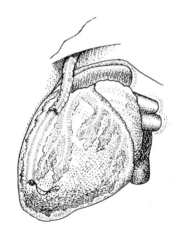

gives a later modification of Vineberg's technique) shows how a mammary artery is implanted in a tunnel surgically excised in the heart muscle. If a large area of ventricle is failing, the other mammary artery can be brought down to share the new circulatory burden. Of four hundred Cleveland patients so treated (to 1967) over three hundred and seventy, examined a year or more after surgery, had improved muscle, less pain, and better exercise tolerance. The best results were achieved in those whose muscle, though short of blood, had not yet begun to deteriorate.

When large areas of muscle have died in a major attack, the therapy depends on how soon the victim can be got into theatre. If within hours, so that the muscle is still dying, there is a good chance that the modified Vineberg technique can restore at least some muscle function. If the area is dead, no surgical or medical technique can revive it. These dead areas, which scar and become fibrous, are a constant menace to the rest of the heart. They can swell and turn into little balloon-like annexes of the ventricle, swelling when it pumps, emptying while it fills, thus shunting blood uselessly back and forth and consuming the energy of the remnant muscle. They can also harbour clots. The best technique then is straightforward excision. It results in dramatic recovery of efficiency and reduction of arrhythmias. From 1963 to 1968 the Cleveland Clinic operated on 130 critically ill patients in this way. Of the 117 who survived, over eighty-five went back to work. Without excision most would have died or the survivors would have faced the life of an invalid on the borders of heart failure.

Such results stem only from the closest cooperation between physicians and surgeons, for by no means all coronary patients are suited to this kind of surgical intervention. For instance, it makes little sense trying to save the heart if the rest of the body has degenerated.

Heart and heart-lung transplantation

If all other surgical and medical remedies fail, the only remaining course is a heart transplant or a heart-lung transplant. The surgical technique is fairly easy, certainly easier than a triple valve replacement, for instance. In the heart-only transplant, the technique devised by Norman Shumway of Palo Alto, California, and used in almost every transplant to date, is to cut out the useless recipient heart, leaving only part of the back atrial wall (with its four pulmonary veins) and the front-atrial wall linking the venae cavae. The donor heart is similarly pared, but left with its SA node intact. Then it is sutured to the remnant (see figure 2·7 on page 37).

I was once a strong advocate for leaving the recipient SA node intact and innervated; but this means leaving quite a bit of the original heart intact. Post-operative experience (with over one hundred patients throughout the world) has taught us to leave as little of the recipient heart as possible, for its coronary supply is lost with the removal of the useless heart and the remnant soon scars and turns fibrous. In so doing it loses all ability to contract and its surface properties change, two factors that make it become a possible source of clot. The back atrium wall is a little more favourably placed, for as you will remember, it is embryologically derived from vein tissue and so has its own (though rather tenuous) supply.

Another valid reason for cutting out the recipient's own SA node is that this effectively isolates the new heart from the vagus nerve. In many ways a denervated heart recovers better from an operation than one at the mercy, so to speak, of minute-by-minute vagal inhibition. A heart separated from the vagus beats steadily on with its own sinus rhythm – a little faster than normal, between 80 and 100 beats per minute, but steadily, whatever crisis may be taking place elsewhere in the system.

Although it has no nerve supply, the transplanted heart is remarkably responsive to changes outside it. It responds to temperature, of course, since its metabolism – like all body chemistry – is temperature dependent. Thus V_{max} and rate both increase with fever. It also responds to the Starling mechanism: any extra venous return, when the veins contract for any reason, stretches the muscle, raises V_{max}, and raises the arterial output and pressure.

The Bainbridge reflex (increase in heart rate when the front atrial wall is stretched) also works well, though not so well as in the intact heart. This could be because the reflex is partly central-nervous and partly local, but more probably the remnant of the recipient atrium takes some of the strain, diminishing the effect on the donor atrium.

The only case where lack of nerve connection is damaging is when the pressure inside the chest rises greatly: when, for instance, the transplantee strains to defecate. The natural system adjusts to this pressure without significant loss of cardiac output. The transplanted heart, lacking the autonomic pathways through which the adjustment occurs, cannot respond; the patient may faint momentarily through loss of cardiac output when he strains in this way.

Where you and I have one cardiovascular system, the transplantee has a cardiac system and a vascular system. The only mechanism which unites them is that of the circulating hormones, especially those that reinforce sympathetic nerve activity: adrenalin and noradrenalin. Adrenalin constricts the peripheral circulation, dilates the coronaries, and raises V_{max}. Isopropylnoradrenalin (isoprenalin), a man-made derivative, dilates all the vessels and raises V_{max}. Digitalis has its normal effect on the transplanted heart. since its activity does not depend on autonomic nerve pathways.

All these drugs help to bring the heart through difficult postoperative episodes.

The greatest problem is undoubtedly rejection of donor tissue by the recipient body (and, to a more limited extent, vice versa). The mechanism is not at all well understood. It involves two of the body's defence mechanisms: the circulating antibodies, which combine with free foreign antigen (protein) and render it less toxic; and the plasma cells, which attack invaders at the cellular level, destroying foreign endothelial lining and disrupting the metabolism of foreign cells, eventually killing them.

Of these two mechanisms, the plasma-cell response is far and away the most lethal to the donor tissue. It can be diminished somewhat by choosing donor tissues which match the host's as closely as possible. Five or six genes are responsible for the factors that make one person's proteins unacceptable to another's defences. The potential number of combinations is thus quite large, but many are in practice, fortunately, rare. In a way it is misleading to talk in terms of genes, for science is not yet advanced enough to deal with the problem at the genetic level. When we type tissues we do not, in fact, discover what genes are present in our donors and recipients. Our technique is akin to the unscientific method of colour matching by holding up labelled samples of different colours until we find a close fit. We separate the donor's white blood cells and divide them into a number of samples, each of which we mix with a different pure serum. The tissue-type report reads something like: 'Your recipient reacts against 4, 14, 17, and 21.' This means his white cells aggregated in a lump or were killed outright when placed in the pure typing sera labelled 4, 14, 17, and 21. Suppose we then get a potential donor who reacts against 4 and 14. This means that the donor possesses whatever factor is represented by 17 and 21, and so his cells do not react to it. The recipient, however, reacts strongly against these two, so that the donor is unacceptable to him. A single incompatibility, experience has taught, is acceptable; two or more are not. But suppose the situation were reversed:

Recipient reacts against 4, 14;

Donor reacts against 4, 14, 17, and 21.

This is an acceptable match for a heart transplant, or a kidney, or any organ that does not make white cells, for the only white cells the donor can put into the system are those in the blood while the organ is lifted from donor to recipient, and such blood is soon replaced in the natural course of events. The rejection by *its* white cells of the recipient is a trivial event that passes unnoticed amid the general trauma of the operation. In a heart-lung transplant, however, such a match would be less acceptable because the donor lung would manufacture replacement white cells antagonistic to the recipient. This quite minor reaction could be adequately controlled with drugs, but it would be better to avoid it if possible.

Even with well matched tissue (except that from identical twins, or from fraternal twins whose blood mingled in the womb) there must still be drug therapy to control the multiplication of plasma cells and prevent them from massing for an assault on what is still recognisably foreign tissue, despite the 'perfect match' according to our present crude typing system. The chief drugs are the cytotoxic agents which hamper or prevent cell division by preventing the formation of new protein: azathioprene, butazolidene, 6-mercaptopurine, and others. The more recently developed antilymphocyte sera also reduce the rejection.

Figure 7·15 shows all the parameters that are normally monitored post-operatively in a transplantee (one who has survived forty-five days). The drugs given are a good guide to the patient's state on any particular day. Thus increases in the dosage of azathioprene and butazolidene mark rejection episodes. The first (day 6) was worse than the second (day 28) since it called for doses of isoprenaline, to increase heart rate, extra digoxin, a digitalis compound to strengthen the heart-beat, hydrocortisone, to promote general well-being, and frusemide, a diuretic. The terminal episode (from about

7·15 This graph combines all the parameters monitored in a postoperative heart transplantee who survived 45 days, with rejection episodes on days 6 and 29. Most are around normal until the terminal episode, which was due to infection, not rejection. For each parameter the maxima and minima (except where minimum was zero) are given in the commonly used units — which need not concern the nonspecialist reader. Two suspect readings are marked with a query. A word about the drugs: azathioprene and butazolidene are immunosuppressives. Prednisone and prednisolone are steroids, used for unsticking the platelet aggregates that form around antigen-antibody complexes. Hydrocortisone is to combat general illness. Isoprenaline stimulates the pulse rate. Digoxin (given intravenously from day 38) is a heart stimulant. Frusemide is a diuretic. (Chlorothiazide and adrenaline were given only in the terminal stage and are not included.) The bars in *fluid balance* represent daily intake and output; the solid line is the cumulative balance; the dotted bars (days 43 to 45) are blood transfusions. From day 38 the respiration was mechanically assisted. ESR (erythrocyte sedimentation rate) is a nonspecific index of general illness — the higher, the worse; unreliable when drug therapy is as complex as here. The platelet count normally falls after heart-lung bypass; its persistent low level is a sign of rejection. The eosinophil percentage, in figures below the bars, is also symptomatic of rejection. The hymphocyte RNA count (labelled RNA) was an experimental procedure designed in the hopes of forecasting rejection — in which it failed. In general this graph reveals the amazing return to normality brought about by transplantation. Before it this patient was hardly able to cross a room without severe pain; after it he achieved, on one occasion, 600 straight-leg-raisings without pause.

day 33) was due not to rejection but to other complications.

If only we could overcome rejection, the transplantation of the heart would become as routine as valve replacement now is (and that was rare enough only five years ago). Nothing is more encouraging than the *immediate* betterment that follows the replacement of a worn-out heart by one that is young and vigorous. Men and women who could not cross the room without the most crippling and undignified pain are younger and more sprightly almost from the moment they gain consciousness. Livers and kidneys severely compromised by the original failing heart show immediate improvement with the new one. Few surgical procedures offer such a rapid and deep-reaching improvement.

In this account I have concentrated on heart-only transplantation, because it is the operation of which we have the most experience. Even so, I have long advocated heart-lung transplantation as a more logical and, in fact, simpler operation. The heart and

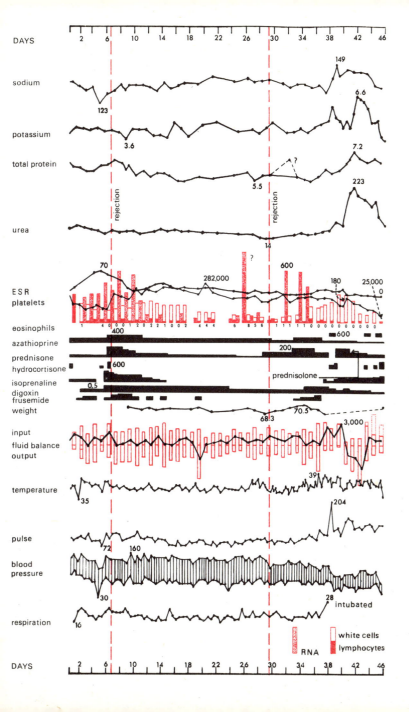

lungs, as I have stressed at many points in this book, grow up together; they are perfectly adapted to one another. *Your* pulmonary arteries expand and contract to preserve maximal flow for minimal effort from *your* front ventricle. Mine respond differently, but they achieve the same optimisation for *my* front ventricle. The two organs also share a rich plexus of autonomic nerves, which is severed unless the two are taken together. Also we must remember that low-output failure can cause lung damage; if we leave damaged lungs in the recipient, we risk matching them against a vigorous heart whose strength may do further damage.

The major problem of heart-lung transplantation is the risk that surfactant production will be impaired. The lung needs its autonomic nerve pathways if it is to keep making surfactants; if those paths are damaged, surfactant production stops, leading to severe lung damage and death from respiratory failure.

However, that is by the way. The point I want to stress is that whether we perform a heart or a heart-lung transplant, the improvement in the patient is dramatic and thought-provoking. Airline pilots are grounded the moment they have a detectable coronary. If we groundlings were to be judged by similar criteria; for example, if we compulsorily retired everybody earning more than three times the national average (that being a good guide to responsibility) who had a detectable coronary, the rule would cripple our civilisation. Heart disease, as we saw in chapter 5, has assumed such gargantuan proportions that gargantuan measures – and budgets to match – are now needed.

When we have solved the rejection problem, and there can be no doubt that we *will* solve it, there will still be a shortage of donor material. As roads grow safer and drivers find other outlets for aggression, the number of accident victims will fall, so we must earnestly hope. At the moment the young man with a high-output sports car is the hope of the older man with low-output failure.

As supply dwindles and demand grows we will certainly turn to animals as the source of donor hearts. The problem there is not just one of tissue matching but also of electrolyte balance, since each animal has its own characteristic concentration of sodium, calcium, potassium, and so on. Pigs' hearts, for instance, fail to contract in humans; they seize up when they meet human electrolyte concentrations. We are already starting to work on the problems of animal-to-man transplantation, and we have found a number of animals with similar electrolyte ranges to man. Now we must look for other possible physiological incompatibilities.

Medicine's place in the bioscience revolution

And what then? The surgeons will have run out of demands: time, normal temperature, direct vision, techniques, spare parts, patching materials, an unlimited supply of viable hearts, the ability to induce tolerance to foreign tissue, all will have been won. Then we shall remember the vascular part of the cardiovascular system. And what will we do about it? Speculation in this chapter has already brought us to the useful limits of guesswork; this question, in the light of present knowledge, takes us beyond that limit.

Indeed, many doctors would say that guesswork of any kind not only has no useful limits, it has no use at all. 'Sufficient unto the day are the problems thereof . . .', and so on. One of the problems of medicine all over the world is that so few doctors project the future for themselves in any but the most trivial ways, if, indeed, they do so at all. I have heard one of the greatest living pioneers of modern surgery talk to other surgeons about a new technique of fundamental importance, devised by himself. And when the question session came, what did those other surgeons want to know? What, perhaps, did the great man think would be the next logical extension of his technique? No, they were not interested in that.

Did, perhaps, the technique call for any change in diagnostic method or refinement? That did not occur to them either. The first question they asked was: 'Did you use a 6–0 suture?'! It set the tone for the rest of the session.

Responses like this from senior medical men reinforce a conviction which sometimes overcomes me that medicine and its practitioners are like a primitive tribe about to be overrun by a culture of greater technical superiority. Like many peasant peoples we are staunch individualists; we tend our own patch, fight for our own territory, band strongly against the rustler and poacher, grumble about administrators and taxes, and take a most unpassionate interest in the great world beyond our horizons. If one of our areas lags – mental health, say, or the care of the chronically sick, or geriatrics – there is no general medical effort to redress the balance. We act as if we were quite unaware of the organisational changes that technology is forcing on all sectors of civilisation.

As far as heart surgery is concerned, I think that this book has indicated where the greatest need for such changes lies. But they form only one part of the enormous advances called for within medical science as a whole, many of which will rely on fundamental discoveries in bioscience – especially in our understanding of genetic control, of self-recognition, self-regulation, and self-repair in living tissue, and of the active sites in the traffic between living cells and bioactive chemicals.

These advances are not going to be made willy nilly; they will come only out of the closer coordination of basic research and clinical care. In short, they will depend on the application of financial and technical criteria that are still a little foreign to medicine, though now quite common in industry and other areas of government. In Britain, where the central organisation of medicine fosters the illusion that its progress is centrally directed, we are going to face an acute problem in dismantling ancient empires and establishing a new commonwealth. In America, where the disarray is more naked (but hardly more severe) a start has already been made. In 1966, when President Johnson introduced Medicare, he pointed specifically to the need 'to get our knowledge fully applied ... to zero in on the targets.' A year later the Surgeon General recommended closer ties between the National Institutes of Health (NIH) and Medicare activities within the Public Health Service and pointed to an undue emphasis on basic research at the expense of community health work. A congressional subcommittee later castigated the NIH for irresponsible administration, weak management, favouritism in awarding research grants, support of bad research, and the launching of programmes that lacked care in formulating objectives and priorities. And on a more global scale – but one that surely includes medicine – President Nixon has recently urged the creation of an Atlantic committee at ministerial level, charged with exploring 'ways in which the experience and resources of the Western nations could most effectively be marshalled toward improving the quality of life of our peoples.'

On every hand we sense this swelling chorus of concern for the quality of our future. More and more we are aware that the complex problems that beset us are all interconnected, even if we cannot yet penetrate the full subtlety of their relationship. Quite properly then the involvement of people who cannot put MD after their names in the direction of biomedical endeavour is certainly not going to diminish. For those of us who would like to retain some say in the direction of medicine the writing is on the wall.

Appendix

The following pages are intended more for the would-be specialist than for the lay reader. They contain a select list of cardiovascular diseases taken from the International Standard Classification of Diseases (ISCD – 7th revision) together with some notes on each entry. Like all attempts to classify diseases this list is a compromise – and a fairly uncomfortable one at that. To start with, its cardiovascular entries were determined before the days of open-heart surgery and so reflects little of the knowledge we have gained since we have been able to *see* lesions *in situ* in the living heart. Even to open the heart with confidence, let alone to work on it surgically, we have have had to learn vastly more about its dynamics and about the origins and courses of disease than is reflected in this list. Secondly, its compilers had to bear in mind that many diagnoses of death have to be made in circumstances where little of the patient's history is available, where no post-mortem examination is contemplated, and where diagnostic machines are either not available or – because the patient is dead – useless anyway. Thus we have catch-all entries beginning with words like 'general' and 'other', which may reflect no fundamental condition or disease. Many of the deaths entered under these headings would have been put elsewhere if the doctor had had time, equipment, or the legal obligation to make a more precise diagnosis. Thirdly, it is a list of effects rather than of causes and of the intervening processes.

In the modern context this is the gravest deficiency of all, for it both reflects and encourages an inadequate view of the whole business of disease and diagnosis. In the seventeenth and early eighteenth centuries there was very little diagnosis in medicine; doctors had literally thousands of remedies but next to no means of matching them accurately to their patients' ailments. The late eighteenth and early nineteenth centuries saw a most sensible reaction: 'no treatment without diagnosis' became the watchword. Unfortunately the reaction was so overdone that diagnosis became an end in itself – a fit occupation for the great men of medicine. Treatment was left in the hands of lesser mortals. In certain ways this unhealthy tradition persists, though things are not nearly so bad as they were. Increasing success at therapy, together with our increasing understanding of the complexity of the systems we treat, have together made it essential for diagnostician and therapist to unite in one person or one team. For instance, it is no longer valid for a surgeon to act on a general diagnosis of, say, mitral valve stenosis; he must know exactly how severe it is, exactly what form it takes, how it was caused, how it has been deteriorating recently, as well as many other facets of the patient's personal and familial medical history. He must also know, of course, what to do about it once he has entered the heart. It is impossible in such a case to separate the diagnostic function from the therapeutic.

Is it fanciful to see in this the seeds of a new revolution in clinical medicine? I think not. I believe we are approaching a state in which we will cease to think of diagnosis as a process of tracking cause and effect phenomena through a simple maze and arriving at boxes labelled, for instance, 'mitral stenosis' or 'dissecting aneurysm of the aorta'. Instead we are beginning to see disease as physicists 'see' fundamental particles (a cloudy sort of meeting place of charges and probabilities) or as mathematicians think of multidimensional space. In our multidimensional *diagnostics space*, to coin a phrase, the axes will represent causes, processes, and degrees of severity. Inside this space we will see that groups of diseases do not each occupy precise points but that, for instance, patients with mitral stenosis will fit a whole cluster of points congregating in a *region* labelled mitral stenosis. Assigning a disease to the correct region (the traditional business of diagnosis) will then be only a small part of true diagnosis; it will be much more important to find his precise whereabouts within the bounds of that cluster, for that precise position will determine his subsequent therapy.

Every part of this diagnostics space will map, point for point, on to an equivalent *therapeutics space* and in this way disease, diagnosis, and therapy will be precisely linked. How we label each point in any given cluster so that their identification is universally possible is not yet an urgent issue. Obviously we shall have to attempt some such labelling before we can compile an alternative to the ISCD list; but I believe we should resist for quite a long time the temptation to start constructing elegant labelling systems. At this point in time it is far more important for us to realise the greater intellectual liberation that will come when we are freed from the tyranny of pat diagnosis – and any conscientious houseman or intern who has sat far into the night trying to fit what he knows about a patient into the procrustean boxes of the ISCD (something he must do on a patient's discharge or death) will know how great that tyranny is.

Like all liberations it will bring a fresh challenge – in this case to our organising ingenuity. The emphasis in diagnosis has shifted from effects to causes and processes; it is a shift from mere empirical observation to one based on growing fundamental understanding. Thus, like the surgeon I mentioned a few paragraphs ago, we are not so much concerned with what a patient *has* (i.e., the effect) as with how he got it, and how its course has run. When we look at diagnosis in this light we operate, as it were, a sieve that leads inexorably to one region in what I have called diagnostics space – the region that includes whatever condition(s) our patient has. The sieve is most easily grasped in diagram form (figure A1). Such a sieve covers all forms of disease. For cardiovascular disease we must add two further branches (other specialisms would use other branches) (figure A2). *Anomalous pathways* includes arteriovenous shunts and all other misroutings of blood and nerve

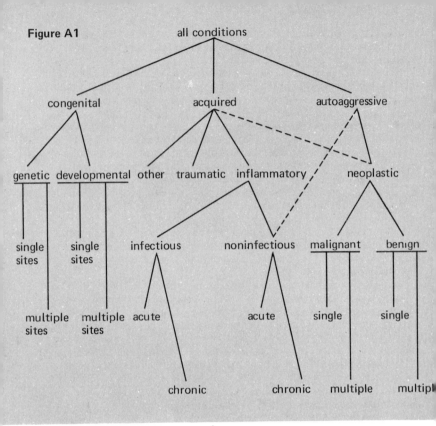

Figure A1

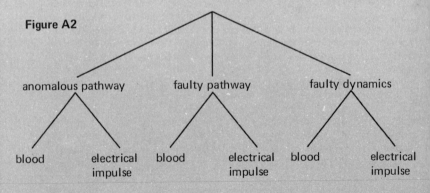

Figure A2

220

impulses. *Faulty pathways* includes all coarctations, hypertrophies, stenoses, and forms of incompetence as well as analogous conduction faults such as blocks. *Faulty dynamics* includes all aneurysms, balloons, thromboses, electrolyte-induced failures – again with analogous conduction failures.

Sieves of this kind have long been taught in medical schools. The newcomer in the main diagram is the entry *Autoaggressive*, which is almost certainly not a true alternative to *Congenital* and *Acquired*. Autoaggressive diseases occur when the chromosomes of the cells that control tissue growth, maintenance and repair undergo a somatic mutation – to which they are genetically susceptible. These diseases thus have both a genetic and an acquired component. They include neoplastic conditions and they almost certainly include some noninfectious inflammatory processes as well as many that we now classify under other headings. Dr Philip Burch of Leeds University, one of the discoverers and leading proponents of the autoaggressive theory of disease, has produced evidence that even such a classically traumatic lesion as a fracture of the femur has an autoaggressive component – that is, the site of fracture is autoaggressively weakened before the mishap that causes the fracture occurs.

Nevertheless, despite the radical alterations that the autoaggressive theory will produce in this traditional sieve, the principle is unshaken. If we use such a sieve, however, reconstituted, to guide us in taking a patient's history and planning his physical examination, we arrive at an accurate diagnosis. But more than that, because the method presupposes that the doctor has a good current understanding of the processes that lead to the condition, the sieve also suggests a basis for treatment. To put the argument another way: at any given moment of its recent history medical practice is and has been a mixture of empirical knowledge and fundamental understanding. There are still a few areas where we have no fundamental understanding whatever; treatment in these areas is based on empirical rules ('In nine cases out of ten with this disease such-and-such a treatment is effective – but for heaven's sake don't ask me why.' Convulsive brain therapy is a good example here.) Until about two hundred years ago most medical practice fell into this category. Today, in most areas, we have achieved at least a partial fundamental understanding (enough to know how much we still have to learn) and our treatment is a mixture of empirical experience guided by that deeper insight. The various treatments for hypertensive heart disease are examples of this mixed approach. Nowhere is our fundamental knowledge *total*; yet there are areas where it is adequate enough for us to say that our therapy has very little empirical element left. Insulin therapy for diabetes and various immunisation techniques are examples. The virtue of the diagnostic sieve is that it focuses our thoughts on the fundamental processes of disease and so encourages understanding at the expense of empirical medicine.

The tragedy of the ISCD is that it offers no such encouragement. Why then, having said all this, do I use it as a basis for this appendix? The main reason is that it *is* international. It is the basis for all available statistics. It is being widely written into medical-computer programmes. There is no doubt that today and for many years to come we are lumbered with it; so we had better learn to use it well until our collective dissatisfaction is deep enough to wring some changes in its basis. Here and there in the list I make comments on the specific entries to underline this point.

Each entry has a standard format: ISCD number; ISCD name of disease; United States male/female deaths followed in parentheses by the death rate per million males/females; England and Wales (E&W) male/female deaths followed in parentheses by the death rate per million males/females. In some cases the statistics are not comparable, in which case attention is drawn to the fact in the text. For both countries the statistics refer to 1967. The notes on the diseases are my own. (No great moment should be attached to differences – even order-of-magnitude differences – between British and American rates. As I say, the list is a clumsy sorting box, and there are also differences in diagnostic tradition and fashion on both sides of the Atlantic.)

022 **Syphilitic aneurysm of the aorta**
US 1,176/473 (12/5)   E&W 358/183 (16/11)
A result of untreated syphilis. The spirochaetes attack the adventitia and deplete the blood supply to the media. This leads to fibrous scar replacement, which, under aortic pressure (average 100 mm Hg), stretches. The aorta may swell to many times its normal diameter (aneurysm) and press on nearby structures: (1) bronchi → lung damage; (2) vertebral column → bone erosion and severe pain; (3) superior vena cava → high venous pressure in head and neck and possible oedema. Abdominal aneurysms (about 10 per cent of all aortic aneurysms) are usually degenerative, not syphilitic, in origin. Aneurysms may rupture into nearby structures, usually fatally. Average *course* is about eighteen months, though much longer survivals are reported. *Treatment:* routine antisyphilitic therapy; surgical replacement with homograft or prosthesis.

Other cardiovascular syphilis
US 291/123 (3/1)   E&W 64/55 (3/2)
See also 022. The lesion may weaken the aortic root → dilatation and aortic incompetence. The valves become rolled, thickened, and dwarfed. The coronary orifices may also be partly blocked → myocardial ischaemia and fibrosis; possibly also → angina; rarely → heart block (see 433·0). *Course:* in advanced cases, with back ('left') ventricular failure and low-output failure, prognosis is bad; with survival around two years. Symptom-free patients, treated, have a 50 per cent chance of surviving ten years. *Treatment:* see 022. Damage cannot be undone except by valve and aortic root replacement.

401 **Rheumatic fever with heart involvement**
US 185/164 (2/2)   E&W 6/10 (0/0)

Rheumatic fever is an autoaggressive disease usually following an infection by haemolytic streptococcus. It is commonest in childhood and adolescence, rare in infancy and old age. The streptococci themselves do not attack the cardiovascular system but, seemingly, trigger a polyarthritis (of which rheumatic fever is one form). Polyarthritis is currently thought to be a sign that part of the body's routine control and maintenance systems are disturbed. The rheumatic attack has several possible consequences. It includes the whole heart – muscle and pericardium as well as valves. Normally, because there is such a huge reserve of muscle, the damage shows most readily in the valves. But where the muscle is already weakened or vulnerable, it can be badly damaged. Diagnosis of rheumatic carditis rests on: (1) signs of inflammatory process (fever, leucocytosis, raised erythrocyte sedimentation rate); (2) evidence of rheumatic origin – (a) polyarthritis; (b) streptococcal infection; (c) response to salicylates; (d) chorea (see 402.1); (e) possible skin lesions; (f) possible pulmonary signs, especially pleurisy; (g) raised ASO titre; (3) evidence of carditis – (a) mitral valvitis; (b) aortic valvitis; (c) rarer pulmonary and tricuspid valvitis; (d) possible heart block; (e) pericarditis; (f) heart failure – almost always with gross aortic or mitral valve disease. *Course:* after fever about 65 per cent of patients have residual valve damage; but 10 to 15 per cent of these recover completely, while between 20 and 40 per cent of those who appear to be free of damage later develop chronic rheumatic heart disease (figures relate to ten and twenty years, respectively). Also, 40 per cent of adults with chronic rheumatic heart disease had no diagnosed rheumatic signs in childhood. *Treatment:* the rheumatic fever is alleviated by steriods, salicylates, aspirin, and other drugs. Carditis requires absolute bed rest, especially in heart failure. Nothing can reverse the cardiac effects of rheumatic fever. Extended convalescence (aimed at minimising exertion, exposure, infections of all kinds, emotional upset, cold, and damp) can minimise the risk of relapse and thus of later effects. Prophylactic antibiotic therapy is essential. Despite such precautions, however, relapses are not uncommon. Rheumatic pericarditis → fusion and thickening of the pericardium and surrounding tissues is never constrictive and has no clinical consequences. Thus it does not figure in the ISCD.

402·1 **Chorea with heart involvement**

US 0/0   E&W (0/0)

Chorea (St Vitus dance) is a motor disturbance similar to a nervous tic and other kinds of hysteria, but differing in these respects: (1) its movements are rapid, elaborate, irregular and varied – particularly in facial grimaces; (2) when the hand is held out, the wrist flexes and the fingers hyperextend; (3) the knee-jerk reflex may show prolonged contraction. Chorea usually occurs without other signs of rheumatic fever – even with a normal erythrocyte sedimentation rate. There is no demonstrable brain lesion. About 20 per cent of chorea patients later develop rheumatic heart disease. *Course and treatment:* see 401. Chorea lasts six to twelve weeks and patients may need heavy sedation in the most active phase. It rarely figures as a direct cause of death because the onset of the consequent heart disease is slow and late.

410 **Diseases of the mitral valve**
US 2,089/3,448 (22/34)   E&W 1,263/2,704 (54/109)
For nonrheumatic diseases, see 421·0. In a ten-year-old child the peak normal pressures (resting) sustained by the four heart valves are of this order: mitral 100 mm Hg, aortic 60, tricuspid 15, pulmonary 5. Exertion may quadruple these figures but does not change the order. Rheumatic valvulitis affects these valves in this order: mitral 85 per cent of all cases, aortic 44 per cent, tricuspid about 13 per cent, pulmonary 1 to 2 per cent. This striking correlation may explain the different incidence of the disease in the four valves. *Course:* in the acute stage the valve (which is more vascular in the child than in the adult – especially the mitral) is inflamed and becomes damaged at the free edge. Thrombi form, leading to small pink nodules. Later there is secondary sclerosis affecting the cusps, tendinous cords, papillary muscles, and valve root. Slight initial damage leads to fusion and mitral stenosis between two to eight years after the attack. Gross initial damage leads at once to regurgitation, with thick, disorganised leaflets. When the valve is well scarred, however, further deterioration is slow. *Treatment:* see 401. A stenosed valve can often be relieved *in situ* by surgery; a grossly regurgitant valve is dealt with by autograft, homograft, or prosthetic replacement.

411 **Diseases of the aortic valve specified as rheumatic**
US 1,050/528 (11/5)   E&W 282/180 (12/7)
Rheumatic aortic valvulitis usually → quickly to a permanent aortic regurgitation. It may also cause stenosis. See notes under 410.

412 **Diseases of the tricuspid valve**
US 10/13 (0/0)   E&W 11/12 (0/0)
Rheumatic valvulitis in general is discussed under 410. With the tricuspid valve it usually causes stenosis and/or regurgitation (found at necropsy in up to 20 per cent of cases of chronic rheumatic heart disease). It is almost always accompanied by mitral stenosis. It prevents the front ('right') ventricle from filling properly and so lowers cardiac output; however, this can diminish the effect of pulmonary congestion (and haemoptysis, paroxysmal cardiac dyspnoea, orthopnoea, and winter bronchitis) due to mitral stenosis. Thus tricuspid stenosis often

causes remarkably little disability. The commonest early symptom is a visible or palpable jugular pulse (*a* wave). The patient does not complain until cardiac output is so low as to cause fatigue or engorgement of the liver. *Treatment:* prosthetic replacement or surgical modification of both valves when the condition is severe.

413 Diseases of the pulmonary valve specified as rheumatic
US 1/2 (0/0)   E&W No data

Pulmonary valve involvement in rheumatic fever is usually secondary and functional – very rarely the result of direct rheumatic attack on the valve. Mitral stenosis due to rheumatic disease leads to pulmonary hypertension, and this may cause pulmonary valve regurgitation.

414 Other endocarditis specified as rheumatic
US 312/419 (3/4)   E&W 65/134 (3/7)

This category includes those cases where the three most commonly involved valves (mitral, aortic and tricuspid) are all more or less equally damaged. There is always myocardial involvement and endocardial involvement, too, though this is less frequently fatal because there are such great reserves of myocardium.

415 Other myocarditis specified as rheumatic
US 71/92 (1/1)   E&W 14/25 (0/1)

The rheumatic process (see 401) attacks muscle as well as valve material, though valve damage predominates in about 95 per cent of all cases. Myocardial damage includes the formation of inactive fibrous tissue among the muscle fibres and a consequent loss of power and efficiency → in advanced cases to low output failure. Aschoff nodes, one of the signs of rheumatic heart disease, are present in 50 per cent of all fatal cases of chronic rheumatic heart disease.

416 Other heart disease specified as rheumatic
US 2,259/3,506 (23/35)   E&W 329/694 (14/28)

Most deaths in this category would have been placed in others of 410 to 415 if more adequate diagnosis had been possible. Rheumatic pericarditis has no category of its own because – in the absence of other rheumatic carditis — it has no clinical consequences. Rare cases of heart block due to rheumatic carditis belong here.

420·0 Arteriosclerotic heart disease, so described
US 79,196/81,641 (819/807)   E&W 641/868 (27/35)

There is obviously a great difference in diagnostic tradition here in the two countries! Arteriosclerosis (or atherosclerosis) is a slow degeneration of the arteries. Up to forty years of age it is overwhelmingly a male disease; at fifty it attacks 8 males for each 1 female; between sixty and seventy the ratio is 3 to 1; and after seventy the incidence is equal. The causes of atherosclerosis are still obscure, despite an enormous amount of research; they are known to include disordered fat metabolism and hypercholesterolaemia. The disease results in patchy and irregular accumulations of lipoid material in the arterial wall. The pressure of these deposits → atrophy of underlying tissue and even narrowing of the vessel lumen. Later these deposits become vascular and may bleed into the vessel wall. They may also calcify, converting the arteries into bony tubes. Ulceration or erosion → sites for thrombosis → sudden coronary occlusion. Massive blockage of a major coronary artery → massive myocardial infarction and heart failure. Even a small infarct can become an irritable focus of atrial and ventricular rhythm disturbances and, by triggering a contractile stimulus during the refractory phase → ventricular fibrillation and death. Usually the occlusion is less dramatic and only a patch of muscle is infarcted; results vary from mild irritation, passed over as 'indigestion', to rhythm disturbances and permanent cardiac insufficiency. Most cases have many coronary attacks before heart failure occurs. Not all coronary atherosclerosis leads to occlusion and myocardial infarction; and occlusion can occur without atherosclerosis – for instance, by emboli from a fibrillating back ('left') atrium or in autoaggressive disease like polyarteritis nodosa. Dying or blood-starved myocardium produces a localised or spreading chest pain, angina pectoris, but – because it can be confused with other chest pains – angina pectoris is not a confirmation of heart disease. *Treatment:* rapid diagnosis and surgery (Vineberg-type implantation of arterial grafts into infarcted areas) can revive dying muscle. A heart in failure can be replaced by transplantation. Medical treatment is palliative – using drugs to stimulate remaining coronary circulation, control fluids and electrolytes, combat rhythm disturbances, combat heart failure by resting the heart as much as possible, allowing the damage to scar and heal with minimum strain. Development of a long-term heart-lung machine, now very close to realisation, will enable the heart to rest and so recover more function than is possible when it has to keep working. For myocardial degeneration with atherosclerosis see 422·1.

420·1 Heart disease specified as involving coronary arteries
US 265,798/146,229 (2,749/1,445)   E&W 69,076/44,544 (2,932/1,794)
The majority of deaths in this category would have been listed under 420·0 if more adequate diagnosis had been possible at the time of death. Congenital coronary anomalies are dealt with under 754·5.

420·2 Angina pectoris without mention of coronary disease
US 160/129 (2/1)   E&W 86/77 (4/3)
Angina pectoris (chest pain) is usually a symptom of myocardial

ischaemia, myocarditis, and cardiomyopathy. However, in thyrotoxic patients there may be an excessive demand on a nonischaemic heart → angina. Similarly traumatic damage to and other lesions of the chest may produce the symptoms of ischaemia and angina. It is important to realise that angina pectoris is not itself a disease but always a symptom of some deeper-lying cause. Its appearance in diagnoses of death can only mean that deeper diagnosis was impossible or for some reason not attempted. A few deaths in this category will be hysterical.

421 Chronic endocarditis not specified as rheumatic

US 2,229/1,507 (23/15)   E&W 1,427/1,554 (61/63)

The various forms of chronic endocarditis often accompany myocarditis of similar kinds, and this entry should be read in conjunction with entries under 422·2 and 431. Some are caused by inflammations of unknown origin and are possibly autoaggressive. They are marked by necrosis and fibroelastic repair; when the endocardium is involved it is white and thick as in congenital fibroelastosis – which is a developmental failure probably due to anoxia (being common with coronary and valve defects that lead to ischaemia). Other forms, similar in effect, are due to collagen diseases and allergies: (1) *periarteritis nodosa*, a hypersensitivity provoked by a number of antigens, may involve both myo- and endocardium; effects are similar to isolated myocarditis; (2) *disseminated lupus*, a widespread necrosis of connective tissue, may produce myo- and endocarditis, which often affects the tricuspid, mitral and aortic valves; less damaging than bacterial endocarditis; (3) *scleroderma*, a diffuse collagen disease of the connective tissue (skin, joints, oesophagus, heart, and occasionally lungs and kidneys). *Course and treatment:* see 431. Deaths and rates for specific endocardial sites are given in the following entries.

421·0 Chronic endocarditis of mitral valve, specified as nonrheumatic

US 57/81 (1/1)   E&W 76/229 (3/9)

Mitral regurgitation may be secondary to ischaemic heart disease with damaged papillary muscles or to severe back (left') ventricular failure with dilatation.

421·1 Chronic endocarditis of aortic valve, not specified as rheumatic

US 1,587/827 (16/8)   E&W 1,239/1,095 (53/44)

Apart from causes mentioned elsewhere in these pages, aortic valve disease is caused by: (1) rheumatoid arthritis; (2) ankylosing spondylitis, a fusion (probably autoaggressive) of the spine and joints, leading terminally to pneumonia and/or valve disease;(3)Reiter's syndrome, an autoaggressive condition (probably venereal, too) marked by urethritis, possible kidney disease, and inflammation of the joints; (4) congenital defects.

421·2 Chronic endocarditis of tricuspid valve, specified as nonrheumatic
US 0/2 (0/0)   E&W 1/2 (0/0)

421·3 Chronic endocarditis of pulmonary valve, not specified as rheumatic
US 80/36 (1/0)   E&W 4/2 (0/0)

421·4 Chronic endocarditis, other and ill-defined, not specified as rheumatic
US 505/561 (5/6)   E&W 107/226 (5/9)

422·0 Myocardial degeneration, fatty
US 15/22 (0/0)   E&W 26/50 (1/2)
Replacement or enlargement of the myocardium by fatty tissue – in the absence of atherosclerosis – is uncommon. It can occur in athletes who suddenly give up, or have to give up, heavy training; it can also, but rarely, accompany diabetes mellitus. It is part of normal ageing.

422·1 Myocardial degeneration with arteriosclerosis
US 19,990/21,860 (207/216)   E&W 5,288/9,342 (224/376)
This category is identical, as far as origins go, with 420·0. However, this is, so to speak, the chronic form of the condition, with gradual myocardial death and replacement → low output failure. It is part of normal ageing.

422·2 Other myocardial degeneration
US 3,653/3,421 (38/34)   E&W 5,372/10,518 (228/424)
Again there are obvious differences in diagnostic tradition between the two countries. This category includes many deaths that, for various reasons, could not definitely be assigned or certified under 420, 421 and other 422 categories. This is a convenient point at which to classify the various cardiomyopathies. There are two bases for such classification – first by clinical picture:
    congestive, with back ('left') ventricular failure due to dilatation of the ventricle;
    constrictive, producing a picture similar to restrictive pericarditis;
    hypertrophic, in which the ventricle, usually the back ventricle, obstructs itself by virtue of its own excessive enlargement.
The second classification is based on aetiology; many of the diseases in the following list are described elsewhere in this appendix:
    endocrine diabetes, Cushing's disease, thyrotoxicosis, myxoedema;
    infection bacterial, virus, tubercular;
    infestation Chagas' disease, toxoplasmosis;
    granulomata sarcoid;
    infiltrations amyloid, lukaemia, haemochromatosis;
    storage diseases Gaucher's disease (abnormal production and storage of the lipoid kerasin in lymphohaematopoietic system → death by

haemorrhage), Niemann-Pick disease (abnormal storage of the lipoid sphyngomyelin in reticular cells and histiocytes, course similar to Gaucher's), von Giercke's disease (abnormal glycogen storage in liver and heart → ventricular hypertrophy);

biochemical porphyria;

autoaggressive polyarteritis nodosa, scleroderma, rheumatoid arthritis, disseminated lupus erythematosis;

drug sensitivities;

irradiation;

myopathies muscular dystrophy (especially Duchenne), dystrophia myotonica, Friedreich's ataxia.

Primary cardiomyopathies include: viral infection of the heart alone; endomyocardial fibrosis; complications of alcoholism, pregnancy, and puerperium; endocardial fibroelastosis; hypertrophic obstructive; and cardiomyopathies of unknown aetiology.

430·0 Acute and subacute bacterial endocarditis

US 476/248 (5/2)   E&W 167/86 (7/4)

Nonrheumatic endocarditis is usually due to infection either acutely by pyogenic bacteria or subacutely by organisms such as *Streptococcus viridans*. There is often arteritis as well. Almost always there is an underlying fault – a congenital or acquired anomaly that leads to turbulent blood flow. Thus atrial septal defects are rarely involved, while ventricular septal defects, bicuspid aortic valves, and patent ductus are often attacked. So, too, are the sutured roots of prosthetic and homograft valves. Often there is an old rheumatic history, and active bacterial endocarditis can sometimes superimpose on active rheumatic carditis. In fatal cases there is always myocardial infiltration, too. The bacteria invade the surfaces of damaged or congenitally deformed valves and defects. Elsewhere in the body such colonies are soon granulated and cleared away by leucocytes. But where the blood flow is turbulent, granulation is inefficient and thrombi form, providing a good culture medium. At onset endocarditis is often put down as a stubborn influenza; this, together with recent dental history (ulceration or extraction) is always suspect. The effects are widespread in the body and include fever, anaemia, capillary fragility, splinter haemorrhages, septic infarcts (Osler's nodes) on the pads of fingers and toes (from which the organism may be cultured), peripheral emboli (which can lead to mycotic aneurysms), pulmonary emboli (when the front ventricle is involved an apparent subacute haemorrhagic bronchopneumonia), and various renal lesions. Such signs and symptoms, together with suspicious heart sounds on the appropriate side of the heart, are grounds for provisional diagnosis – confirmed, unless there has been antibiotic therapy, by positive blood cultures from four to six samples (with the usual precautions in patients with a dental history).

Course: untreated acute cases die in days or weeks; subacute cases in months, rarely years, with bouts of fever and remissions. Death is due to septicaemia, embolism, heart failure, haemorrhage, uraemia, and other less frequent causes. *Treatment:* antibiotics have revolutionised the treatment of bacterial endocarditis in developed countries, allowing most patients to recover without after-effect. Those who still die are either diagnosed late (still a common misadventure), have resistant infections, or are patients whose underlying heart defect is already so serious that they have no reserve. Death correlates with presence and degree of heart failure, malnutrition, and the virulence of the attack.

430·1 Other acute endocarditis

US 13/15 (0/0)   E&W 0/2 (0/0)

Vary rarely infections by bacteria, toxoplasma, fungi, rickettsiae, and other parasites have secondary effects on the myocardium. As antibiotics select out the more common sources of bacterial endocarditis, this group may grow in relative importance, be recognised more readily, and so seem to be on the increase in morbidity charts.

431 Acute myocarditis not specified as rheumatic

US 453/407 (5/4)   E&W 81/58 (3/2)

Many of the causes of myocarditis, acute and chronic, with endocardial involvement are discussed under 422·2 and 430. The commonest cause of acute myocarditis is the benign Coxsackie B virus. Other forms are secondary to bacterial infections, especially with diphtheria. There is hyaline degeneration and necrosis in the muscle fibres, followed by fibrous repair. Often the first sign is a rhythm disturbance, followed by a partial or complete heart block and bundle branch block (both usually transient). Deterioration leads to sinus tachycardia, cardiac enlargement, gallop rhythm, and systemic congestion. Sudden death from ventricular fibrillation or low output failure is common. Survivors usually develop severe polyneuritis. *Treatment* includes antitoxic serum, total bed rest, and light diet limited in sodium and fluids. Pneumococcal and streptococcal myocarditis takes a similar form but is rarely fatal unless there is already severe mitral or aortic incompetence. A tropical equivalent is myocarditis accompanying South American trypanosomiasis (Chaga's disease). Very rarely there is myocarditis with toxoplasmosis, schistosomiasis (effect via pulmonary damage), trichiniasis (by allergic reaction), actinomycosis (usually spreading inward from the pericardium), and coccidiodo-mycosis. There are also collagen diseases discussed under 421, to which must here be added sarcoidosis, a rare and little-understood condition. It usually involves the lungs (→ cor pulmonale, see 433·2) and may also

→ a myocarditis. Also, apart from the metabolic disorders listed under 422·2, there are these rare conditions: (1) *haemochromatosis*, in which iron is absorbed to an abnormal degree and deposited in the heart, liver, skin, adrenals, testicles (95 per cent of cases are men) and pancreas. Cases present with obvious symptoms and appear to have isolated myocarditis, with low output failure, heart block, and ultimately ventricular fibrillation; (2) *primary amyloidosis*, in which amyloid material is accumulated in the interstices between atrophied muscle fibre – in the heart, and perhaps the tongue and skeletal muscle (biopsy of which aids diagnosis); diagnoses of Pick's disease should always exclude amyloidosis to save the patient the discomfort and hazards of a needless thoracotomy. Finally, *endocrine disorders* (myxoedema, thyrotoxicosis, acromegaly), *neuromuscular dystrophies*, secondary effects of *cardiac neoplasms, cysts, abscesses, chronic alcoholism, drug overdose, and malnutrition* can all → forms of myocarditis. (There are fashions in diagnoses of 'myocarditis' – often meaning no more than that the physician has excluded the typical forms of everything else the patient could possibly have.)

432 Acute pericarditis specified as nonrheumatic
US 52/32 (1/0)   E&W 26/18 (1/0)

Rheumatic pericarditis is never constrictive and has no clinical after-effects. Other infective and allergic forms are similar in origin to the endo- and myocardiac lesions discussed in earlier sections – that is, they may be allergic, pyogenic, tuberculous, uraemic, or endocrine. Acute pericarditis may also follow or accompany rheumatoid arthritis, acute viral myocarditis, infarction, toxic overdose, general ischaemia, or trauma. When dry (fibrinous) there is often considerable pain and an audible friction rub. When it is effusive there is often still an audible rub and there may also be discomfort, reflex cough, and breathlessness. Effusion constricts the heart and reduces ventricular filling, reducing the arterial pressure and stroke volume → tachycardia. If deterioration continues, coronary flow is critically reduced (cardiac tamponade) and there may be permanent failure. *Chronic constrictive pericarditis* (Pick's disease) is a later complication of tuberculous (75 per cent of cases), pyogenic, and other forms of pericarditis. The fibrous tissue deposited in the acute phase contracts as it matures and often calcifies, immuring the heart in a stone-like cast, which must be removed by painstaking surgery. Pulsus paradoxicus is an invariable accompaniment (it also occurs in tamponade). *Treatment* of the other forms depends on their origin and includes surgical drainage, antibiotics, drug therapy, and so on. Pericardial effusion can partly counteract malignant hypertension that does not respond well to drugs; but in other cases, where the effusion is great and reaccumulates rapidly after drainage, partial or total pericardectomy is advisable.

433·0 Heart block

US 2,951/2,687 (31/27)
E&W For all causes labelled 433: 4,684/5,773 (58/97)

Heart block has four degrees of severity: (1) delayed atrioventricular
conduction; (2) missed beats; (3) ratio blocks; (4) total atrioventricular block. Delayed conduction is associated with most forms of
active carditis, drugs (especially digitalis), coronary blockage, and
other events. Missed beats are usually a temporary block and recover
spontaneously; some deteriorate to total block. The Wenckebach
phenomenon (progressive atrioventricular delay over a few beats until
the delay is so great that one beat is dropped entirely – the whole
sequence being repeated cyclically) belongs here; but there are also
cases where the dropping of beats is random. In ratio blocks there are
2 (or 3 or 4) atrial contractions to every ventricular contraction; such
blocks are commoner with ischaemic heart disease than with carditis.
Total heart block, which affects 4 males to every female, is associated
with ischaemic and hypertensive heart disease, severe calcification of
the aortic leaflets or mitral roots (producing a fibrous lesion of the
bundle and/or branches), infective secondary carditis (especially
syphilis and diphtheria), digitalis poisoning (especially where there is
atrial fibrillation), haemorrhage, trauma, and neoplasms. Sometimes
there is no obvious cause, so there is a possibility of an autoaggressive
factor with some forms of heart block. It is usually permanent. Ventricular stroke volume is at least doubled and the heart enlarges; output
pressure is high but, because of extensive vasodilation, the pulse
collapses. Venous pressures are also high and low-output failure
develops early. When a partial block degenerates to a total block the
patient is very susceptible to Stokes-Adams attacks (ventricular
asystole or tachycardia or fibrillation for varying periods, usually a
few seconds, producing abrupt syncope). If an attack is prolonged,
there is cerebral anoxia and twitching. When the ventricles beat again
there is widespread reactive hyperaemia and the CO_2-depleted blood
that lay stagnant in the lungs can produce a transient cyclic disorder in
the respiratory centre (Cheyne-Stokes breathing). Ventricular fibrillation is a complication of Stokes-Adams attacks; occasionally normal
rhythm may return spontaneously, but usually, unless patients are
defibrillated within minutes, they die. (It is worth noting that in a few
patients with total block the idiopathic ventricular pacemaker can be
faster than the atria, reaching a pulse of 100, and is remarkably resistant
to all normal cardiac accelerators and decelerators.) Partial blocks are
rarely the primary causes of death; they are best treated by drugs,
electrolyte manipulation, and, in some cases, demand pacemakers.
Total blocks, both permanent and transient, are best treated by demand
pacemakers. (In passing: some authorities use a threefold classification
of blocks; 1st degree (prolonged PR interval), 3rd degree (total, 2nd

degree (everything else).

433·1 Other disorders of heart rhythm

US 2,444/2,550 (25/25)   E&W see 433·0

We will consider these by sites in the order of the passage of the pace-making impulse: SA node → atrial conduction → AV node → bundle of His → branches. (Heart block is covered under 433·0.) *Sinus arrhythmia* is a normal phenomenon when associated with the natural breathing rhythm, emotion, exertion, and other normal aspects of living, especially in children. It is abnormal when associated with other arrhythmias discussed below. *Sinus tachycardia*, commonly associated with raised venous pressure and the consequent Bainbridge reflex (increased atrial stretch → vagal inhibition). It is a normal response to effort and pregnancy, and is also found in Paget's disease, thyrotoxicosis, beri beri, anoxic pulmonary heart disease, arteriovenous shunts, anaemia, and low output failures. As long as the heart remains in the optimum reaches of Starling's curve, sinus tachycardia is a helpful adaptation to normal and abnormal stresses – despite the reduction it brings to the diastolic rest period and coronary blood flow. But when the heart goes 'over the top' and into the descending part of the curve, the tachycardia becomes a grave embarrassment. The same is true from the onset of tachycardia where there is a pre-existing mitral stenosis or hypertension. With pericarditis (see 432), the tachycardia is the sole means of maintaining output. Where the cause is vagal (i.e., no Bainbridge reflex), as in anxiety, drug-induced vagal inhibition or sympathetic stimulation, and convalescence, the fall in venous input can counteract the raised heart rate and so merely embarrass the heart. However, the heart tolerates all kinds of sinus tachycardia better than it tolerates high output and hypertension. These qualifications must be borne in mind when one talks loosely of tachycardia 'causing' heart failure. *Sinus bradycardia* is normal in athletic training and in individuals with congenitally low pulse rate; it is an adaptive response to acutely raised blood pressure (e.g., in acute nephritis) and raised intracranial pressure. It is a feature of obstructive jaundice, myxoedema, and convalescence from some fevers. Stroke volume rises so as to maintain output, which is doubled at a pulse of 40; if bradycardia is prolonged, the ventricle may hypertrophy, as in athletic training. The AV node is less affected by the depressor influences on the SA node and, at 40/minute, may occasionally take over (ventricular or nodal escape). SA *block* is equivalent to AV block, with randomly missed beats, cyclically missed beats (Wenckeback type), and ratio blocks (here 2:1 only). The equivalent of total block is, of course, nodal rhythm. The first two kinds are common in sinus bradycardia. SA blocks are due to excessive vagal stimulus and can cause short periods of cardiac arrest. *Nodal rhythm* promotes a heart rate of 120–160/minute and is due to the abnormal elevation of the AV-nodal rate above that of the SA node, as a result of which the AV node becomes *the* pacemaker. Both nodes continue to fire with varying asynchronicity, giving the impression that there is a single 'wandering pacemaker' (misleadingly so described in much of the literature) loose in the atria. Nodal rhythm is commonly caused by digitalis therapy; it is occasional in health, and not rare with active carditis and coronary occlusion near the SA node. It is harmless. *Bundle branch blocks* are caused by congenital, organic, traumatic, or functional lesions affecting either of the branches of the bundle of His, which conducts the impulse from the AV node to the fine network of Purkinje fibres that ramify throughout the myocardium. In either case the ventricle whose branch is blocked receives a delayed stimulus from the ventricle with the still-functioning branch. Front ('right') bundle branch block is sometimes found in health and is then of no clinical significance. It is also associated with atrial septal defect, mitral stenosis, and gross pulmonary embolism. Back ('left') bundle branch block is associated with hypertensive heart disease, aortic valve disease, or myocardial ischaemia. Either kind of block is found with active carditis, neoplasms, trauma, thyrotoxicosis, and any kind of fibrous repair of the myocardium. Both kinds may be partial (usually progressive) or total; also transient, paroxysmal or permanent. The defects are not responsive to drug therapy and (because of transventricular conduction) not very significant for prognosis – which is always related to the severity of the underlying condition.

433·2 Other functional diseases of the heart

US 23/15 (0/0)   E&W see 433·0

Far and away the most important heart disease not covered under other ISCD entries is *cor pulmonale*, a chronic response of the heart to a long-standing pulmonary lesion. It is predominantly a disease of the over-50s and is five times more common in men than in women. Since it is usually unsuspected until its acute phase is triggered by acute bronchopneumonia or bronchitis, it is most often treated in general hospitals where the cardiac involvement may go unrecognised until there is acute heart failure. Thus it is certainly more common than the figures suggest – possibly accounting for 10 per cent of all cases of low output failure. The two causes are hypoxia and partial obliteration of the pulmonary vascular bed. Such obliteration (with emphysema or interstitial pulmonary fibrosis) rarely advances so far as to cause pulmonary hypertension at rest; usually the crisis comes on effort or with the onset of bronchitis, virus or bronchopneumonia, asthma, and so on. Barriers to O_2 diffusion may also aggravate the condition: silicosis, asbestos or beryllium inhalation, sarcoid or scleroderma, diffuse carcinoma, and x-ray therapy. With these there may be no CO_2 retention. Whatever the cause, the hypoxia raises the heart rate, the typical sign of cor pulmonale. The acute event or trauma further lowers alveolar $PO_2 \rightarrow$ transient pulmonary vasoconstriction and raised pressure (up to 50mm Hg). This intolerable double burden on the front ('right') ventricle $\rightarrow$ low output failure. Diagnosis is often complex, especially in emphysematous cases with alcoholism or Paget's disease, also with hyperthyroidism and liver carcinoma. Where there is toxic vasomotor collapse with pneumonia the possibility of mitral stenosis, Pick's disease, Eisenmenger's syndrome, tumours, and other kinds of pulmonary hypertension must also be taken into account. General hypertensive heart disease may also complicate the picture. *Course:* if the patient is referred to a cardiac clinic for 'heart failure' before there is an acute crisis, and if he is properly diagnosed, the prognosis is obviously better than if the condition is either not recognised at all or only detected in acute failure. Cardiac catheterisation and respiratory function tests (both impossible when the patient is desperately ill) make the diagnosis certain. *Treatment:* symptomatic treatment for bronchial spasm; antibiotics for underlying infection; cardiac muscle stimulants and coronary dilators; oxygen tent (or ventilators for patients with no remaining response to arterial PCO_2); and physiotherapy. Reduction in venous pressure by diuretics is advisable. In extremis it can be treated by transplantation of the whole heart-lung complex.

434·0 Kyphoscoliotic heart disease
US 75/101 (1/1)
E&W For all diseases labelled 434 4,684/5,773 (199/233)
Kyphoscoliosis (pigeon chest) has no direct bearing on the heart. It used to be thought that this condition would leave inadequate room for heart development, but as an active muscular organ the heart will poach space from all surrounding structures, chiefly the lung. However, kyphoscoliosis can cause severe pulmonary problems and produce the secondary heart lesion known as cor pulmonale (see 433·2). Kyphoscoliosis is associated with other blueprint or metabolic failures, such as atrial septal defect and dissecting aneurysm of the aorta (see 451).

434·1 Congestive heart failure
US 5,685/5,286 (59/52)   E&W See 434·0
Heart failure is the inability of the ventricle(s) to respond to variations in the filling pressure and volume. In the main body of this book the two forms of 'congestive' heart failure are considered under their more helpful titles: low output failure and high volume failure (or shock). In the ISCD, however, they share a single subentry, so we begin with a word on their differences. Low output failure is associated with some barrier to circulation, such as a valve stenosis or general hypertension, or with a poor ventricular muscle. Back ('left') ventricular failure, for

instance, often follows hypertension or aortic valve disease. At onset there are compensations: raised heart rate, peripheral shutdown, possible raised venous pressure, and so on. Symptoms first show in response to effort – chiefly dyspnoea. Later (often complicated by paroxysmal cardiac dyspnoea and orthopnoea) they show even at rest; this is heart failure in common parlance. X-rays show venous congestion in the lung fields, and there is often pulsus alternans, gallop rhythm, and Cheyne-Stokes breathing. Front ('right') ventricular failure often accompanies pulmonary hypertension and pulmonary valve stenosis or it may be secondary to back ventricular failure; fatigue and hepatic or general oedema are common results of compensatory adjustments (though general oedema is often absent in acute failure, especially in children). The lung fields are often clear on x-ray, unless the front ventricular failure is secondary to failure of the back ventricle. Various kinds of myocarditis can also lead to either or both kinds of ventricular low output failure. In both kinds the cardiac output and peripheral circulation are reduced. High-volume 'congestive' failure is associated with anaemia, hyperthyroidism, cor pulmonale, liver disease, Paget's disease, arteriovenous fistulae, beri beri, and so on. Here, although cardiac output is raised it is still insufficient to meet demand, so the symptoms of low-output failure (oedema, dyspnoea, etc.) are coupled with symptoms of raised peripheral flow: warm extremities, venous distension, marked pulse, and so on. Congestive failures are the result of many of the conditions covered under other entries in this ISCD list, so nothing further will be said under this entry about other causes. Apart from the signs and symptoms already mentioned, there may be findings of: (1) venous thrombi and pulmonary infarcts; (2) oliguria, with urine high in albumin, blood cells, and casts; (3) jaundice secondary to hepatic congestion (with hepatic damage) or haemolytic jaundice (with pulmonary damage); (4) polycythaemia with hypoxia (only in cor pulmonale); (5) loss of weight, often noticed only after diuresis; (6) hydrothorax; (7) psychic disturbances ranging from loss of short term memory to frank psychoses. *Treatment* Treatable underlying causes (e.g., stenoses, bronchopneumonia) should, obviously, be treated urgently. Partial or total rest, control of fluid and sodium intake, cardiac and coronary stimulants, diuretics, control of rhythm disturbances, and dialysis are also part of the treatment. Venesection, currently unfashionable, may stage a partial comeback.

434·2 **Left ventricular failure**

US 275/197 (3/2)   E&W See 434·0

Considered under 434·1. The back ('left') ventricle, being the main pumping chamber of the heart, is more frequently the site of attacks of various kinds, from systemic hypertension and ischaemia to the rarer cardiomyopathies.

343·3 Other diseases of the heart

US 205/142   E&W See 434·0

This is, ideally, not a separate classification. With perfect conditions for diagnosis all heart lesions should be referrable to other categories. However, in real life diagnostic conditions are not perfect. Hence entries like this and 434·4.

434·4 Unspecified disease of the heart

US 4,628/2,325 (48/23)   E&W See 434·0

As for 434·3.

440 Essential benign hypertensive heart disease

US 36/59 (0/1)   E&W 35/48 (1/2)

The ISCD categories for dealing with hypertensive disease really make rational discussion impossible. Firstly the distinction between hypertension with (440–443) and hypertension without (444–447) heart involvement reflects no fundamental condition; there is *always* heart involvement, even if it is safely adaptive until the episodes leading up to death. Secondly the term 'benign' (440, 444) masks a variety of causes – including some that are in themselves quite normal adaptations – all of which can degenerate into a true malignant state. Thirdly the term 'essential' (440, 441, 444, 445) is merely a mask for ignorance; it means 'hypertension we cannot yet explain'. Fourthly the bald inclusion of arteriolar nephrosclerosis (442, 446) begs the question of whether the renal signs are causes or effects or a mixture of both. And finally the last category (447) is difficult to countenance unless you believe that some organ other than the heart is responsible for the circulation (especially in view of the fact that all other possible causes have their own ISCD categories: adrenal disease (274), acute and chronic nephritis (590, 592), pyelonephritis (600·0), and hypertensive disease arising during pregnancy (642·0)). In view of these inadequacies, hypertension in all its forms will be discussed only under this present heading. *Hypertension* is not simply a matter of abnormally high blood pressure. An anxious young adult pacing around a room, say, may have a mean arterial pressure of 200mm Hg and a cardiac output of 12 litres/minute – both around double the normal for the same person when walking calmly. From these data we can calculate his total peripheral resistance to be about 1,400 dynes.sec/cm – well inside the definitely normal range of 800 to 1,600 dynes.sec/cm. (Total peripheral resistance is, of course, the true measure of hypertension.) But if his cardiac output were only 6 litres/minute at the same arterial pressure, his peripheral resistance would be 2,800 dynes.sec/cm – well above the definite hypertensive mark of 2,000 dynes.sec/cm. A reliable estimate or BCG measurement of cardiac output must always be used to qualify apparently high blood pressures before hypertension of any kind can be confirmed.

(Incidentally, such considerations eliminate the possibility of a chronic hypotensive condition. To qualify as hypotensive, a heart putting out, say, 4 litres/minute would have to have a mean arterial pressure of *below* 40 mm Hg!) Hypertension may be paroxysmal with certain lesions of the suprarenals, e.g. phaeochromocytoma, which causes excess secretion of adrenaline and noradrenaline. It may be transient with toxaemia of pregnancy and acute nephritis; in these cases the condition may be due to humoral and nervous stimuli traceable ultimately to the kidney. Acute heart failure, when it occurs, is probably biochemical in aetiology. Hypertension in pregnancy may be prolonged and develop into persistent hypertension. With chronic nephritis, pyelonephritis, and 'surgical kidney' the resultant hypertension is probably humoral, originating in the kidney. And, of course, transient hypertension is normal in anxiety; but if the anxiety itself is neurotic and chronic, the hypertension may become permanent. A so-called 'benign' hypertension is one that cannot be assigned to any of these causes. All kinds of hypertension, if the stimulus is prolonged, can result in an 'essential' hypertension that persists after all known causes are removed or excluded – the result, according to one hypothesis, of a 'resetting' of the baroreceptor mechanisms in the cardiovascular system. And we must not neglect the possibility that such resetting may occur autoaggressively. This hypertension is 'benign' where it deteriorates slowly, 'malignant' when it deteriorates rapidly. (Actually, the term 'malignant', though used in the ISCD, is not now common; most cardiologists refer to 'accelerated' hypertension.) In women the degeneration is generally slower than it is in men. Complications include ventricular hypertrophy, arteriosclerosis, cerebral haemorrhage, acute pulmonary oedema, retinal haemorrhage, and rhythm disturbances culminating in ventricular fibrillation. Patients susceptible to hypertension can be selected on a familial basis (around 90 per cent probability if both parents were hypertensive, around 45 per cent if one was hypertensive). Early diagnostic tests include pressor tests such as the immersion of one hand in cold water or holding the breath. *Course:* if the patient has a good back ('left') ventricle to begin with and a good coronary flow, with little familial history of coronary attack, and if he is naturally calm and sedentary, the deterioration may be so slow as to be clinically insignificant. At the other extreme, the excitable, active patient with a history of myocardial infarction and coronary occlusion has no real hope. Between these two extremes every grade exists, and for many hypertensives the deterioration is so slow that some other cause of death intervenes. They are, however, vulnerable, for a single myocardial infarct can worsen the prognosis overnight. The typical malignant course is several attacks of low output failure leading to a slow stuporous death within 8 months to 2 years of the first attack. Strokes and uraemia each account for about 10 per cent of all deaths. *Treatment:* If the patient puts prolongation of life above all else, he must avoid stress, overwork, excitement, smoking, sudden cooling, lack of sleep, and constipation. Medical treatment includes psychotherapy, drugs, initial bed rest (to investigate renal function, stabilise the condition, and restore morale), low sodium diet (except where renal function is already poor), sympathectomy, dialysis, and nephrectomy. Not all these treatments, of course, are appropriate in all cases. Though treatment delays rather than halts the deterioration, its rate is often so slow that a doubling or trebling of life expectancy is no mean benefit.

441 **Essential malignant hypertensive heart disease**
US 239/180 (2/2)   E&W 53/33 (2/1)

442 **Hypertensive heart disease with arteriolar nephrosclerosis**
US 4,893/5,396 (51/33)   E&W 29/48 (1/2)
The differences between the two countries partly reflect diagnostic tradition but also show that 'diagnostic resolution' is finer in the US than in Britain.

443 **Other and unspecified hypertensive heart disease**
US 16,374/22,798 (169/225)   E&W 2,950/4,351 (125/175)

444 **Essential benign hypertension**
US 1,050/1,746 (11/17)   E&W 1,166/1,510 (49/61)
Differences in diagnostic tradition again.

445 **Essential malignant hypertension**
US 838/640 (9/6)   E&W 396/153 (16/6)

446 **Hypertension with arteriolar nephrosclerosis**
US 3,637/3,095 (38/31)   E&W 206/226 (8/5)
See comments under 442.

447 **Other hypertensive diseases without mention of heart**
US 58/85 (1/1)   E&W 3/1 (0/0)

450·0 **General arteriosclerosis without mention of gangrene**
US 15,430/19,825 (160/190)   E&W 3,919/6,304 (166/254)

450·1 **General arteriosclerosis with mention of gangrene as a consequence**
US 1,159/1,150 (12/11)   E&W 425/506 (18/20)

451 **Aortic aneurysm, nonsyphilitic, and dissecting aneurysm**
US 8,448/3,176 (87/31)   E&W 2,099/1,501 (89/60)

452 **Other aneurysms, except of heart and aorta**
US 457/345 (5/3)   E&W 77/50 (3/2)

453·0 **Raynaud's disease**
US 4/6 (0/0)   E&W 0/3 (0/0)

453·1 **Thromboangiitis obliterans**
US 67/17 (1/0)   E&W 18/3 (0/0)

453·2 **Chilblains**
US 0/1 (0/0)   E&W For all 453·2 and 453·3 82/62 (4/3)

453·3 **Other peripheral vascular disease**
US 81/66 (1/1)   E&W See 453·2

454 **Arterial embolism and thrombosis**
US 656/490 (7/5)   E&W 65/99 (3/4)

455 **Gangrene of unspecified cause**
US 184/183 (2/1)   E&W 39/51 (1/2)

456 **Other diseases of arteries**
US 633/981 (7/10)   E&W 209/223 (8/9)

460 **Varicose veins of lower extremities**
US 104/195 (1/2)   E&W 49/157 (2/6)

461 **Haemorrhoids**
US 23/14 (0/0)   E&W 7/9 (0/0)

462 **Varicose veins of other unspecified sites**
US 271/133 (3/1)   E&W 25/22 (1/1)

463 **Phlebitis and thrombophlebitis of lower extremities**
US 619/789 (6/8)   E&W 94/169 (4/7)

464 **Phlebitis and thrombophlebitis of other sites**
US 521/667 (5/7)   E&W 18/31 (1/1)

465 **Pulmonary embolism and infarction**
US 2,960/3,609 (41/36)   E&W 1,087/1,339 (46/54)

466 **Other venous embolism and thrombosis**
US 1,120/1,287 (12/13)   E&W 940/1,615 (40/65)

467·0 **Hypotension**
US 39/34 (0/0)   E&W For all diseases labelled 467 54/72 (2/3)
Hypotension occurs as a sign in: aortic stenosis, myocardial infarction, low output failure, chronic constrictive pericarditis (Pick's disease), hypothermia, hypovolaemia, and all cardiomyopathies; it also occurs with mitral stenosis and all obstructive lesions, pulmonary embolism, and various physiological disorders. Vasodilators, neglectfully given during high output failure, can also → hypotension. There is, however, no category of 'chronic essential hypotension', as this heading might suggest – see 440.

467·1 **Diseases of capillaries**
US 18/19 (0/0)   E&W See 467·0

467·2 **Other unspecified circulatory disease**
US 398/325 (4/3)   E&W See 467·0

754 **Congenital malformations of the circulatory system**
US 8,472/4,772 (49/39)   E&W 1,182/914 (50/37)
Notes on specific malformations follow but individual morbidities for E&W are not published.

754·0 **Tetralogy of Fallot**
US 276/204 (3/2)   E&W See 754
The two blueprint failures of the tetralogy are pulmonary stenosis and dextroposed aortic root; both arise from a failure of the embryonic heart bulb to develop and twist properly. The other two defects are contingent upon them: a ventricular septal defect caused by the riding aorta, and a front ('right') ventricular hypertrophy due to the fact that both ventricles must work against the full systemic pressure. Since the front ventricle 'grew up' with this pressure it does not face a cor-pulmonale-type situation. The tetralogy is very nearly twice as common among males as among females. The severity varies with the degree of pulmonary stenosis, which may be infundibular (50 per cent of cases), valvular (30 per cent), or both. If pulmonary stenosis is so mild that its resistance is below systemic resistance, the defect is well tolerated, with no cyanosis at rest; but effort intolerance is still no better than grade 2B. A patent ductus also makes for tolerance since it promotes normal pulmonary irrigation. Other compensatory changes include enlargement of the bronchial vascular bed and polycythaemia. Normally the pulmonary resistance is greater than the systemic resistance; then there is central cyanosis at rest, polycythaemia, clubbing, squatting, and effort intolerance of grade 3 or poorer. Squatting cuts off the venous return from the lower half of the body, decreasing the front ventricular load and the front-to-back shunt.

Syncope is common in 20 per cent of cases in infancy and childhood. Atypical cases can present diagnostic problems, particularly in differentiating from: (1) pulmonary stenosis with reverse atrial shunt (confirmed by cardiac catheterisation for PCO_2 and pressures in the chambers and peripheral arteries); and (2) mild uncomplicated ventricular septal defect (maladie de Roger), confirmed by the heart sounds and lack of effort intolerance with VSD. Complications include cerebral thrombosis (from polycythaemia), cerebral abscess, and reduced resistance to bacterial endocarditis. *Course:* prognosis depends on the severity and complications of the defect, expectancy reaching late middle age in mild cases. *Treatment:* open-heart surgery has dramatically improved the chances of severe cases.

754·1 **Patent ductus arteriosus**

US 136/164 (1/2)   E&W See 754

Patent ductus arises when the duct fails to close (or closes and reopens) during the first six weeks of life. (The term is tautological since after birth the ductus becomes the ligamentum arteriosum; if it remains a ductus, it is by definition patent.) Blood intended for the systemic circulation is then shunted at high pressure through the lungs and back to the back ('left') side of the heart, causing pulmonary damage, occasional mitral regurgitation or relative mitral stenosis, hypertrophy of the back ventricle, and hyperactivity of the heart. Damage is directly related to the degree of patency. A small patency, equivalent to 6mm diameter or less in adulthood, causes a tolerable hypertrophy of the front ventricle and a tolerable rise in pulmonary pressure; thus it causes no shunt, even on catheterisation. A large patency can lead to intolerable pulmonary pressures, gross hypertrophy, and high output failure. Complications include (1) tricuspid atresia (where a patent duct is essential to the maintenance of pulmonary circulation); (2) coarctation of the aorta; (3) hypertension, which adds to the already burdened heart. Because of turbulent bloodflow the pulmonary artery is susceptible to bacterial endocarditis. *Course:* untreated cases succumb to back ventricular failure (or bacterial endocarditis), the age depending on the degree of patency and severity of complications. *Treatment:* surgical ligation of the duct up to the age of fifty; contra-indicated where pulmonary hypertension causes a reversed shunt through the duct (for then, of course, the hypertension has no means of relief).

754·2 **Interventricular septal defect**

US 304/386 (3/4)   E&W See 754

In 90 per cent of cases the defect lies in the anterior part of the membranous septum. A defect up to 2mm diameter (adult) may escape all routine investigation and be of no clinical significance – except insofar as it makes the pulmonary side of the shunt more susceptible to bacterial endocarditis. A mild VSD (maladie de Roger) measures up to 5mm; there is no pulmonary hypertension and the shunt is 1·5 to 3 l/minute. A moderate VSD measures up to 10mm; pulmonary hypertension is slight and the shunt is 4 to 8 l/minute. A severe uncomplicated VSD measures up to 15mm; pulmonary hypertension is moderate to severe and the shunt is 10 to 15 l/minute. A VSD up to 30mm raises pulmonary resistance to systemic levels, reducing the shunt to 3 to 5 l/minute. Strain on the heart is severe in any defect over 5mm – only the front ('right') atrium escapes the burden of handling shunted blood. Systemic output and oxygenation are normal. Complications include Eisenmenger's complex, bacterial endocarditis, pulmonary stenosis, and aortic regurgitation (one cusp of the valve being defective or tied by a fibrous band to the defect). *Course:* prognosis depends on the severity of the defect and its complications. *Treatment:* a VSD can be closed routinely in any clinic equipped for open-heart surgery.

754·3 Interatrial septal defect

US 206/239 (2/2)   E&W See 754·0

ASD is the commonest congenital heart condition. Even if we exclude patent foramen ovale (which occurs in 20 per cent of the population at large and has no clinical significance unless there is also pulmonary stenosis or raised pulmonary resistance), it is still the commonest, accounting for almost 20 per cent of all congenital heart disease. Because back ('left') ventricular filling resistance is normally greater than that of the front ventricle there is usually a shunt into the front atrium. The defect typically measures 10 to 33mm. The front of the heart hypertrophies but the back atrial filling pressure usually rises in step, maintaining the direction of the shunt and leading to low output failure. Where there is high pulmonary vascular resistance, however, the shunt reverses and there is cyanosis. Complications include: (1) Marfan's syndrome (arachnodactyly, tall thin build, muscular hypotonia, high palate, slight kyphoscoliosis, hypoplasia of the aorta); (2) Eisenmenger's syndrome (see 754·5); (3) pulmonary hypertension and stenosis; (4) tricuspid regurgitation, with gross hypertrophy and low output failure; (5) bacterial endocarditis (rare unless there is pulmonary resistance of some kind); (6) anomalous pulmonary drainage; (7) mitral stenosis (Lutembacher's syndrome). *Course and Treatment:* prognosis used to be poor for severe complicated ASD, but open-heart surgery has greatly reduced the mortality and improved the prognosis.

754·4 Fibroelastosis cordis

US 157/133 (2/1)   E&W See 754·0

Fibroelastosis is an architectural failure of the endocardium during foetal life – possibly related to periods of anoxia, for it is found with various kinds of valvular atresia and coronary anomalies. Where there is no such obvious link it may be due to transient sealing of the foramen ovale in foetal life. It is marked by ventricular enlargement over a dense white fibroelastic endocardium. *Course:* the baby is born apparently normal but soon develops cyanosis, dyspnoea, ventricular hypertrophy, and low output failure. *Treatment:* only transplantation from e.g. an anencephalic baby could save one with fibroelastosis. Prognosis should be good because of the immunological immaturity of the two systems.

754·5 Other and unspecified malformations of the heart
US 2,662/2,162 (28/21)   E&W See 754·0

The total list of congenital heart diseases not covered by a separate entry in the ISCD list is vast. Only the most significant of them will be discussed here in any detail. Anomalies of the aorta are discussed under 754·6. *Dextrocardia* (0·5 per cent of all congenital heart disease): mirror image transposition of the heart and great vessels (and usually of the viscera, too) is of no clinical significance: the heart is healthy in structure and function. All ECG leads from such cases must be mirror reversed to produce conventional traces. *Congenital aortic valve defects:* (1) regurgitation, common in Marfan's syndrome (see 754·3), rare with VSD (see 754·2), may also be caused by (2) bicuspid aortic (occurs in just over 1 per cent of population), is commonly associated with 'left heart syndrome' (coarctation of the aorta, bicuspid aortic, and/or VSD); it usually scleroses and regurgitates, and it is prone to infection and rupture; (3) aortic atresia is not compatible with more than a few days' life, during which time the circulation is contrived via ASD, anomalous pulmonary venous drainage, and/or anastomotic broncho-pulmonary venous channels; accompanied in any case by fibro-elastosis (see 754·4); (4) stenosis, due to fusion or incomplete in-corporation of the bulbus cordis; degree of severity varies, mild cases usually succumbing to rheumatic attack or other forms of endocard-itis. *Congenital mitral stenosis* is rare. *Cor triatrium*, also rare, may produce symptoms identical with mitral stenosis – a perforated septum divides the back ('left') atrium between the orifices of the pulmonary veins and the mitral valve; the perforation may be only a few mm in diameter, through which the whole cardiac output must flow. *Ebstein's disease* (malformation and deformation of the tri-cuspid valve) is also rare, though (since many cases have no cyanosis, normal effort tolerance and little dyspnoea and paroxysmal tachy-cardia) the incidence may be higher than suspected. Typical cases, however, have gross dilatation of the front heart, clear lung fields, mild hypotension, cyanosis, small pulse, and partial or complete front bundle branch block. Prognosis varies with the degree of cyanosis. *Eisenmenger's complex* (3 per cent of all congenital heart disease) is a VSD with pulmonary hypertension great enough to reverse the shunt or make it bidirectional. The VSD is always 10mm or more and the high pulmonary resistance – which is helpful and probably life-saving in these circumstances – exists at birth. (The term Eisenmenger's *syndrome* is often used to describe similar pulmonary hyper-resistance with shunts at other levels – e.g., at ASD or patent duct level.) Cases present with cyanosis (differential when the ductus is patent), effort intolerance, occasional angina, syncope, haemoptysis, clubbing of the fingers, mild hypotension, and small pulse. *Pulmonary stenosis* (16 per cent of all congenital heart disease) is next in frequency to ASD among congenital heart defects. Cases complicated by shunts in tetralogy of Fallot, patent duct, VSD, and ASD are discussed under 754·0 to 754·3 respectively. With mild to moderate cases ventricular pressures at rest of 50 to 100mm Hg maintain normal post-stenotic pressure and flow. With severe cases even ventricular pressures of 300mm Hg cannot maintain normal pressure and flow. Depending on the degree of stenosis patients present with peripheral cyanosis, moon facies, mild hypotension, and faint pulse. X-rays show post-stenotic dilatation (less common when the stenosis is infundibular) and front ventricular hypertrophy. *Pulmonary atresia* is always associated with ASD and broncho-pulmonary anastomosis – on which life depends. *Tricuspid atresia* is associated either with ASD or patent foramen ovale (here the lungs are ischaemic) or with transposition of the great vessels (where the lungs are plethoric). *Transposition of the great vessels* (aorta and pulmonary artery) is incompatible with life unless there is a shunt – usually by ASD *and* VSD as well as broncho-pulmonary anastomosis. *Persistent truncus arteriosus* (very rare) arises from a failure of aorta and pulmonary artery to differentiate, so that a single great riding vessel with an anomalous (often 4-cusped) valve serves both circulations; with normal pulmonary resistance, hyper-trophy → low output failure is common; with resistance high enough to prevent plethora and ventricular overload, prognosis is fair to good. *Total anomalous pulmonary venous drainage* in which the original single embryonic pulmonary vein flows into the front atrium or one of the venae cavae is compensated by patent foramen ovale (otherwise life is impossible); if patency is small, prognosis is poor; if it is adequate, prognosis is fair to good. *Partial anomalous systemic drainage* (SVC or IVC) into the back atrium (rare) leads to cyanosis but little other disability. *Cor triloculare biatriatum*, in which the interventricular septum fails to develop, results in complete arterio-venous mixture; haemodynamics and prognosis resembles persistent truncus. *Cor biventriculare triloculare* (extremely rare) is which the atrial septum fails to develop, resembles gross ASD; death in untreated cases usually occurs before the fifteenth year. *Cor biloculare* (rarest of all), in which both atrial and ventricular septa fail to develop, produces a situation like that of cor triloculare biatriatum. *Congenital artery anomalies:* (1) a single coronary artery, which quickly divides into a back and

245

front branch or into atypical branches serving the whole heart, is rarely fatal unless associated with other congenital defects; (2) a back coronary artery arising from the pulmonary artery is inadequate, despite anastomotic connections, in pressure and oxygenation to serve the back ventricle, which becomes fibrous and partly calcified; death is usual in early infancy unless diagnosed and treated; very difficult to recognise without catheterisation; (3) a front coronary arising from the pulmonary artery is far less serious because front ventricular pressures (15/7mm Hg) are low enough to permit flow, and even though the blood is only 80 per cent oxygenated, the muscle appears unaffected; often unsuspected until autopsy; has no effect on life expectancy; (4) arteriovenous fistulae (which may also be traumatic) lead to inadequate coronary perfusion; (5) ruptured sinus of Valsalva (which may also be traumatic, acquired, or infectious) also leads to inadequate perfusion; (6) congenital coronary atresia, partly compensated during foetal life by alternate pathways, leads to such poor perfusion that death in early infancy is inevitable. *Treatments:* many congenital defects that were once fatal or severely disabling are now treatable by surgery. Defective or missing parts and valves can be replaced; septal defects are routinely patched and septal atresias made good; anomalous vessels can be returned to their rightful place. But, obviously, gross and multiple anomalies, especially those involving high pulmonary resistance and/or a multitude of anomalous anastomotic pathways, are difficult to set to rights.

754·6 Coarctation of the aorta
US 168/107 (2/1)   E&W See 754·0

The infantile type, in which the aorta is constricted or closed just above the ductus, is not compatible with more than a few years' life. In a rare infantile variation, also incompatible with survival past infancy, there is actual or functional aortic atresia with a patent ductus carrying the whole systemic output. In the common adult type the constriction is beyond the ductus. Anomalous thoracic arteries develop to carry the systemic output and give the ribs on chest x-ray a characteristic notched appearance (which may be absent if the ductus is patent). Other associated anomalies are fibroelastosis (with the infantile type, fatal); bicuspid aortic valve; aortic stenosis (left heart syndrome); and mitral stenosis. Uncomplicated coarctation is often remarkably symptom-free; in women it is commonly unnoticed until the routine tests made during pregnancy. Complications are almost always fatal and include: dissection or rupture of the aorta, bacterial endarteritis or carditis, cerebral vascular lesions, and hypertrophy → low output failure. *Treatment:* surgical excision with direct anastomosis or replacement. *Other congenital aortic defects:* (1) right-sided aorta is of no clinical significance; it is, however, associated with tetralogy of Fallot and

Eisenmenger's syndrome but not with uncomplicated pulmonary stenosis or pulmonary hypertension with reverse shunt through patent ductus or ASD – and so it may aid diagnosis; (2) aortic hypoplasia is also of no clinical significance unless part of Marfan's syndrome (see 754·3); (3) persistent primitive aortic arches or an aberrant right sub-clavian artery may press on the trachaea and oesophagus, causing respiratory and swallowing difficulties; not usually fatal unless compli-cated by bronchopneumonia. Symptoms disappear after infancy, when the vessels lengthen, but there may be a return with arteriosclerosis in later life.

754·7 **Other circulatory malformations**
US 863/575 (9/6)   E&W See 754·0

782·4 **Symptoms, senility, referable to acute heart failure, undefined**
US 1,200/883 (12/9)   E&W 51/56 (2/2)

Acknowledgments

To Murray Brooks, Senior Lecturer in Anatomy at Guy's Hospital, London, whose grasp of the subject was most useful at one or two tricky moments in the writing of chapter 3. To Professor C. P. Wendell-Smith, who, though he played no direct part in this book, sowed the seeds of it some years ago. To Professor Roger Warwick, Mark Patterson, Henry Light, Eunice Lockey, Donald Ross, Keith Ross, and Keith Jefferson for help, advice, and encouragement. To Miss Daphne Beauchamp for her splendid selection of X-ray plates and angiograms. To Simon Joseph for unstinted and painstaking help with the chemotherapy charts and parts of the appendix. To Ray Gosling, Dennis Deuchar, Henry Light, Denis Melrose, and Norah Burns, all of whom put valuable time at my disposal, freely discussed their work with me, and allowed me to report it here. And to Vernon Mills, who did most of the illustrations and made several helpful suggestions and improvements, beyond what one normally expects of an illustrator.

For pictures my thanks are due to Messrs Smith, Kline, and French Laboratories for the USCG picture on page 158; to Dr H. A. Becker of Queen's University, Kingston, Ontario, for the photograph on page 76; to the Wellcome Foundation for the Vesalius print and the diagram from Harvey's classic studies – both in chapter 1; and to Barry Roberts and his assistants at the National Heart Hospital who took all the other photographs in the book. Mr Dewar of GU Instruments, London, kindly provided historical references for the diagram on page 189.

The British Heart Foundation, the National Heart Hospital, and the National Health Service have all contributed in various ways to this book and to the work on which it is based; to them also my thanks are due.

Selected book list

The history of cardiology is well covered in *Classics of Cardiology* by Frederick A. Willius and Thomas E. Keys (Dover Publications Inc.); it contains papers by fifty-one leading researchers from the time of Harvey onward – including the whole of Harvey's 'De Motu Cordis'. There is a good analysis of work before Harvey in *The Origins of Modern Science* by Herbert Butterfield (G. Bell & Sons, London). Physiology is well covered in *The Physiological Basis of Medical Practice* edited by Best and Taylor (E. & S. Livingstone, Edinburgh and London; Williams and Wilkins, Baltimore); a shorter version of this book, suitable for senior school work, is *The Human Body* (Chapman & Hall, London; Holt Rinehart and Winston, New York). Other good physiologies: *Review of Medical Physiology* by William F. Ganong (Lange, California; Blackwell, Oxford), and *Clinical Physiology* by E. J. M. Campbell *et al.* (Blackwell, Oxford; F. A. Davis & Co, Philadelphia).

The embryology of the heart has not yet been satisfactorily described in any book. Good books on human embryology in general include *Developmental Anatomy* by Arey (W. B. Saunders Company, London and Philadelphia) – not now in print but available in all good medical libraries; *Human Embryology* by W. J. Hamilton, J. D. Boyd and H. W. Mossman (Heffer & Sons Ltd, Cambridge); and, as a good introduction to the subject, *Basic Human Embryology* by P. L. Williams and C. P. Wendell-Smith (Pitman Medical, London). The heart's own physiology and control mechanisms are well described in *Cardiovascular Physiology* by R. M. Berne and M. N. Levy (C. V. Mosby Co, St Louis; Henry Kimpton, London). Cardiovascular disease and diagnosis and therapy are covered in *The Year Book of Cardiovascular Disease* by various authors, published annually by Year Book Publishers; in *Cardiovascular Pathology* by R. E. B. Hudson (Edward Arnold, London) – it is pricey at £48 but contains every worthwhile reference there is, as well as Professor Hudson's own valuable comments and descriptions; and in *Paul Wood's Diseases of the Heart and Circulation* by his colleagues (Eyre and Spottiswoode, London).

The heart's anatomy is well described in *Quain's Anatomy* (Longmans, London and New York); *Gray's Anatomy* (Longmans, London and New York); the *Ciba Collection of Medical Illustrations, volume 5: The Heart* by F. H. Netter (Ciba Foundation, London); *Lehmann's medizinische Atlanten* by J. Sobotta (J. F. Lehmann's Verlag, Munich); *The Anatomy of the Coronary Arteries* by Thomas N. James (Paul B. Hober Inc., New York); and *Les Cavités Cardiaques* by E. Henry, R. Courbier and P. Rochu (Mason & Cie Editeurs, Paris). Books of especial interest to surgeons include: *Anatomy for Surgeons* by Hollinshead (Cassell, London); *Surface and Radiological Anatomy* by Apple, Hamilton and Simon (Heffer, Cambridge); *A Method of Anatomy* by J. C. B. Grant (Bailliere, Tindall and Cassell, London and New York); *Pathology for Surgeons* by Boyd (Saunders); *Cardiac Surgery* by Rodriguez (W. B. Saunders Company, London and Philadelphia); *Biology and Surgery of Tissue Transplantation* edited by Maxwell Anderson (Blackwell, Oxford); and *Experience with Heart Transplantation* (The 1968 Cape Town symposium) edited by H. A. Shapiro (Butterworth Press, London and New York).

Indices

Illustrations Index

Subject Index

Of the appendix material only the headings are referred to in this index

250